MANAGING TECHNOLOGY IN HIGHER EDUCATION

The Jossey-Bass Higher and Adult Education Series

Managing Technology in Higher Education

Strategies for Transforming Teaching and Learning

A. W. (Tony) Bates and Albert Sangrà

 JOSSEY-BASS
A Wiley Imprint
www.josseybass.com

Published by Jossey-Bass
A Wiley Imprint
989 Market Street, San Francisco, CA 94103-1741—www.josseybass.com

Readers should be aware that Internet Web sites offered as citations and/or sources for further information may have changed or disappeared between the time this was written and when it is read.

Limit of Liability/Disclaimer of Warranty: While the publisher and author have used their best efforts in preparing this book, they make no representations or warranties with respect to the accuracy or completeness of the contents of this book and specifically disclaim any implied warranties of merchantability or fitness for a particular purpose. No warranty may be created or extended by sales representatives or written sales materials. The advice and strategies contained herein may not be suitable for your situation. You should consult with a professional where appropriate. Neither the publisher nor author shall be liable for any loss of profit or any other commercial damages, including but not limited to special, incidental, consequential, or other damages.

Jossey-Bass books and products are available through most bookstores. To contact Jossey-Bass directly call our Customer Care Department within the U.S. at 800-956-7739, outside the U.S. at 317-572-3986, or fax 317-572-4002.

Jossey-Bass also publishes its books in a variety of electronic formats. Some content that appears in print may not be available in electronic books.

Tierney and Hentschke quotes on pages 195 and 232 from Tierney, William G., and Guilbert C. Hentschke, *New Players, Different Game*, pp. 13–14, 135. Copyright © 2007 The Johns Hopkins University Press. Reprinted with permission of The Johns Hopkins University Press.

Library of Congress Cataloging-in-Publication Data

Bates, Tony, date.
  Managing technology in higher education : strategies for transforming teaching and learning / A. W. (Tony) Bates, Albert Sangrà.
      p. cm. – (The Jossey-Bass higher and adult education series)
    Includes bibliographical references and index.
    ISBN 978-0-470-58472-9 (hardback); ISBN 978-1-118-03854-3 (ebk); ISBN 978-1-118-03855-0 (ebk); ISBN 978-1-118-03856-7 (ebk)
  1. Education, Higher–Effect of technological innovations on.   2. Information technology–Management.   I. Sangrà, Albert, date.   II. Title.
    LB2395.7.B376 2011
    378.1′01–dc22

                                                                                    2011002090

Printed in the United States of America
FIRST EDITION
HB Printing   10 9 8 7 6 5 4 3 2 1

To students everywhere

Contents

FIGURES AND TABLES

PREFACE

THE ORIGIN OF THE BOOK

Albert Sangrà and I worked closely together for five years (2002–2007) while I was a part-time chair of research in e-learning at the Open University of Catalonia (UOC) in Barcelona.

During that time, he was collecting data for his thesis on the integration of technology in the university based on six case studies from Southern Europe. When I read the thesis, I was struck by the similarities of the results from his study and my own experience working with North American universities and colleges, despite the large differences in language, culture, and history between the two continents. In particular, we shared a common interest in using technology to improve the quality of teaching, to increase access to learners, and to improve the cost-effectiveness of universities and colleges. We decided therefore to join forces, and look in an international context at the issue of managing technology for transforming teaching and learning, based on actual practices from different institutions.

THE PURPOSE OF THE BOOK

It is 20 years since the development of the World Wide Web and 15 years since the first uses of the Web for teaching and learning. In North America, over 90% of postsecondary institutions are using a learning management system such as Blackboard or Moodle. Over the same period, most postsecondary institutions have made massive (in a few cases, financially crippling) investments in administrative software systems for student, financial, and human resource services. In recent years, there has been an increasing move to Web-based student self-service, such as online admission and registration, payment of fees, and student portals, and to integration of services, through the use of enterprise resource planning systems (ERPs) and business intelligence. Information technologies are now a core resource for nearly all postsecondary educational institutions, not only for administrative purposes, but also to support teaching and learning.

Nor does the rate of technological change show any signs of abating. The emergence of Web 2.0 tools provide learners with as much control over the technology as the instructors. Cloud computing allows individual administrators and faculty to bypass centralized IT services, with implications for strategic priorities, network load, quality, security, and privacy.

However, evidence that will be reported in this book indicates that universities and colleges are still struggling to fully integrate information and communications technology (ICTs) within their activities. Particular issues are the lack of clear vision for the academy in a technologically rich environment, setting clear and measurable goals for IT investment and applications, the governance and management of information and communications technology within the academy, poor returns on ICT investment, educational program design, strategies for coping with the pace of technological change and development, security and privacy, and measurement of performance. This book will examine the causes of these difficulties, and will make concrete and practical recommendations to improve performance in all these areas.

WHO IS THE BOOK FOR?

This book is aimed first of all at senior academic university and college administrators, such as presidents, vice presidents, and deans. However, because of the critical role of faculty in university and college decision making, we also hope to reach a substantial number of professors and instructors. Their understanding of the issues, and their willingness to address them, will be critical if the changes needed to make institutions fit for the twenty-first century are to be implemented. We also hope that the book will be of particular value to government officials in ministries or departments of education, and to postgraduate education students studying or researching the role of technology in postsecondary education.

WHAT ISSUES DOES THE BOOK ADDRESS?

The book examines the rationales for the use of technology in universities and colleges. A major feature of the book is the relationship between the use of information and communications technologies for teaching and learning, and the needs of learners in a knowledge-based society. In particular, it focuses on how the planning and management of technology can be used to transform teaching and learning within the institution.

The book examines current practice in managing technology in postsecondary education, based on empirical studies of practice in over twenty universities worldwide, and in-depth study of 11 universities and colleges (six in Europe and five in North America). These studies identify a range of issues that inhibit the effective integration of technology in universities and colleges. The book also argues that to manage technology effectively, all instructors and senior administrators need professional development specifically directed at using technology for teaching and for the management of technology. This book provides some of the knowledge base for such training. It also examines the barriers to change and makes recommendations for overcoming these barriers.

Most important, the book argues that because the application of technology is now a core activity in teaching, research, and administration, institutions need to look at investment in technology from a strategic perspective. This means integrating technology planning as a major component of the overall vision and strategy for the academy.

WHAT'S IN THE BOOK?

First, because administrators like to cut to the chase, we provide a very brief executive summary of the main recommendations coming from the book. However, we strongly recommend that readers follow up on the reasons for these recommendations, and the evidence behind them, that are contained in the book, as some recommendations are strongly based on data, and others are more speculation on our part.

Most of the chapters start with a scenario of a particular individual—a student, faculty member, or administrator—facing a typical situation regarding the use of technology for teaching and learning. The characters and institutions in the scenarios are fictional, but provide concrete contexts for many of the issues covered in this book (not all necessarily discussed in the chapter where the scenario appears). Nor have we provided our own solutions or recommendations for the scenarios. We do not believe there are simple, "off-the shelf" solutions for many of the management decisions required to transform teaching and learning through technology. The scenarios then are mainly a heuristic device, to encourage analysis and discussion of the findings and recommendations in the book, and could be used to encourage participants in workshops or courses on educational management to find their own solutions or determine their own positions regarding the use of technology for teaching and learning.

Chapter One provides an analysis of the changes in society, and their impact on postsecondary educational institutions. There is a particular emphasis on the development of a knowledge-based society, and the skills and knowledge associated with this. Another related factor is the rapid growth of postsecondary education (massification), and the implications for teaching.

Chapter Two looks at developments in technology over the last twenty years that have relevance to the operations of universities and colleges. On the administrative side, the chapter discusses the impact of data-based services, technology integration, and the move to student and academic self-service. It also discusses the impact of the Web and the Internet on teaching and learning, such as blended, online, and mobile learning; the implications for student access; and the development of skills and competencies. It discusses particularly the development of Web 2.0 technologies, and their implications for teaching and learning. Then it discusses issues of security, privacy, and the potential impact of cloud computing.

Chapter Three describes how we collected data and analyzed it. This includes a review of relevant literature, an international survey of strategies for managing technology in 25 universities worldwide, 11 in-depth case studies, and the personal experience of the authors. We provide brief thumbnail sketches of each of the case study institutions' strategies for technology integration over a period of years. We also developed a set of questions that allowed us to rank the case studies in terms of the extent of technology integration.

Chapter Four examines leadership and strategic planning. How did the case study institutions do technology planning? What is the best way for leaders to work to support technology integration? How are goals and priorities set for the use of technology? Who should decide on what technologies are used for teaching? How useful is strategic planning?

Chapter Five looks at organizational structures and projects that were implemented in the case studies, including attempts to build administrative and teaching software systems in some institutions; the roles, mandate, structures, and effectiveness of technology committees; what permanent organizational units were established to support technology integration; and finally the need for a comprehensive governance structure for technology.

Chapter Six discusses quality assurance for technology-based teaching and looks at how the case study institutions went about this, and we discuss the effectiveness of quality assurance processes for technology-based teaching.

Chapter Seven takes a hard look at how technology is financed and the costs of technology-based learning. Because of a lack of information about the relative costs of different kinds of teaching in the institutions, and a concern over the unintended consequences of funding technology-based teaching, we recommend a methodology for tracking costs of different forms of technology-based and face-to-face teaching.

Chapter Eight seeks to explain why institutional strategies are generally so conservative regarding the goals for technology, and so slow in changing. It suggests that substantial change will not happen without much more extensive and comprehensive training of instructors and administrators. This chapter also suggests some roles for government in stimulating change.

Chapter Nine, the final chapter, pulls together the main conclusions and recommendations, and discusses the implications for institutions.

Although the focus of the book is the strategic management of information and communication technologies, it inevitably raises fundamental questions about the role of postsecondary educational institutions in the twenty-first century, the culture and management of institutions, and the implications for faculty and administrators of an increasingly technological environment. Above all, we argue that new visions for the organization and management of universities and colleges are needed, built around the potential of technology, if we are to properly serve the needs of society in the twenty-first century.

ACKNOWLEDGMENTS

It is hard to know where to begin, as so many people have contributed to this book. First we must thank the staff and senior administrators of the eleven case study institutions. Some may not be aware that their institutions were the subject of a case study for this book, because we have used already published secondary sources for some of the studies. Others were approached and allowed us completely open access and total cooperation. We have drawn heavily on the work and ideas of professional colleagues, administrators, faculty, and distance education/learning technology support staff, at the University of British Columbia and the Open University of Catalonia. Most of the good suggestions and recommendations have come from colleagues with whom we worked in several of the case study institutions. The bad suggestions are ours entirely.

Publishers have been generous in allowing us permission to quote from other works. We would like to thank Springer and IGI Global particularly for permission to reproduce material previously published in U-D. Ehlers and D. Schneckenberg (eds.) (2010) *Changing Cultures in Higher Education: Moving Ahead to Future Learning*, Heidelberg/London/New York: Springer; and M. Lee and C. McLoughlin (eds.) (2010) *Web 2.0-Based E-Learning: Applying Social Informatics for Tertiary Teaching*, Hershey, PA: IGI Global. The John D. and Catherine T. MacArthur Foundation kindly allowed us to adapt for the scenario at the start of Chapter Two the summary from the report by M. Ito et al. (2008) *Living and Learning with New Media: Summary of Findings from the Digital Youth Project*, Chicago, IL: The John D. and Catherine T. MacArthur Foundation.

We would also like to thank Andrew Higgins, Tom Prebble, and the New Zealand Centre for Tertiary Teaching Excellence for allowing us to use the full list of questions that administrators need to ask when making decisions about e-learning that Andrew and Tom developed from their research.

We drew heavily from a study by the U.S. State Higher Education Executive Officers and the American Center for Quality and Productivity on best practices in faculty development for teaching with technology, that also provided a host of data about other important elements for good management of learning technologies. Barbara Truman at the University of Central Florida, and Jeff Miller at UBC, provided the most recent statistics on their universities' use of technology.

Mercé Gisbert of Universitat Rovira i Virgili and Gabriel Ferraté of the Open University of Catalonia provided critical advice on research in general and specifically on the design and interpretation of the Spanish and Italian cases. Finally, we both owe profound thanks to our families, who have had to put up with distracted and inattentive writers for long periods.

We hope you find this book both stimulating and helpful.

March 2011   Tony Bates
                                                 Vancouver, BC, Canada

Executive Summary

This executive summary pulls together the main recommendations from the book and provides some of the context for these recommendations. However, it is also important to assess the evidence and reasoning behind these recommendations because their value will vary depending on the context of the reader, and this will require more detailed reading of the book.

Purpose of the Book

This book examines strategies and actions that support the integration of technology into the core activities of universities and colleges. In particular, it explores ways to transform teaching and learning through the use of technology.

Context for the Book

Technology is an essential component of any modern postsecondary educational institution, not only for supporting administrative activities, but also increasingly for the core activities of teaching and learning.

Although the core missions of universities and colleges are even more relevant today, radical change is needed in their organization and in their design and delivery of teaching, if they are to respond adequately to the challenges they are facing. The integration of technology and its use to transform teaching and learning are key strategies for such change.

Methodology

The book draws heavily on information collected from case studies of 11 public sector postsecondary educational institutions, six in southern Europe and five in North America, including seven campus-based universities, two community colleges, and two open universities. All the cases were chosen because of the stated intention of the senior administration in the institutions to make technology integration an important goal.

We examined a number of indicators of technology integration and, on this basis, we ranked the 11 case studies by the extent to which technology had been integrated within the organization. This enabled us to look for strategies and activities in the top-ranked institutions and compare them with the strategies and policies used in the lower-ranked institutions. We also compared strategies across the 11 institutions with our analysis of the challenges facing higher education institutions, and in the final chapter we make a number of recommendations for change in the institutional management of technology, to support a more radical transformation of teaching and learning to meet twenty-first-century needs.

MAIN FINDINGS AND RECOMMENDATIONS

INSTITUTIONAL PLANNING AND STRATEGY (CHAPTERS FOUR AND NINE)

In general, institutions were too cautious in their goals for technology. In particular, most seemed content to use technology to enhance traditional classroom teaching, rather than to use technology to transform the way teaching is designed and delivered. Using technology to enhance classroom teaching merely adds cost to the system, with no measurable learning benefits. Most of our case study institutions had no institutional plan for learning technologies. Institutions were not usually clear enough about the different goals for learning technologies. When defined, they were not usually stated in measurable terms.

Recommendations

1. Set "innovation in teaching" as a priority goal in the Academic Plan. Fund, evaluate, and reward it.
2. A high-level technology committee (see the Organizational Structures section) should be mandated to develop long-term goals and strategies for learning technologies. In addition to

supporting innovation in teaching, we suggest the following as possible long-term goals for learning technologies:

- Increasing flexible access for a more diverse student body
- Increasing interaction between instructors and students, and allowing for more individualization of learning
- Developing student skills in identifying, collecting, analyzing, and applying knowledge
- Teaching students how information technology can be used within a particular professional or subject domain
- Using technology to support the development of twenty-first-century skills of independent learning, initiative, communication, teamwork, adaptability, collaboration, networking, and thinking skills within a particular professional or subject domain
- Greater cost-effectiveness: more students at a higher quality and less cost through the use of technology

Institutions should track and measure their performance on such goals.

LEADERSHIP (CHAPTER FOUR)

Leadership is critical for technology integration, but rather than a strongly directive leadership from an individual, it needs to be of a style that facilitates a collective approach to the setting and implementation of goals. In particular, all members of the executive team need to be on the same page regarding the need for change in teaching, and the importance of technology for transforming teaching and learning. They also need to understand the financial implications when making this commitment. The key role for the executive team is to ensure that there is a comprehensive governance strategy in place for technology, which includes its use for teaching and learning.

Recommendations

3. All the executives should actively promote the importance of technology for transforming teaching and learning, through public announcements, the strategic plan, and personal example in decision making about resources.

4. The senior executive team should guide, facilitate, and be responsive to the wide range of technology decision makers within the organization.
5. The senior executive team should develop a clear, coherent, and comprehensive governance structure for technology decision making and policies. The design and maintenance of this governance structure should be a direct responsibility of the senior executive team. (For more detail, see Chapter Nine.)

Planning at the Program Level (Chapters Four and Nine)

Generally, there was a lack of imagination on the part of both instructors and administrators about the potential of technology for teaching and learning. A critical area for developing vision for the use of technology is at the academic program planning stage, when programs are being planned or renewed following review. Choice and use of technology is best made at the program planning level. This means integrating decisions about technology with other academic decisions, such as content, method of teaching, and how the program will be delivered (the mix of face-to-face, hybrid, and distance learning).

Recommendation

6. There should be in place an annual program planning process that is integrated with the allocation of resources and financial plan. As part of this process, program proposals should contain a clear vision of how the program will be designed and delivered, including the use of technology.

Organizational Structures (Chapter Five)

Organizational structures to support the use of learning technologies have evolved over time in a somewhat ad hoc way in many institutions. The main development has been the growth of learning technology support units, either central or located within large faculties, with professional staff to support the design and delivery of technology-based teaching and learning. These units are increasingly being integrated with faculty development and distance education activities and units.

A single technology project (such as the development or adaptation of software for teaching) was sometimes the main strategy for learning technologies in some of the case study institutions. Technology projects work best when they are part of a more general strategy for technology implementation that includes training of instructors, and a focus on teaching and learning. In our case studies, these single technology projects were not successful in bringing about sustainable e-learning.

Technology for teaching and learning is now used throughout the institution. This has led to a range of committees and decision-making bodies for the management of learning technologies, but rarely in a comprehensive or coordinated way. Because of the dynamic nature of technology, a governance structure needs to be designed that enables decisions about technology to be made on an ongoing basis. The structure should ensure that the right decisions are made by the right people at the right level.

Recommendations

7. The senior executive should put in place a comprehensive committee structure to support technology integration, and give the committees power to establish priorities and policies for technology integration. In particular, a high-level technology committee should be established with a mandate to set strategic goals and strategies for technology (including learning technologies), allocate resources, approve projects, and evaluate the effectiveness of technology strategies. (See Chapter Nine for more details.)

8. Institutions should create a unit combining faculty development, learning technology support, and distance education management, under a single director reporting to the VP of academic affairs, with an annual service contract to locate specialist staff in academic departments based on their annual academic plans. (The establishment and management of units located within large faculties may be more decentralized in very large research universities.)

QUALITY ASSURANCE AND EVALUATION (CHAPTER SIX)

Quality assurance methods are valuable for accreditation agencies concerned about institutions using e-learning to cut corners or reduce costs without maintaining standards. They can be useful for providing instructors new to teaching with technology, or struggling with its use, with models of best practice to follow.

However, the best guarantees of quality in e-learning are a commitment by the leadership to supporting innovation in teaching, instructors well trained in both pedagogy and the use of technology for teaching, highly qualified and professional learning technology support staff, adequate resources (especially regarding instructor-student ratios), appropriate methods of working (teamwork, project management), and systematic evaluation. Generally, the same standards that apply to online learning should also apply to face-to-face teaching.

Recommendation

9. Use standard methods of program approval, review, and evaluation, slightly adapted for the special circumstances of online learning. Ensure that learner support is provided in suitable ways for off-campus students. Use a team approach, with instructional designers and Web support staff, and best practice in online course design, for hybrid and distance courses. Ensure that the course design is adapted to meet the needs of off-campus learners. Begin applying some of these techniques to the redesign of large face-to-face classes.

Financial Management (Chapter Seven)

Because technology has mainly been added to conventional face-to-face teaching rather than replacing activities or generating new revenues, because new categories of staff have been hired to support learning technologies, and because instructors have not been comprehensively trained in using technologies for teaching and are therefore spending more time on teaching, costs have almost certainly increased substantially. No institution had a handle on the true costs of teaching with technology. One problem is that postsecondary institutions do not usually track the costs of activities, such as programs. Activity-based costing is essential to understand the true costs of learning technologies. Another way to control costs is to set standard workloads for instructors that apply to all forms of teaching.

Recommendations

10. The design of teaching needs to be changed to control costs and obtain the benefits when technology is introduced; merely adding technology on to old processes will not produce the desired benefits.
11. Traditional department-based financial reporting systems need to be combined with activity-based costing methods to enable the costs of different teaching models to be accurately analyzed. Details are provided in Chapter Seven.

ORGANIZATIONAL CULTURE AND BARRIERS TO CHANGE (CHAPTER EIGHT)

Senior administrators are often aware of the need to change, and would like to introduce some of the recommendations we are making, but are constrained by the barriers of organizational culture, and, in particular, by faculty's strongly held beliefs about traditional teaching methods, the privileging of research over teaching, and the mistrust of formal training in teaching. These barriers will not easily be overcome by short-term financial incentives, and may need strong external pressure, as well as strong internal leadership.

Nevertheless, formal training in modern teaching methods is an essential requirement for the effective use of technology in teaching, as well as for ensuring the development of the kind of graduates needed in the twenty-first century.

Also, senior academic administrators rarely have any formal training in the management issues around technology decision making, and indeed sometimes have little familiarity with the technology itself.

Recommendations

12. All instructors who have regular teaching commitments should receive comprehensive training in teaching at a post-secondary level before appointment (even or especially in research universities), and continuous professional development that includes regular learning activities around new developments in teaching and technology.

13. All middle and senior managers and administrators should be provided with an individually adapted orientation program about technology issues and technology expertise available in the institution that could assist them with technology decisions within their area of responsibility.
14. Institutions need to find stronger incentives to encourage instructors to innovate in teaching, otherwise the investment in technology will be wasted.

ROLES FOR GOVERNMENT (CHAPTER NINE)

In general, we support a hands-off approach by government in postsecondary education, but there are some key roles for government that could immensely help the introduction of necessary changes that will support the effective use of technology for teaching in postsecondary education.

Recommendations

15. In consultation with institutions and other key stakeholders, governments should develop a strategic plan setting priorities and strategies for information and communications technologies for their postsecondary education system.
16. Governments should use funding to drive innovation in teaching and the use of technology within their postsecondary education systems. In particular, they should require all instructors with regular teaching loads to be qualified through a government-approved postsecondary teacher training program.
17. Governments should create new postsecondary institutions based on hybrid delivery models with a footprint centered on but wider than the local community, with a focus on the development and support of local high-tech industries.

CONCLUSION

This is a very brief summary of the book. Each chapter provides a full discussion of the findings from our case studies, a discussion of the issues, and detailed recommendations.

CHAPTER ONE

THE CHALLENGE OF CHANGE

Today, everyone, if they are to have a job, needs the kind of higher order thinking skills that only those in managerial or professional positions formerly needed. We can only achieve this through major structural reform of our education system.
—JANE GILBERT, 2005, P. 67

Meet Samantha, a Twenty-First-Century Student

Samantha is 25 years old, with a one-year-old baby, and lives with her boyfriend, Shaun, who works as a trainer in a fitness center. She works part-time at a local day care center. She has an old Honda Civic, a "smart" mobile phone, and her own laptop computer with broadband Internet access. She regularly uses Twitter, Skype, Google Search, Google Mail, Facebook, Flickr, iTunes, and YouTube, as well as standard PC software such as Word and Excel.

Material in this chapter first appeared in Ehlers, U-D., and Schneckenberg, D. (eds.) (2010) *Changing cultures in higher education: Moving ahead to future learning.* Heidelberg/London/New York: Springer. Reproduced with permission of the publisher.

She is taking the fourth year of a bachelor of commerce degre[e] from her local college, which is a 35- to 45-minute drive from h[er] home. This is her fifth year in the program. She was unable [to] complete all her courses in her third and fourth years, because her classes often clashed with her day-care hours, and she kept getting behind with her studies. She is taking almost all her classes on campus, but she managed to find one course in her program that was offered online, which she is enjoying.

In her first year, there were around a hundred students in most of her classes, but this year there are about thirty per class. The college prides itself on its high-technology classrooms, with Smartboards, wireless access, clickers, and three screens in most classrooms. Some of her instructors have started to record their lectures, so she can download them, but others refuse to do so, because if they do, they fear students won't come to the classes (and she agrees with them).

Samantha often uses Facebook to discuss her courses with friends who are in the same class, but most of the instructors don't use anything more than e-mail outside class for communication with students, although one of her instructors has organized online discussion forums. On the whole, she likes being on campus, especially meeting the other students, but the lectures are often boring, so she sometimes joins in the class Tweets about the instructors while they are lecturing, which she finds amusing, if distracting.

She worries about the stress her studies are causing in her relationship with Shaun. She is always studying, driving, working, or looking after the baby. She particularly resents the eight hours a week she spends driving to and from the college, which she would rather spend studying. Shaun has a friend who has moved out of state who wants Shaun to join him as a partner in running a fitness center, but this would mean giving up her studies at her local college, and she doesn't want to do that, as she may have problems getting credit for her courses at a college in another state. The thought of having to start her studies all over again fills her with dread. If that happens, she will enroll with either the University of Phoenix Online, or another of the fully online for-profit universities. They seem to understand her needs better than her local college.

This student is unique, but nor is she atypical of today's students, the majority of whom are 24 or older, working at least part-time, and commuting on a regular basis to college. With new course designs and the proper use of technology, we could do much better for students like Samantha.

CREATING HIGHER EDUCATION INSTITUTIONS FIT FOR THE TWENTY-FIRST CENTURY

Universities are resilient. The concept of the university has remained largely unchanged for over 800 years. Universities have always had to balance an uneasy tension between cloistered independence and relevance to society at large, but they have successfully thrown off or resisted control by church, princes, state, and commerce to remain on the whole fully autonomous, at least in Western society. In eight centuries, they have undergone massive expansion, the introduction of fundamentally new areas of scholarship, and radical restructuring, while protecting their core mission. As a result, universities appear to be more strongly established today and certainly more numerous than at any other time in history. Yet often when institutions appear to be all-powerful, they can be extremely vulnerable to changes in the external environment.

Indeed, today universities and colleges are facing strong pressures for further change. For cultural and historical reasons change is likely to be slow, at least for most public institutions. Nevertheless, economic development has been and will continue to be strongly linked to the ability of education systems to adapt to the demands of a knowledge-based society. Thus those postsecondary educational institutions that do change appropriately are likely to gain a strong competitive advantage, both for themselves and for the societies in which they operate. In other words, we need strong universities and colleges that are adapted to the needs of the twenty-first century.

UNIVERSITIES: FAILING IN TECHNOLOGY

Technology is a key factor for bringing about such relevant and necessary change in higher education institutions, but we will produce evidence that suggests universities and colleges still don't really "get it" as far as technology is concerned. In particular, universities and colleges in general are underexploiting the potential of technology to change the way that teaching and learning could be designed and delivered, so as to increase flexible access to learning, improve quality, and control or reduce costs, all core challenges faced by higher education institutions today.

Although managing technology in a way that leads to the transformation of teaching and learning is the primary focus of this book, any discussion of information and communications technologies must be placed within the overall context of the role and mission of postsecondary educational institutions. We start then by examining the issues and challenges facing universities and colleges today, and suggest that although their core mission and values should remain largely unchanged, radical change is needed in their organization and in particular in the design and delivery of their teaching, if they are to be "fit for purpose" for the twenty-first century.

We will also argue that information and communications technologies have a crucial role to play in such changes, but for technology to be used fully and effectively, major changes are needed in the prevailing culture of the academy and the way in which it is managed. The aim of this book, therefore, is to examine how best to manage information and communications technologies, so that universities and colleges can appropriately address their main challenges and goals, can provide the kind of teaching and learning needed in the twenty-first century, and thus better serve students like Samantha.

UNIVERSITIES AND COLLEGES IN AN INDUSTRIAL SOCIETY

The organization and structure of the modern university began to form in the mid- to late-nineteenth century. The forces leading to these changes were complex and interrelated. The growth of the nation state and the extension of empire required a large increase in government bureaucrats, who tended to be taught the classics (philosophy, history, Greek, and Latin). The rise of science, and the recognition of its importance for economic development through the Industrial Revolution, was another factor. Thomas Huxley in Britain and Wilhelm von Humboldt in Germany were two key figures who promoted the growth of science and engineering in the university. Indeed, Huxley had to start his own program for teaching biology at the Royal School of Mines— which later became Imperial College—because neither Oxford nor Cambridge University was willing to teach scientific biology at the time (Desmond, 1997).

Consequently the number of universities and colleges in Europe and North America expanded considerably toward the end of the nineteenth century. The land-grant universities in the United States in particular were developed to support agricultural expansion, and "red brick" universities were opened in the industrial cities of Britain to meet the increasing demand for engineers and scientists for local industries. Despite this expansion, though, entrance to university in many countries was limited largely to a small, elite minority of upper-class or rich middle-class students. As late as 1969, less than 8% of 18-years-olds (children born in 1951) were admitted to university in Britain (Perry, 1976).

As a result, teaching methods in particular were suited to what today would be considered small classes, even at the undergraduate level, with seminar classes of 20 or less and smaller group tutorials of three or four students with a senior research professor for students in their last year of an undergraduate program. This remains today the ideal paradigm of university teaching for many professors and instructors.

In the United States and Canada, the move to a mass system of higher education began earlier, following the Second World War, when returning servicemen were given scholarships to attend university, and for the last half of the twentieth century, access to university and colleges was expanded rapidly. For a mix of social and economic reasons, from the 1960s onwards, governments in Europe also started again to rapidly expand the number of university places, so that by the end of the century, in many Western countries more than half the 19-year-old cohort are now admitted to some form of postsecondary education. The figure for Canada in 2004 was 52% (Statistics Canada, 2009), and currently there are over 18 million students in postsecondary education in the United States (U.S. Census Bureau, 2009).

This represents a massive increase in numbers, and not surprisingly, governments, although spending ever more each year on postsecondary education, have not been able or willing to fund the staffing of universities and colleges at a level that would maintain the low class sizes common when access was limited. Thus in many North American universities, there are first- and second-year undergraduate courses with more than 1,000 students, taught mainly in large lecture classes, often by nontenured instructors or even graduate students. However, at the same time, completion rates (that is, the proportion of students who enter a degree program who go on to complete the degree program within six years) in undergraduate four-year degree programs remain below 60% in the United States for many public universities (Bowen, Chingus, & McPherson, 2009). In other words, universities are failing a significant number of students each year.

The widening of access has resulted in a much more diverse student population. The biggest change is in the number of older and part-time students (including students who are technically classified as full-time, but who are in fact also holding down part-time jobs to pay for tuition and other costs, like Samantha). The mean age of students in North American postsecondary education institutions now stands at 24 years old, but the spread of ages is much wider, with many students taking longer than the minimum time to graduate, or returning to study after graduation for further qualifications. Many are married with young families. For such students, academic study is a relatively small component of an extremely busy lifestyle.

By definition, many of the students who now attend university or college are not in the top 10% of academic achievers, and therefore are likely to need more support and assistance with learning. With the growth of international students, and increased immigration, there are now wider differences in language and culture, which also influence the context of teaching and learning. Yet the modes of teaching have changed little to accommodate these massive changes in the nature of the student body, with lectures, wet labs, and pen and paper examinations being the norm rather than the exception.

Finally, in most economically advanced countries, the unit costs of higher education have steadily increased year after year, without any sign of abating. Between 1995 and 2005, average tuition and fees rose 51% at public four-year institutions and 30% at community colleges in the United States (The College Board, 2005; Johnson, 2009). The average cost per student per year in tertiary education (excluding R&D costs) in the United States in 2006 was just over $22,000 per student, compared with an average of $7,500 per student for European countries (OECD, 2009, p. 202). Thus although there are now many more postsecondary students, the average cost per student continues to increase, putting excessive pressure on government funding, tuition fees, and hence costs to parents and students. More disturbingly, these increases in overall costs have not been matched by similar proportions of spending on direct teaching and learning activities (such as increasing the number of faculty). Most of the increased expenditure has gone into other areas, such as administration, fund raising, and campus facilities (Wellman, Desrochers, Lenihan, Kirshstein, Hurlburt, & Honegger, 2009). Thus postsecondary education has become larger, more costly, but less efficient.

Despite these challenges, modern universities and colleges still have many features of industrial organizations (Carlton & Perloff, 2000; Gilbert, 2005). Classes are organized at scheduled times in a fixed location on the assumption of full-time attendance. Students receive (at least within the same course) a standard or common product, regarding the curriculum (same lectures, same reading lists, and so on, for each student in the course). The institution is divided into departmental silos, with a hierarchical management structure. The Spellings Commission in the United States (U.S. Department of Education, 2006) even pushed (unsuccessfully) for standardized measurements of output, to allow comparison in performance between institutions, reflecting a classic industrial mentality of standardized products.

THE GROWTH OF THE KNOWLEDGE-BASED ECONOMY

It is debatable whether the expansion of postsecondary education led to the growth of a knowledge-based economy or vice versa, but the two are inextricably linked. Peter Drucker (1969) is credited with coining the term "knowledge-based economy." He made the simple but powerful distinction between people who work with their hands and those who work with their heads. Typical knowledge-based occupations can be found in biotechnology, telecommunications, banking and insurance, computing and electronics, health, entertainment, and education. These enterprises depend heavily on information and communications technologies for the creation, storage, transmission, analysis, and application of information in ways that create knowledge.

Labor is a major cost in industrial organizations. Cheaper labor means lower costs and hence competitive prices. In a globalized market, factories move to the lowest cost labor market. Thus we have seen to a large extent the deindustrialization of former industrial economies. (The shift is not quite that simple. Manufacturing remains important in advanced economies, but manufacturing itself is becoming increasingly dependent on innovation and knowledge-based components. For instance, Volkswagen estimates that over 70% of the cost of their cars comes from research, design, digital technology, and marketing, all knowledge-based activities. As a result, manufacturing in advanced economies is becoming increasingly focused on high-end manufacturing with a strong knowledge-based component.)

It is probably no coincidence however that as the numbers of graduates from universities and colleges increased year by year, so did the expansion of the knowledge-based economy, thus balancing to some extent the jobs lost in the industrial sector. Knowledge-based jobs of course require large numbers of people with higher levels of education, and this to some extent compensates more economically advanced economies for their lost of industrial jobs. Knowledge-based work is generally classified as service industries. The Canadian Services Coalition and the Canadian Chambers of Commerce (2006, p. 3) report:

> The amount of employment represented by the services sector as a percentage of total employment, in comparison to the agriculture and industry sectors, has been steadily increasing over the last 25 years. In fact, according to Statistics Canada, 80 percent of all new jobs within Canada between 1992 and 2005 were in the services industry.

Similar data would apply to other economically advanced countries, but on a different time scale; whereas the crossover between people employed in service industries surpassed those employed in manufacturing in Canada in 1991, this crossover occurred in Britain, the heartland of industrialization, in 2007 (Financial Times, 2009). (Note that services include both high-paid knowledge-based work and low-paid unskilled work.) Thus, to maintain the high living standards of economically advanced countries, it is essential to develop knowledge-based industries, and the large proportion of the population receiving postsecondary education helps to feed and stimulate that market.

Skills and Competencies in a Knowledge-Based Economy

Industrially based businesses revolve around the manufacturing and distribution of goods. Because of the benefits of economies of scale in manufacturing—the same product using the same manufacturing process operating on a very large scale to offset the high capital costs of a production line—goods are produced in large factories, with relatively unskilled manual workers organized around a strict division of labor, with separate, narrowly defined jobs and even different unions for each step in the industrial process. Management of course is hierarchical, with owners, managers, supervisors, and workers.

Knowledge-based businesses operate very differently. They are often small—two or three people, sometimes recent graduates who start their own company—and even when they grow large, such as Microsoft, Apple, or Google, they employ far fewer workers than the large industrially based companies. The majority of knowledge-based companies employ less than 100 people, so the spread of work is much flatter. In such companies, workers have to be multiskilled. A typical worker in a small computer software company has to be an entrepreneurial manager, an accountant, a software specialist, and a marketer.

Because knowledge-based companies do not need direct access to raw materials, they can be located wherever there are good Internet services. However, because of their need to access highly qualified workers, such companies are often found in clusters around universities. Nevertheless, knowledge-based companies are often virtual in that they work primarily over the Internet. Small companies tend to build networks and partnerships with other companies that can provide added-value services, allowing a small company to focus on its core business, such as a software product. Workers in knowledge-based industries need to continue to learn throughout life, to keep up to date in their fields and indeed to develop new knowledge that can be applied to their work.

The skills and competencies in knowledge-based companies have been clearly identified (see, for example, Conference Board of Canada, 1991; The Partnership for 21st Century Skills, 2009). Workers in such industries are expected to have the following:

- Good communication skills (reading, writing, speaking, listening)
- Ability to learn independently
- Social skills (ethics, positive attitudes, responsibility)
- Teamwork
- Ability to adapt to changing circumstances
- Thinking skills (problem solving; critical, logical, and numerical thinking)
- Knowledge navigation (where to get information and how to process it)

In particular, knowledge-based workers need to be entrepreneurial, not necessarily in the sense of being skilled at making money, but in seeing an opportunity, and doing what is necessary to make it happen. Knowledge-based companies depend on innovation—creating, modifying, and improving products and services—rather than reproducing the same product all the time, as in an industrial organization. Thus knowledge-based workers need to be creative and risk takers.

Most universities would claim to develop thinking skills such as problem solving and critical thinking (the basis for training mandarins in the civil service, for instance), but these are not generic skills: they need to be embedded within the professional discipline, because problem solving in business is different from problem solving in medicine. Not only does the content base differ between medicine and business, but so too does the approach to problem solving. We shall see that the need to embed skills within a subject domain applies also to information and communications technology skills.

RATIONALES FOR THE USE OF INFORMATION AND COMMUNICATION TECHNOLOGIES IN TEACHING AND LEARNING

Most people understand the importance and influence of information and communications technologies in modern society. Information and communications technologies can be thought of as the raw materials of a knowledge-based economy, in that they provide the means for creating, storing, analyzing, transferring, reproducing, and transforming information.

However, it would be a mistake to see information and communications technologies merely as modern tools for preserving and reproducing knowledge, as if knowledge is somehow separate from or independent of the technology. The technology of the mass-produced, printed book led to great changes in society, economics, and the development and dissemination of new knowledge. The new information and communications technologies are having a similar effect. For this reason, then, we need to examine carefully the reasons or rationale for the use of information and communications technologies for teaching and learning (or e-learning, as it is often called, for the sake of brevity).

1. ENHANCING THE QUALITY OF TEACHING AND LEARNING

The choice of wording here is deliberate. One of the authors was working at one institution on a committee trying to set down the key goals or the rationale for their use of e-learning. A colleague suggested: "to improve the quality of teaching." This was rejected by other members of the committee, who argued that the quality of the teaching was already excellent—technology would enhance it, but not improve it.

It is difficult to find good data on the extent to which technology is being used to enhance the quality of teaching and learning.

However, survey evidence by the Sloan Consortium (Allen & Seaman, 2006, 2008) and anecdotal evidence from learning management system (LMS) managers and data extracted from learning management systems suggest that enhancing classroom teaching is still the major form of e-learning in postsecondary education.

The big question that needs to be asked though is whether the quality of teaching in our postsecondary institutions is already of high quality and thus merely needs to be enhanced with technology (the icing on the cake), or is there major room for improvement in how we teach?

Can the high investment in technology be justified if it is merely added on as an enhancement to what is already being done? For instance, in many large research universities, lecture theaters or even small seminar rooms now have at least three screens—one on each side at the front of the room, and one in the middle at the back so the lecturer can see what students are seeing. Certainly this enables everyone in the room to see what is going on, but nothing else changes. The teaching goals are the same, the student-teacher ratio is unaffected, and is there any suggestion that students will learn more because of this? Lecture capture—the video recording of a lecture, stored on a server for later downloading by students—is another example. Can the investment of $6,000 per classroom be justified in terms of better learning? If not, cost is being added without any measurable benefits.

Universities and colleges generally follow a form of teaching that is largely historical in origin, and which has not accommodated well to the major shift that has occurred as a result of opening up access to postsecondary education. It has accommodated even less well to the opportunities (or affordances) that new technology offers. Using technology to enhance the quality of teaching is just accommodating technology to the old ways of doing things. We are adding quadraphonic sound and a GPS system to a horse and cart, but it's still a horse and cart. We believe new models for teaching and learning are needed that build on the strengths and opportunities that technology provides, and, incidentally, also build on the tremendous research advances made over the last 60 years in understanding how students learn, and how best to teach (Christensen Hughes & Mighty, 2010).

Thus, using technology to enhance the quality of learning merely increases costs without any measurable benefits. It does not address the need to change a teaching model that poorly serves mass higher education. It does not make the best use of technology. It may be a necessary first step to engage faculty in the use of technology for teaching. Nevertheless, we shall see that using technology this way does not usually lead to more fundamental changes.

2. ACCOMMODATING TO THE LEARNING STYLE OF MILLENNIALS

One of the goals sometimes claimed for e-learning is that it accommodates better to the learning styles or needs of Millennial students, or put another way, these students will learn better through e-learning because it fits their experience and ways of behaving.

Who are the "Millennials"? This is a term used for those born between the mid-1970s to early 1990s inclusive. Other terms for people born in these years are Generation Y, the Net Generation, or Digital Natives. The term describes learners who have grown up with technology such as computers and the Internet all through their life. They are assumed to be technology-savvy, are able to multitask, have developed specific skills such as video game playing, and are sometimes described as having a sense of entitlement ("it's all about me")—after all, they are the children of the Baby Boomers (Alsop, 2008).

More specifically, with regard to higher education, Oblinger and Oblinger (2005a) identify the following characteristics as being typical for Millennials:

- Digitally literate in the sense of being comfortable and familiar with digital technology
- Connected to friends and the world through technology
- Immediacy: rapid multitasking, fast response to communications
- Experiential: they prefer to learn by doing rather than being told
- Highly social: "they gravitate toward activities that promote and reinforce social interaction"

- Group work: they prefer to work and play in groups or teams
- A preference for structure rather than ambiguity
- Engagement and interaction: an orientation toward action and inductive reasoning rather than reflection
- A preference for visual (that is, graphics, video) and kinesthetic learning rather than learning through text
- Active engagement in issues that matter to Millennials

Writers such as Prensky (2001) and Oblinger and Oblinger (2005b) argue that education needs to be adapted to meet the needs of these learners. Millennials need to be actively engaged, need to be motivated and interested to learn, and above all need to be immersed in a technological environment for learning.

Bullen, Morgan, Belfer, and Qayyum (2009) challenge these findings:

> A review of literature on the millennial learner and implications for education reveals that most of the claims are supported by reference to a relatively small number of publications. . . . What all of these works have in common is that they make grand claims about the difference between the millennial generation and all previous generations and they argue that this difference has huge implications for education. But most significantly, these claims are made with reference to almost no empirical data. For the most part, they rely on anecdotal observations or speculation. In the rare cases, where there is hard data, it is usually not representative.

Bullen and his colleagues are right to draw attention to the source of such claims. Going back to the original research is always a good idea, and often on this topic the empirical database is very weak, with small samples and often with samples skewed toward high users of technology. However, it is also important to look at what exactly is being claimed. For instance, Oblinger and Oblinger (2005b) comment:

> Although these trends are described in generational terms, age may be less important than exposure to technology. For example, individuals who are heavy users of IT tend to have characteristics similar to the Net Gen.

In another paper in the same publication, Hartman, Moskal, and Dziuban (2005) report on a survey of students at the University of Central Florida. The University of Central Florida (UCF) regularly conducts formative and summative surveys of students' online learning experiences (UCF has a high proportion of blended and fully online courses). In the 2004 survey there were 1,489 online student responses, representing a return rate of approximately 30%. They found for a start that there was "substantial age diversity in the distributed learning population in metropolitan universities" (Hartman, Moskal, & Dziuban, 2005). Over half the students (55%) were in fact Generation X students, and almost as many students were Boomers (22%) as Millennials (Net Gens) (23%). Over five years the proportion of Millennials will have increased, but in most institutions they are likely to remain a minority of students, because of the increasing number of older students returning to postsecondary education. However, these older students will in most cases also have had an increased level of exposure to technology than their predecessors.

Another finding from the Hartman, Moskal, and Dziuban paper is that Millennials indicated less engagement with online learning than their older counterparts. Although this may be counter to the argument that Millennials are more comfortable with technology and therefore need technology-based teaching, it is consistent with the finding that older or more mature students do better at online and distance learning.

There are really three separate issues here. Are Millennial learners distinctly different from other students currently in college? Millennial students exist, of course, as they are defined by age. However, Millennials are not a majority of students in many postsecondary educational institutions and there is evidence to suggest that exposure to technology is equally as important as age in determining the learner characteristics described by Oblinger and Oblinger. So one should not put too much emphasis on date of birth as a determining characteristic of today's learner. Also, there is a danger in stereotyping. Not all Millennials behave the same way or have a total immersion in technology.

Are students in college today different from students in college 25 years ago? Despite the lack of rigor of the claims for Millennial learners, it would be surprising if current students are the same as students 25 years ago, given the exposure of all students to technology over the last 25 years. Thus the characteristics described by Oblinger and Oblinger are likely to apply to many students today. However, there are also other differences that are even more important educationally, such as a much greater proportion of students today being older, studying part-time, and requiring more flexible access to learning.

If students are different, what should instructors do? This is a much more difficult question to answer. Although there is some merit in the argument that students entering postsecondary education now are qualitatively different from previous generations of students—some commentators go so far as to argue that their brains are "wired" differently—one needs to be careful in interpreting this argument in education. Research has shown that skills developed in one context (for example, problem solving in video games) do not necessarily transfer to other contexts (for example, problem solving in business). In particular, students' use of the Internet for social and personal purposes does not necessarily prepare them adequately for academic applications of the Internet, such as searching for reliable sources of information (CIBER, 2008). Finally, there are some inherent requirements in education—such as a disciplined approach to study, critical thinking, evidence-based argumentation, for example—that cannot or should not be abandoned because they do not fit a particular student's preferred learning style.

Nevertheless, instructors should take into account the needs of all the learners they are dealing with. Young people see technology much the same way they see air and water—part of everyday life. It is natural then that they will see technology as a normal component of teaching and learning. Full-time Millennial students on campus have frequently reported that they do not expect technology to replace face-to-face contact with their teacher, and that they expect teachers to help them to know how best to use technology for learning (JISC, 2009). There is not an automatic transfer of technology skills from social and personal use to academic use, and most students are aware of this. The important issue here is that instructors need to understand how technology can be appropriately used for studying, and need to ensure that teaching makes the best use of technology possible. Some students will need more help than others in their use of technology for learning, but all students will need to learn how to integrate technology successfully within their subject discipline.

Finally, Prensky (2001) and others argue that teachers need to change their strategies, because Millennials are used to being stimulated and engaged outside school, and therefore need to be engaged inside school. This may be true, but why is it special to Millennials? Should not all our students be engaged and challenged, stimulated by learning, and find the joy and excitement of discovery? Intelligent use of technology can help, certainly, but it is not sufficient on its own; it needs to be harnessed to effective teaching strategies, such as collaborative learning, problem- and project-based teaching, and enabling students to take responsibility for their own learning. This should apply to all students, not just the Millennials.

However, with respect to using technology to engage students, there is continuing evidence that students think instructors are not doing well. For instance, a recent report (CDW-G, 2009) found that

- Students rate faculty lack of tech knowledge as the biggest obstacle to classroom technology integration and see it as a growing problem.
- Just 32% of students and 22% of faculty strongly agree that their college/university is preparing students to successfully use technology when they enter the workforce.

Thus we are not failing just Millennials; we are failing *all* our students if we do not use technology to its full potential.

3. TO INCREASE ACCESS TO LEARNING OPPORTUNITIES AND TO INCREASE FLEXIBILITY FOR STUDENTS

There are several aspects to using technology to increase access and flexibility. There is reasonably good data (at least from the United States) on the use of technology for fully online learning. Systematic, large-scale surveys conducted by the Sloan Consortium (Allen & Seaman, 2006, 2008), and by the Instructional Technology

Council (2008) indicate that growth in enrollments in fully online learning in postsecondary institutions in North America has been averaging approximately 12–14% per annum over the last five years, compared with 2–5% for enrollments in solely campus-based teaching.

The bulk of this growth has come from conventional, public campus-based institutions moving a proportion of their courses and programs to fully online delivery, often as an option to the regular campus-based courses. Many two-year colleges in the United States for instance now require campus-based students to take at least one fully online course. Cerro Coso Community College, a traditionally campus-based two-year college in California, now has more than 50% of its enrollments in distance courses (Jaschik, 2009). As a spokesperson for the college said, "The students are voting with their mice." Thus fully online courses have demonstrated that even conventional, campus-based students appreciate the flexibility and access that fully online teaching provides, though these students still take most of their program through conventional campus-based teaching. The private, for-profit sector, represented by the University of Phoenix Online, Kaplan University, Nova South Eastern University, Full Sail University, and several others in the United States that offer all their programs online, is expanding even faster than the public sector, with 32% of the online market in 2009 (Garrett, 2009).

However, there is still probably unmet demand for even more online programs (*eSchool News*, 2009). There is evidence that the trend toward more online learning will intensify over the next five years. For instance, Ambient Insight Research (2009) suggests that by 2014, 20% of all students in postsecondary education in the United States will take all their studies online (compared to 5% in 2009), and 70% of students in postsecondary education in the United States will take some of their classes online (compared to 40% in 2009). Only 20% will take all of their courses in a physical classroom in 2014, compared to 45% in 2009.

The growth is likely to come particularly from lifelong learners, those who have already graduated and are now in the workforce, but returning for more courses and programs. Indeed, with aging populations and the need for continuous learning in knowledge-based jobs, lifelong learners could soon become the majority in formal postsecondary education, exceeding the numbers coming from high schools, in many economically advanced countries.

Unfortunately the focus of many public universities is not on lifelong learners. The focus is still on getting the best students from high school and moving them into graduate studies to become researchers. Lifelong learners are often seen as "extra" students in an already overloaded system. Universities and, more so, colleges are responding to the lifelong learning market, but not aggressively enough. The lifelong learning market may need new business models that enable tenured faculty to be hired from the revenues generated by full-cost tuition fees for professionally oriented online graduate programs, but if public universities continue to ignore the lifelong learning market, their loss of direct revenue from tuition fees, and loss of public support for failing to meet demand from what is increasingly now their major market, will be damaging.

In conclusion, there is strong evidence that e-learning has been successful in increasing flexibility and thus making postsecondary education more accessible. Enrollments in online courses are increasing far more rapidly than enrollments in campus-based courses, and there are indications that demand for online learning far exceeds the supply, at least in North America. There is also evidence that the trend toward more online learning will intensify over the next five years.

The reason for this has as much to do with the changing nature of the student demographic in North America as it has to do with the greater effectiveness of online learning (although there is some evidence for this as well—see Means, Toyama, Murphy, & Bakia, 2009). Because of increases in tuition fees (inevitable given the increased access to higher education and reluctance to increase taxes to pay for it), more and more students are like Samantha, working at least part-time to pay for their initial undergraduate and graduate education. Furthermore, because of the demands of knowledge-based occupations such as health, telecommunications, and computer software engineering, there is increasing demand from lifelong learners to return for postgraduate studies and continuing education that leads to further qualifications. Thus, students are increasingly combining work, family, and study. Online learning clearly provides the flexibility that such students need.

4. TO DEVELOP THE SKILLS AND COMPETENCIES NEEDED IN THE TWENTY-FIRST CENTURY

Several commentators have discussed the difference between learning outcomes suitable for industrial and knowledge-based societies (see for instance, Gilbert, 2005; Conference Board of Canada, 1991). Indeed, in the United States, the Partnership for Twenty-First Century Skills (2009) is an organization set up to promote the development of such skills, which were outlined earlier in this chapter.

These skills can be classified as being "process-oriented" rather than "subject-oriented." However, it would be a mistake to see these skills as being independent of the subject or topic domains in which they need to be used. Skills need to be embedded within a subject or knowledge domain. Thus there are implications for setting learning goals (what is to be learned), curricula (what is to be taught), teaching methodology (how it is taught or learned), and assessment (what is to be examined or assessed). Each of these areas must be adequately addressed, if learning goals for a knowledge-based society are to be achieved.

Where does e-learning fit into this? One of the core competencies now required in nearly all subject domains, and more specifically in different occupations and professions, is embedded digital literacy. This is the ability to use information and communications technologies in ways that are specific to a particular knowledge or occupational domain.

Because digital technology is now so pervasive, all areas of human activity are increasingly being touched by it. Academic knowledge is no different. Almost all subject areas have been affected by the development of information and communications technologies in terms of the content of the curriculum.

To be a scholar now means knowing how to find, analyze, organize, and apply digital information. Studying without the use of technology is increasingly like learning to dive without water. This is not an argument for teaching generic computer literacy skills, such as how to keyboard or use a word processor, but for using computers for digital imaging in medicine, for graphical information systems in geology, for using wikis to teach writing skills, for knowing which databases hold information relevant to solving a particular medical problem. Thus information and communications technologies are essential for developing these skills. However, without using technology embedded within the teaching, it will not be possible to develop core digital literacy within a particular subject domain.

This has significant implications for the way students are assessed. If we are setting examinations (or other forms of assessment) that do not explicitly assess problem solving, critical thinking, digital literacy, and communications skills within the subject domain, then students will not focus on developing these skills. And as well as assessing such skills, we also need to design our teaching to give students the opportunity to develop and practice such skills.

Most academics are aware of the increasing importance of digital technology within their subject discipline. Information technology is no longer just a useful tool that supports university and college administration and, to a lesser extent, teaching and learning; rather it is now an integral and essential component of almost all core higher education activities and as such needs to be used, managed, and organized accordingly. However, using technology for teaching is a necessary but not sufficient requirement for developing the knowledge and skills needed in the twenty-first century. It has to be accompanied by curriculum reform (the content), by changes in teaching methods that facilitate the development of skills in a particular subject domain, and by changes in assessment, to ensure those skills are evaluated.

5. To Improve the Cost-Effectiveness of the System

Institutions and governments face the challenge of balancing the conflicting pressures of increasing access, improving quality, and controlling costs. Can technology provide the fourth side of the square? Can information and communications technologies provide opportunities and potential for both improving effectiveness, through better qualified graduates and higher completion rates, and also for reducing unit costs, that is, the cost of each graduating student?

The old-style university is built around the delivery of programs through campus residence, the physical attendance of students at lectures, seminars, libraries, and labs. Information and communications technologies now, however, enable students to access information and services, including interaction with instructors and other students, at any time and any place. Programs can now be delivered in a variety of ways to an increasingly wide variety of students, through face-to-face, blended, or fully online learning. Can we use technology to not only improve the quality of services to students, but also to enable students to study in a more effective way?

The majority of university and college instructors (tenured or contracted) work very hard at teaching, if course and lesson preparation, student assessment, hiring and supervising adjunct faculty, and counseling students are all included. In research universities, teaching is supposed to count for no more than 40% of their activities, and there are strong arguments to be made that good teaching and research reinforce each other in higher education. Time must be found for both. Because the proportion of contract to tenured professors has rapidly increased, the senior, experienced research professor is an extremely scarce and valuable teaching resource, as we shall see in Chapter Seven. Can ways be found to make more effective use of "star" research professors' teaching time? Can technology be used to enable instructors to work smarter, rather than harder, as in many other professions? These are some of the questions we will be exploring in this book.

CONCLUSION

Daniel (1999) claims that the modern university has to balance three competing forces: access, quality and cost. Can access—or the number of students—be increased without additional cost or a reduction in the quality of teaching? We see technology as one of the key factors that help to balance these three pressures, as illustrated in Figure 1.1.

FIGURE 1.1. TECHNOLOGY AS A BALANCING FACTOR FOR THE FORCES IMPACTING ON HIGHER EDUCATION

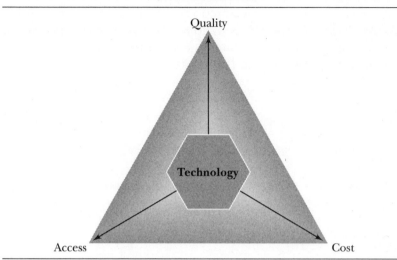

Source: Adapted from Daniel, 1999.

Our view is that the main reason for investment in technology should be to improve the cost-effectiveness of universities and colleges by increasing flexible access for students, helping develop certain core skills and competencies required in today's society (improving quality), and enabling administrators and teachers to work more effectively.

It is now 20 years since the creation of the World Wide Web and 15 years since universities and colleges started to take a serious look at how information and communications technologies should be managed for teaching and learning. The use of digital technology for finance, student information systems, and other administrative functions is now over 30 years old. So how are higher education institutions responding to the potential and challenge of technology? How are they strategically managing their technological resources? Are they being managed so as to achieve the goals of increased flexibility for students, the development of students with the necessary knowledge and skills for the twenty-first century, and greater cost-effectiveness?

This book explores these questions by looking at a relatively random sample of eleven institutions from five countries and two continents. But first, we need to look at developments in technology. As always, technology is in constant flux, and it is important to understand how these changes are influencing higher education, or will influence it in the future.

CHAPTER TWO

RECENT DEVELOPMENTS IN TECHNOLOGY AND EDUCATION

Educators are fond of saying: "It is not about the technology." Sorry, but it has everything to do with the technology!
—DONALD CLARK, LINE COMMUNICATION, UK, 2009

Meet Danny, a Net Gener

Danny is 19 years old and has just started his first year in a state university. He uses new social media to extend friendships within the familiar contexts of college, sports, and other local activities. Danny is "always on," in constant contact with his friends via texting, instant messaging, mobile phones, and Internet connections. This continuous presence requires ongoing maintenance and negotiation. With these "friendship-driven" practices, Danny is almost always associating with people he already knows in his

---

Material in this chapter first appeared in Lee, M., and McLoughlin, C. (eds.) (2010) *Web 2.0-based e-learning: Applying social informatics for tertiary teaching.* Hershey, PA: IGI Global. Reproduced with permission of the publisher.

"offline" life. He uses new media to "hang out" and extend existing friendships in these ways.

Danny also uses the online world to explore interests and find information that goes beyond what he has access to at college or in his local community. His participation in selected online groups enables him to connect to peers who share specialized and niche interests of various kinds, whether that is online gaming, creative writing, video editing, or other artistic endeavors. In these "interest-driven" networks, Danny finds new peers outside the boundaries of his local community. He also uses this network to publicize and distribute his work to online audiences and to gain new forms of visibility and reputation.

In the process, Danny has acquired various forms of technical and media literacy by exploring new interests, tinkering, and "messing around" with new forms of media. Through trial and error, he has added new media skills to his repertoire, such as how to create a video or customize games or his Facebook page. He then shares his creations and receives feedback from others online. Sometimes he "geeks out" and dives into a new topic or talent. He seeks out specialized knowledge groups from around the country or world, with the goal of improving his craft and gaining reputation among expert peers. While both teens and older adults participate, Danny does not automatically recognize the resident experts by virtue of their age or reputation. Geeking out in many respects erases the traditional markers of status and authority.

New media allow Danny a degree of freedom and autonomy that is less apparent in his classroom settings. He finds he has to "gear down" in class and finds it hard to "do nothing" except concentrate on what the instructor is telling him, so he is constantly texting and receiving texts during class, which occasionally gets him into trouble with his instructors. When he's online, he respects the other participants' authority, and is often more motivated to learn from his online peers than from his college instructors. His efforts online in social media are also largely self-directed, and the outcome emerges through exploration, in contrast to classroom learning that is oriented toward set, predefined goals. As a result, he often feels he is living in a different world when in class at college.

Source: Adapted with permission from Ito et al. (2008).

INTRODUCTION

In this chapter, we describe the major developments in technology that are affecting teaching and learning, administrative and operational activities, and increasingly strategic decision making and management. Although many readers will be familiar with most of the technologies described, the implications for teaching and learning, and for the organization and management of post-secondary educational institutions, may be not so well understood. We will examine here in particular the implications for Danny as he tries to work his way through college.

USING INFORMATION AND COMMUNICATIONS TECHNOLOGIES TO IMPROVE ADMINISTRATIVE FUNCTIONS

Although we focus in this book mainly on the management of technology for teaching and learning, technology in universities and colleges has historically been focused primarily on administrative functions. There is a synergistic relationship between technology applications in administrative and teaching areas, so we need to begin by looking briefly at the administrative uses of technology.

COMMERCIAL ADMINISTRATIVE SYSTEMS

Most postsecondary educational institutions made substantial investments in the 1990s to digitalize and integrate core administrative services such as admission procedures, student and financial records, payrolls, and human resource management (ERP—enterprise resource planning—systems). For many educational institutions, this was a fraught and sometimes financially disastrous process. Most of the companies providing ERP systems developed their core products for the business sector. Although there are similar administrative functions between universities and businesses, such as payroll management, other areas are quite different. For example, a student information system has some fundamentally different requirements from a customer services system for a large business. Major software adaptation and major changes to core administrative processes were usually needed to make the software fit to the requirements of an educational institution, often resulting in cost overruns, poor functionality, and major delays in implementation.

Over time, these problems have been gradually ironed out, but as a result, educational institutions are now locked-in to specific commercial service providers. This leaves little opportunity to change providers without great cost, or to resist updates to software that do not always improve educational administrative services, or to avoid the escalation of license fees. Thus most postsecondary educational institutions have large, rigid, and expensive administrative software systems.

THE INTEGRATION OF ADMINISTRATIVE AND TEACHING SYSTEMS

In addition, with the development of learning management systems such as Blackboard, teaching and administrative functions have become more interdependent. For instance, by linking a learning management system to the student information system, class lists and e-mail addresses of students in the class can be automatically generated for a particular section and instructor. Similarly, grades entered into the learning management system can be automatically transferred to the student information system. However, once integrated, changes to an administrative system can have unanticipated knock-on effects on the teaching side, and vice versa.

WEB-BASED SERVICES

Another major development has been the move to Web-based services, enabling students (and instructors) to enter and maintain their own data, thus reducing the need for central data entry. Content management systems allow administrative and academic departments to create and maintain their own Web-based information sites. In particular, many postsecondary institutions now have student portals, providing students with "one-stop" Internet access to all their study requirements. These Web-based developments usually require another layer of software (middleware) sitting on top of the basic administrative databases. However, increased digitization, integration of different software systems, and accessibility of student records and other information through the Web also increase the risk of security and privacy breaches.

THE LACK OF STANDARDIZATION

There is little standardization between different commercial ERP systems and consequently little sharing of resources and services between institutions. In the past each institution negotiated its own requirements individually with each commercial service provider. There is probably a great deal of room for rationalization of services, sharing of costs, and increased cost-effectiveness, through better coordination and collaboration of administrative services systemwide.

As a result, some states and provinces have been moving toward systemwide solutions for student services and administration, where appropriate. One example is the Alberta Postsecondary Application System (APAS), which is a Web-based system that provides one-stop, secure, online student application and transcript transfer services.

CLOUD COMPUTING

Finally, there have been some recent developments in computing that offer the potential for large savings to institutions, through the outsourcing of services. For instance, cloud computing, where a service provider hosts services that are used by many clients on external servers, offer potential savings compared with managing services internally (Katz, 2008). One example would be moving student e-mails from a university-managed system to Google mail. The disadvantages include concerns over security, especially regarding privacy issues such as access to student information, the concern about cloud computing services disappearing if the hosting company goes bankrupt, and perceived difficulties in adapting services to specific local needs.

OPEN SOURCE ADMINISTRATIVE SYSTEMS

Given these developments, it is perhaps not surprising that in 2009, the Kuali Foundation, a consortium of universities, developed the first open source administrative system designed specifically for postsecondary educational institutions (Parry, 2009a). At the time of writing, its first two products are a financial management system, and a software system for research grant administration (Coeus), with several other projects in the pipeline, including a student information system and a system for library management. For consortium members, there are no licensing fees, although the cost of development and maintenance has to be covered by the consortium members, mainly through dedicating in-house software developers to work on projects, although there are now also an increasing number of companies specializing in supporting open source systems. An increasing number of postsecondary education institutions are beginning to use Kuali products or are becoming partners. Although moving from existing systems requires a major effort, the trend to open source solutions is likely to increase as existing contracts with commercial providers come up for renewal.

Technologies for Teaching

It is against this background of earlier and still-developing administrative systems that we now examine developments in technology for teaching and learning.

Classroom Tools

Technology in one form or another has always been an integral part of teaching. One could argue that the classroom is the technology of face-to-face teaching, with its chalk and blackboard, desks, chairs, books, and other tools for learning.

More recently, computers, projectors and screens in the classroom, and Internet connectivity, have allowed instructors to use PowerPoint slides, links to Web sites, and high-quality graphics within the classroom. Audience response systems such as iClickers enable students to provide instant feedback, and answer questions posed by their instructors (Terris, 2009). Lecture capture systems allow lectures to be digitally recorded, and downloaded later by students (Schaffhauser, 2009). The cost of outfitting a lecture theater with all the digital technology now needed can exceed over $1 million (see, for instance, King, 2008). None of these classroom technologies, however, changes the traditional fixed time and place model of teaching.

THE INTERNET

What has changed is that the Internet enables instructors and learners to access materials and communicate with each other at any time and place, provided they have a computer and connection to the Internet. Because it enables virtual communication independent of time and place, the Internet is a paradigm shift for teaching and learning, to which institutions, administrators, and instructors are still struggling to adapt.

COMPUTER-MEDIATED COMMUNICATION

One of the first recorded uses of online teaching was at the New Jersey Institute of Technology in the 1970s (Hiltz & Turoff, 1978). This was a blended learning model, combining classroom teaching with online discussion between students and teacher. Hiltz and Turoff called the online component computer-mediated communication (CMC). One of the most-used CMC systems in the 1980s was CoSy, developed at the University of Guelph in Canada (McCreary, 1989). An important feature of CoSy was that it enabled threaded discussion, in that postings were linked directly to a specific previous posting to which the student or teacher was replying, rather than just listed by the timing of the posting. This enabled the thread of a discussion to be more easily tracked.

THE WORLD WIDE WEB

Until 1990, though, educational applications of the Internet were limited mainly to e-mail and discussion forums such as CoSy. It was difficult to store or send large amounts of content over the Internet, because of the narrow bandwidth available at the time to most users (56 kbps using dial-up modems), and the difficulty and cost of creating, organizing, and transmitting large amounts of textual material over the Internet.

This limitation was removed by the development of the World Wide Web, launched publicly in 1990, and further assisted by continued improvements in Internet infrastructure, allowing for faster and cheaper communication. Initially, the importance of the Web was that it enabled large amounts of text and graphics to be created, stored, searched for, and transmitted easily and cheaply over the Internet to any connected computer, using common standards and protocols that ensured universal use.

LEARNING MANAGEMENT SYSTEMS

It took postsecondary education about five years to find a standard way to use the Web for teaching and learning. Initially instructors created their own Web pages or online courses using HyperText Markup Language (HTML). In 1994 Murray Goldberg, an instructor in computer science at the University of British Columbia, created a standard Web-based shell, or learning management system (WebCT), that included spaces for learning objectives, for creating content through standard keyboarding, pasting, or uploading of documents; for setting up and organizing threaded discussion forums; and for writing multiple-choice test questions which students could answer with a simple click. Students could access and interact with the learning management system over the Web, and access to the course was restricted to authorized students and instructors. WebCT was eventually bought by Blackboard.

Learning management systems have become the main driver of e-learning in postsecondary education. By 2007, over 90% of two- and four-year colleges in the United States had a learning management system (Lokken & Womer, 2007). In recent years, learning management systems have also been designed to link more closely with student administrative systems. Learning management systems have usually been installed on servers and managed within the institution.

Until recently, the main learning management systems used in postsecondary education have been commercial products. The dominant learning management system is currently Blackboard Inc., which is a commercial, license-based system, with approximately 60% of the postsecondary education market in 2008. Over the last few years, though, there has been a move, particularly by large research universities and some government agencies, toward the development and use of open source learning management systems, such as Moodle and Sakai. Gartner Research (Lowendahl, Zastrocky, & Harris, 2008) estimated that open source learning management systems constituted 26% of the market in 2007 and would grow to 35% by the end of 2008. Open source learning management systems have the advantage of being free, in that, unlike commercial learning management systems, there are no user license fees. However, there are costs in installation, adaptation, and maintenance of open source learning management systems.

Synchronous Technologies

Synchronous learning involves instructor and students interacting at the same time, even though they may be physically apart, through text-based chat, audio-, or video-conferencing. In the past, it also meant accessing a particular center where the necessary equipment was located. However, more recently, software such as Skype, Bridgit, Centra, Elluminate, and Adobe Connect allow teachers and students to participate in real time using a desktop computer, laptop, or, in some cases, a mobile phone from anywhere with an Internet connection. Synchronous technologies allow for multipoint audio conferencing, sharing of desktop documents (such as PowerPoint slides) and high-quality images, although multipoint video (that is video linking several students and an instructor at the same time but each at a different place) is still restricted because of bandwidth limitations. Usually the institution will take out a license for use of such technology, but for end users such as students (or instructors) there are no direct costs.

One advantage of synchronous technologies for many instructors is that the mode of teaching is very similar to that of classroom teaching, with the instructor giving a lecture, and students responding accordingly. It is particularly useful if students are on different campuses. The session can also be recorded and made available for later downloading by students.

WEB 2.0

Web 2.0 is a term used loosely to describe a wide range of relatively lightweight tools accessible over the Internet, usually free or at low cost (O'Reilly, 2005). Web 2.0 tools empower the end user to access, create, disseminate, and share information easily in a user-friendly, open environment. Some have called Web 2.0 the "democratization" of the Web. Examples are as follows.

Blogs

A blog is a Web posting that is usually created without the need to write in computer code. Blogs are often used as a form of diary or daily log of activities (the term is a hybrid of "Web" and "log"). A typical use in education is to enable a student to reflect on their learning, or to comment on areas of interest in their studies.

Wikis

Although most blogs allow comments from readers, the blog can be altered only by the person who created it. Wikis on the other hand enable contributions from several authors. Wikipedia is the best example, a collective, open editing of an encyclopedia of information. Another common use of wikis in education is for group work focused on creative writing or writing joint reports on group projects.

Social and Collaborative Networking

This includes tools such as MySpace, Facebook, LinkedIn, and Twitter. Most of these applications enable participants to provide personal information—such as photos, personal details, and e-mail addresses—on a personal Web site, and to share this with friends or colleagues. Users can also communicate through Web-based e-mails and wall posts, which are entries that can be seen by all those participants that are linked. LinkedIn is similar to Facebook, but focused more on professional contacts, or special topic interests. Twitter is limited to 140 characters and is used more for instant messaging to those following someone's "tweets." Messages from all these tools can be relayed over the Internet using mobile phones as well as desktop or laptop computers.

These social software tools are increasingly being used by instructors, as much for research as for teaching. In the personal networking areas, there are several tools "that are fostering collaboration webs that span almost every discipline. . . . [Collaborative workspaces] are easy to create, and they allow people to jointly collaborate on complex projects using low-cost, simple tools" (New Media Consortium, 2008). They are also places to try out or float ideas for discussion with peers.

Some institutions have started to use social media as a way of communicating with students and providing learner support. Twitter can be useful for alerting students to new online course postings, assignment deadlines, and for enabling students to share newly discovered online sources with fellow students. As well as for commenting on an instructor's lack of street cred, Twitter can also be used during lectures to provide feedback or questions to the instructor (Young, 2009).

Supercool School (www.supercoolschool.com) provides a meeting place within Facebook for those wanting to learn and those wanting to teach. Thus a participant can ask for a course or module on a particular topic and be linked to someone willing to teach that topic, or join an already existing course or module. All this is voluntary with sometimes a participant being both a learner on one course and a teacher on another. No formal educational institution or accreditation is involved. Supercool School has now taken this idea into company training, enabling company human resource departments to identify where the demand is for continuing education and training, and where the resources are within the company to provide that training.

Although social software such as Facebook and Twitter are relatively new, online discussion forums date back to the late 1970s, as we have seen. Both social software and online discussion forums allow learners to test, question, and construct their own, personalized knowledge. The main difference is that instructors control and manage online, asynchronous discussion forums, and limit access to students registered in a particular course or program, whereas with social software it is the end user who decides when and how to participate, in self-managed groups that are usually (but not always) open to anyone.

Thus social media are used a great deal for informal, nonacademic learning, as we saw at the beginning of this chapter. We have argued earlier that academic knowledge is different from everyday knowledge, and hence it may seem that social media do not have a place in the academy. However, informal learning is an increasingly important part of the knowledge economy. Universities and colleges may want to think about how informal learning could be harnessed to further academic knowledge. Social media can be valuable for facilitating informal learning within a particular subject area or discipline, and especially around the boundaries of discipline areas, where students' personal interests mesh with academic knowledge. As Ito et al. (2008, p. 3) comment:

> And rather than assuming that education is primarily about preparing for jobs and careers, what would it mean to think of education as a process of guiding . . . participation in public life more generally, a public life that includes social, recreational, and civic engagement? And finally, what would it mean to enlist help in this endeavor from an engaged and diverse set of publics that are broader than what we traditionally think of as educational and civic institutions?

However, this would require schools, colleges, and universities to think quite differently about the design of teaching and learning.

Multimedia Archives and E-Portfolios

Multimedia archives such as YouTube, iTunes, Flickr, or Google Video, and the increasing access to cheap digital video cameras or integrated video and audio recording in mobile phones, now enable learners to create their own digital e-portfolios of work, incorporating text, graphics, audio, and video. These tools are relatively simple to use. Instructors or students can easily record audio podcasts on their computers or even mobile phones, and upload it to a service such as iTunes, from where it can be downloaded to a variety of devices. YouTube provides a video toolbox that is a set of guidelines for producing good-quality video material. Posting video to sites such as YouTube is free, quick, and easy. Learning management systems such as Moodle are increasingly incorporating plug-ins that enable the management of e-portfolios and learner generated content, thus providing more institutional control than if the information is stored on external servers such as those used by YouTube and Flickr.

Virtual Worlds

Virtual worlds—Massively Multiplayer Virtual Worlds (MMVWs)—enable participants to project a nonphysical presence of themselves—an avatar—into a dynamic, computer-generated environment, and within that environment to interact with other participants' avatars, in real time. Second Life is the most well-known virtual world with the largest number of users. By June 2008 Second Life had 14 million accounts (Parsons, 2008), although active accounts are much fewer. Users can build and modify this world to a large degree, using construction tools within the game. Thus, for instance, a university can create an island that can be explored by participants. Senges, Praus, and Bihr (2007) identified a number of educational applications of Second Life. (See http://sleducation.wikispaces.com/educationaluses for a detailed list of educational applications of Second Life.)

Especially with such a large potential number of participants, a learner in Second Life has a wide array of learning opportunities, enabling knowledge to be constructed in a combination of social interaction, collaboration, exploration, and experimentation. However there are not yet well-established educational designs for exploiting the uniqueness of a virtual world, except as simulations of real worlds (for instance, by interacting with virtual three-dimensional models of human anatomy and physiology). Some applications merely replicate traditional classroom practice (for example by delivering a lecture through Second Life to student participants). There are also no business models yet that set costs against benefits, so it is still very much an experimental environment for learning (Senges, Praus, & Bihr, 2007).

Digital Simulations and Games

Digital simulations electronically represent real-world operations or activities, and allow for inputs from learners that result in changes to the simulation in ways that are similar to the operation of equipment or systems in a real-world context. Simulations are often used when operating real equipment would be too expensive, too dangerous for novices, or when substantial practice is required for mastery. Flight simulators are examples of expensive simulations that nevertheless are cost-effective because of the costs and risks of using real planes for training. However, with recent developments in computer software, simpler and equally effective simulations can be designed to represent less complex systems, such as, for example, gas pipe welding.

Applications in workplace training have shown that simulations when used in appropriate circumstances can substantially reduce training costs. Virtual labs or virtual experiments are being used increasingly in teaching science and engineering, when physical laboratory space is scarce, or actual equipment is too dangerous or costly to use for learning purposes. One example is TheChemCollective, online virtual labs developed by Carnegie Mellon University, downloadable free of cost for educational purposes (http://www.chemcollective.org/about.php). The British Columbia Institute of Technology has developed 3D animations and simulations for instruction in aeronautical maintenance and health education (BCIT, 2009).

Simulations are simplified representations of real-life. Games are distinguished by rules and competition. A few games have been designed or adapted for educational purposes ("serious gaming environments"), mainly for the K–12 sector (Prensky, 2006). However, educational games to date have had limited application and utility, mainly because of the high cost of development and lack of appropriate instructional design (Burgos, Tattersall, & Koper, 2007). Nevertheless, there is strong potential for taking some of the building blocks of games technology, such as off-the-shelf software for scenery animation, hand-eye coordination, and crowd behavior, and adapting them to educational purposes, thereby cutting down the cost of building all software from scratch.

MOBILE LEARNING

The rapid expansion of wireless technology has stimulated interest in mobile learning—delivery of education and training to people on the move. Worldwide, more people have mobile phones than personal computers. The trend in the technology is convergence. Devices are becoming smaller, portable, multimedia, and universally accessible through the Internet. As mobile technology has become more sophisticated, with larger, clearer screens, touch-controlled keyboards, and motion-controlled navigation, the potential for educational applications has also increased.

Mobile learning has been developed in a number of ways. The simplest is the use of RSS feeds to their mobile phones to alert students to college news and information, such as the imminent deadline for the next assignment. One major application is to use mobile phones for student data collection, using real-time polling and interviews, photographs and video for project work, and so forth, that students can then organize and post into a class Web site (Alexander, 2004; JISC, 2005). E-book readers, such as the Kindle, that allow for the downloading and reading of large numbers of books, and the iPad, which also provides access to multimedia content such as books, music, movies, and videos, offer another form of mobile learning, and will help to cut the cost of textbooks for students.

However, at the moment, mobile learning is mainly used as a supplement to either face-to-face or other forms of online teaching. At the time of writing there are relatively few apps (software) designed specifically for teaching. Thus the real potential of mobile learning is still just over the horizon, waiting for the next stage of technology integration that will include low cost, wideband connections, new interfaces (perhaps including voice recognition), software applications that are better suited for study purposes, and above all new designs for teaching that enable the unique advantages of mobile learning to be better exploited.

OPEN EDUCATIONAL RESOURCES

Some institutions in recent years have begun to make digital educational materials available free over the Internet for educational purposes. Cooperative copyright management sites such as the Creative Commons (http://creativecommons.org/) provide instructors with protection against improper or commercial use, while recognizing their contribution to the creation of the content.

Massachusetts Institute of Technology, the United Kingdom's Open University, and Rice University's Connexions are offering digital recordings of lectures, online teaching modules, and collections of video lectures, animations, and simulations for free downloading online. These are not free courses or programs, but materials that can be used individually by instructors or students, or incorporated into other educational programs. For those wanting a qualification, instructors are still needed to identify or assess appropriate content, help define learning outcomes, provide ongoing help and support, and to assess students.

On the other hand, Carnegie Mellon University, through its Open Learning Initiative, makes available to other institutions (mainly community colleges) specially designed software-enhanced online courses that track students' progress and provide them with feedback on problems (Parry, 2009b). If the courses are used in combination with instructors, the courses can feed information to instructors about where students are struggling. The courses are team designed by community college faculty experts, scientists who study how people learn, human-computer-interaction specialists, and software engineers, using open access online course materials.

The move toward open educational resources has important consequences for course design, intellectual property rights of faculty, the role of instructors, and assessment. It could possibly provide a means to improve the cost-effectiveness of higher education. More experimentation, research, and analysis will be needed, however, before open content becomes a staple component of higher education teaching and learning.

THE IMPLICATIONS OF NEW TECHNOLOGY DEVELOPMENTS FOR TEACHING AND LEARNING

In Chapter One we discussed the need to balance the competing pressures of increasing access, improving quality, and reducing costs, and we suggested that technology, accompanied by cultural and structural changes in the academy, could help provide that balance. In this section we will discuss how the creative use of technology can do this regarding teaching and learning. This will require examining the modes of technology-based teaching, and the relationship between different technologies and different approaches to teaching and learning, judged against the changing needs of a knowledge-based society.

MODES OF TECHNOLOGY-BASED TEACHING

E-learning is a common term that describes the use of information and communications technologies for teaching and learning. However, this can include a wide range of teaching, and it is important to be clear in defining and understanding the different modes of e-learning. We see e-learning as a continuum, from no use of technology at one end, to all delivery by information and communications technologies at the other (see Figure 2.1).

On the left side of Figure 2.1, we have face-to-face teaching, with no use of information and communications technologies. Socrates sitting in the shade of the linden tree with a small group of students would be an example. Today in postsecondary education, teaching with no use of technology is quite rare.

In the **classroom aids** mode, the teacher uses a computer mainly to add to the classroom experience, for instance, by using PowerPoint to illustrate lectures, or by creating a course Web site, probably using a learning management system (LMS), where

FIGURE 2.1. DIFFERENT MODES OF E-LEARNING

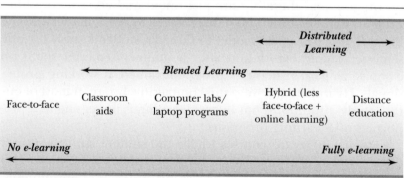

Source: Bates & Poole, 2003; OECD, 2005.

students can access the PowerPoint lecture slides, lists of readings and URLs posted by the teacher, and possibly assignment questions and other online resources. This is still the most common mode of e-learning. However, as instructors gain more experience with using technology, the trend is toward other modes.

With **laptop programs** (where the students bring their own or a leased computer to class), or programs using **computer labs,** where the college provides the computers, the students and the teachers are active users of the computer, but still in a fixed time and place classroom. This mode represents a relatively small proportion of e-learning, possibly around 10% of all e-learning. However, the number of students with their own laptops has now dramatically increased, and alternative, more flexible models of teaching with laptops or portable devices such as mobile phones or iPads are now possible.

In the **hybrid** mode, students still spend some time in class, but class time is reduced to give students more time for online study, and more active learning when not in class. There are several versions of hybrid e-learning. In one version, three class sections a week are reduced to one, with the rest done online. Using virtual labs to reduce time in physical labs is another example. A good example of the increased flexibility that e-learning can provide is Vancouver Community College's Motor Vehicle Repair apprenticeship program, where students do two-thirds of a course online, and the last third—involving hands-on skills—on campus, focusing on the specific skills that the student is lacking. Some students arrive with the skills already acquired on the job, and therefore are just tested and accredited. Other students may need the whole three weeks to reach mastery. In the Royal Roads University model in Canada, students study for one semester online before and after a summer semester spent on campus, as part of master's programs aimed at working professionals. Hybrid models were still comparatively rare in most of our case study institutions, but hybrid learning is increasing as a proportion of e-learning programs.

Finally, there are courses where the student studies entirely online, which of course is one form of **distance education.** This is the fastest growing area of e-learning, in terms of enrollments, in North America, as we saw in Chapter One.

Note that **blended learning** can be any one of the three "middle" modes, and **distributed learning** can be either hybrid or fully online courses (Bates & Poole, 2003).

We can see then that e-learning is no longer a marginal activity for most postsecondary institutions but is now becoming a core means of program delivery. Also the form of e-learning can vary, from ancillary support to traditional classroom teaching to radically different course designs in hybrid learning, to online learning where the student never attends a campus.

Thus, for every course being taught, the following questions arise:

- For this course, and for the students to be taught on this course, where on the continuum of e-learning should this course be?
- What in this course is best taught face-to-face, and what is best taught online?
- How should such decisions be made: by an individual teacher working alone; by collegial decision making at a program level; or by the senior administration for the institution as a whole?
- What policies, principles, or knowledge are needed to make these decisions effectively?

Philosophical and Pedagogical Considerations

The changes in technology are also being accompanied by changes in educational philosophy. We focus on four changes or divides in education that interact with the applications of technology for teaching and learning: a move from an objectivist view of knowledge to a socially constructed view; a move toward developing skills associated with managing a rapidly expanding knowledge base, rather than focusing on learning prespecified facts, principles, and concepts; a move toward more learner-centered teaching; and a view that the Internet and related technologies radically change the nature of knowledge. These are all different facets of an underlying world view about the nature of knowledge in the twenty-first century, and all have significant implications for the management of technology in postsecondary education.

The Social Construction of Knowledge

Epistemology is a philosophical analysis of the nature of knowledge, and in particular the bases, beliefs, or sources that enable us to consider something to be true. A good example of this is the famous argument about the origin of man between Bishop Samuel Wilberforce and Thomas Huxley at Oxford University in 1860. Huxley argued that man was descended from the apes, based on scientific evidence, especially the work of Charles Darwin. Wilberforce argued that man was created by God, based on the scriptures of the Bible. This was not an argument that could be resolved by reason alone, as each came from a different epistemological perspective (an argument which persists today over the theory of intelligent creation).

Within higher education, there are also different epistemological positions. Strongly influenced by the development of science, one dominant epistemological position is objectivism. Objectivists will argue that there exists a reliable set of facts, principles, concepts, and theories that can be consistently demonstrated and proved. Truth exists independently of the human mind. Thus the laws of physics are constant, whether you believe in them or not.

Constructivists, however, argue that knowledge is essentially subjective, constructed from our perceptions and mutually agreed on conventions. Thus even science is merely what scientists believe to be true at the time, and can be interpreted differently (the argument over climate change is a case in point). Knowledge is dynamic and not constant; we continue to assimilate new information that leads to the reconstruction of our understanding. This can occur through individual reflection, although social constructivists strongly believe that the process of knowing is primarily social, through discussion and argument with others (Searle, 1996).

Epistemological positions have direct implications for teaching and learning. Someone with an objectivist view of knowledge will believe that there is a set body of knowledge that must be taught by someone who is expert in the subject. Teaching must be authoritative, informative, organized, and clear. There will be correct or wrong answers to questions. A constructivist, however, will encourage learners to question and discuss issues, to see knowledge as dynamic and changing, and strongly influenced by context. Knowledge is what emerges from the exchange of ideas, and the consensus of people working in groups. Assessment will focus on analysis, comparison of different positions, and contribution to the process of argument and discussion.

These are deliberately polarized positions. Many teachers will operate more functionally, seeing a strongly structured, objectivist approach as appropriate for some topics or students, and a more constructivist approach as more suitable for another part of the course. Figure 2.2 presents a diagrammatic analysis of various e-learning tools. This represents a personal interpretation of the tools, and other teachers may well rearrange the diagram differently, depending on their particular applications of these tools. The position of any particular tool in the diagram will depend on its actual use. LMSs can be used in a constructivist way, and blogs can be very teacher controlled, if the teacher is the only one permitted to use a blog on a course. Indeed, other teachers may prefer a different set of pedagogical values as a framework for analysis of the different tools. However, the aim here is not to

FIGURE 2.2. ANALYSIS OF WEB 2.0 TOOLS FROM AN EDUCATIONAL PERSPECTIVE

Objectivist					Constructivist
Tests	Essays		E-portfolios		Facebook
Books	Simulations	RSS	Google		Portals
	LMSs (e.g., Moodle)		Games		YouTube
Lectures	Discussion Forums/ Seminars			Wikis	Flickr
	Adobe Connect/ Elluminate	Research	Second Life		Blogs
Formal					**Informal**
Teacher Control					**Learner Control**

provide a cast-iron categorization of e-learning tools, but to point out that technologies are not pedagogically neutral. Teachers must decide which tools are most likely to suit a particular teaching approach.

A Focus on Skills Rather Than Content

We have already noted in Chapter One the importance of skills development for knowledge workers. Although constructivists are more likely to focus on developing skills of analysis and argumentation rather than the memorization of facts, an increased emphasis on the development of intellectual skills is also a result of the explosion of knowledge over the last fifty years. Because new knowledge is being created so fast, it is impossible for someone to cover everything within a particular area of study such as engineering or medicine. Therefore the focus must be on the management of information: how to find, analyze, organize, and apply information appropriately. In addition, because the knowledge base continues to change and expand, developing independent and lifelong learning skills is also important.

More Learner-Centered Teaching

Again, although constructivists will also emphasize learner-centered teaching, because of the need to involve the learner in the construction of knowledge, the move toward more learner-centered teaching also comes from research into how people best learn. Learning occurs best when learners are engaged and motivated to learn, when they are active during the learning process, and when they have some control over the learning context.

The Changing Nature of Knowledge

There are also those that argue that as a result of new technologies, the very nature of knowledge is changing. For instance, Siemens (2004) argues that knowledge is no longer generated and validated solely or even mainly by scholarly study, but by the ebbs and flows of discussion among millions of Internet participants, a theory he calls "connectivism." Siemens (2004) argues that

> connectivism presents a model of learning that acknowledges the tectonic shifts in society where learning is no longer an internal,

individualistic activity. . . . The pipe is more important than the content within the pipe.

Lyotard (1984) argues that because of information technologies the idea of acquiring knowledge to train the mind would become obsolete, as would the idea of knowledge as a set of universal truths. Instead, there will be many truths, many kinds of knowledge, and many forms of reason. As a result, the boundaries between traditional disciplines will dissolve, traditional methods of representing knowledge (books, academic papers, and so on) will become less important, and the role of traditional academics or experts will undergo major change.

Others argue that although the Internet affects the speed and effectiveness of communication, and hence facilitates the construction and dissemination of new knowledge, and new forms of knowledge are emerging as a result of new technologies such as virtual worlds, the essential nature of academic knowledge does not change. Laurillard (2002), for instance, argues that academic knowledge is not the same as everyday knowledge. Academic knowledge requires students to go beyond direct experience to reflect on, analyze, organize, and question such experiences (clearly a constructivist approach). All these developments are affecting the way technologies can be used for teaching and learning.

FROM E-LEARNING 1.0 TO E-LEARNING 2.0

From about 1995 through 2005, most online learning, whether as a classroom aid or as a fully distance course, was based on the notion of a teacher-controlled use of technology, using mainly a learning management system. However, whether the Web is used as a classroom aid, or for blended learning, or for fully online courses, nearly all these applications are based on the use of a learning management system.

A learning management system these days, whether commercial or open source, is a heavy piece of software, with a million lines of code or more. It is institutionally driven, linking teaching with administration. The teacher decides on course objectives, content, assignments, and learner activities, loads these into the learning management system, and the students access the knowledge through the Internet. Thus the main teaching model used is the transmission of knowledge from teacher to student (an objectivist approach), although within this overall model, there are wide variations in the amount of student activity through discussion forums, ungraded activities, and formal assessment. This use of the Web as a transmission model of teaching and learning is what Stephen Downes (2005) refers to as e-Learning 1.0. An LMS is a teacher-controlled tool.

Web 2.0 tools, on the other hand, are low-cost tools that empower learners. Web 2.0 tools facilitate more constructivist approaches, with greater emphasis on discussion and the creation of learning materials and knowledge construction by the learners. Furthermore, these tools also facilitate the development of skills needed in a knowledge-based workforce. Finally, there is also the promise of informal learning over the Internet, through networking, interest groups, and social media, outside of any academic institution. Downes (2006) argues that these new tools allow for immersive learning—learning everywhere and at any time, within all aspects of life, without the need for formal, time-and-place-dependent institutions. This kind of learning is what Downes (2005) calls "e-learning 2.0."

What Has Changed

Students now come to university or college already with a wide range of technologies. Students have freedom to use these technologies for study, if they wish, or if instructors design their teaching to make use of such tools. Web 2.0 tools provide learners with much more control over not only the technology but also how and what they will learn. They allow new and powerful ways for learners to demonstrate learning not only of content but also of the application of knowledge. Learners can now do local field work and create digital multimedia Web-based e-portfolios of their work, either individually or collaboratively (Lorenzo & Ittelson, 2005).

The move to more open content also has several implications. Teachers and learners now have an increasing range of quality-assured learning materials that they can access, free of charge, for educational purposes. Teachers no longer need to create all their own material online; learners are no longer restricted to the content and curriculum provided by a college. Thus one can imagine an open content approach to a subject, where the instructor is a guide, providing goals and criteria for assessment, but where the students track down, assess, and organize appropriate learning materials.

For instance, in a course on historiography, students can be taught about basic sources for history, such as registries of births, marriages, and deaths, newspaper clippings, eyewitness reports, and so on, and can be taught about the criteria used to assess the authenticity and reliability of historical sources, how to get permissions, and copyright issues. Students then can be organized into groups, with each group required to write a history of the last fifty years of a city. Online resources, photos, and video clips, as well as copies of text-based historical records, can be collected and used as evidence for the history. Students would be assessed on the range and authority of the quoted sources, on their evaluation of the sources using the criteria provided, and on their ability to create a convincing narrative and set of themes for the history of the city. The group work would then be shared between the groups, with feedback provided online by the other students and the instructor.

The access to multimedia and the use of e-portfolios raises issues regarding assessment as well as the design of teaching and learning experiences (JISC, 2006). Learners can demonstrate what they can do and what they have learned, record their experiences, and allow others—such as potential employers—to access their work through e-portfolios, which could be considered a richer and more authentic form of assessment than traditional pencil and paper assessments, such as essays, tests, or examinations.

Thus Web 2.0 tools, the tools that students are already using for purposes other than studying, also provide opportunities for innovative course design, and in particular can be harnessed to develop the skills needed in knowledge-based work. For this to happen, though, new learning goals, curricula, and teaching methods are required, as well as use of technologies that are not under institutional control. For these reasons, Web 2.0 tools raise issues concerning the role of the instructor, the security of learning and teaching materials, student privacy, the assessment of learners, and in particular who accredits (or should accredit) knowledge.

In conclusion, the context in which academic knowledge is created, disseminated, and learned is what has changed. Content is now open; learners can seek, use, and apply information beyond the bounds of what a professor or teacher may dictate. Increasingly, as more instructors create digital learning materials, and as the Web collects original material from outside academic life but of relevance and importance for learners, quality educational content will be increasingly free, easily identifiable, abundant, and readily accessed, for those who know where to look.

It is not sufficient, then, just to teach academic content. It is equally important to enable students to develop the ability to know how to find, analyze, organize, and apply information or content within their professional and personal activities, to take responsibility for their own learning, and to be flexible and adaptable in developing new knowledge and skills. All this is needed because of the explosion in the quantity of knowledge that makes it impossible to memorize or even be aware of all the developments that are happening in any subject discipline or professional field, and because of the need to keep up to date within the field after graduating.

To do this learners must have access to appropriate and relevant content, know how to find it, and must have opportunities to apply and practice what they have learned. Thus learning has to be a combination of content, skills, and attitudes, and increasingly this needs to apply to all areas of study. This does not mean that there is no room to search for universal truths, or fundamental laws or principles, but such research needs to be embedded within a broader learning environment. Learning should include the ability to use information and communications technologies integrated with the content and skills needed within an area of study.

Conclusion

There is a seething cauldron of new technologies, and new approaches to teaching and learning are being driven by technological development. We shall see that, to date, the response of universities and colleges has been ultraconservative, focusing on protecting and enhancing the traditional model of teaching and learning, even though the context of postsecondary education has changed dramatically. The challenge then for institutions is to find ways to explore new approaches to teaching, learning, and administration that harness the power of technology, and improve the cost-effectiveness of the institution, while at the same time maintaining the core values of the academy.

The choice of technology and the design of the learning experience should be an academic decision that will vary depending on the type of students being taught, the nature of the subject matter, and the affordances of different technologies (what they are and are not suitable for). However, perhaps the most important factor determining choice of the actual tools to be used in online learning will be the educational theory or approach (the pedagogy, for want of a better term) most favored by those responsible for the teaching or learning.

Thus to ensure that technology is being appropriately harnessed to the needs of the academy of the future, the following questions must be asked:

- What kinds of learning are needed in the twenty-first century?
- What teaching philosophy or approach best supports these kinds of learning?
- In what ways do or can different technologies support twenty-first-century learning?
- How can technology best be used to improve the cost-effectiveness of institutional administration and management?
- How can institutions ensure that the best decisions are being made to address these questions?

The rest of this book focuses mainly on the last of these questions, but in the context of the other questions. How should decisions about technology be made? Who should be involved? What strategies seem to work best? This means examining the governance of institutions, but any discussion of governance must always be informed by a discussion of appropriate educational goals and the needs of learners in the twenty-first century. In the next chapter, we explore how institutions are approaching the issue of the governance of technology, and why we think that in the main, current strategies are inadequate.

CHAPTER THREE

TRACKING EXISTING STRATEGIES FOR TECHNOLOGY INTEGRATION

INTRODUCTION

In Chapters One and Two, we described major trends and developments in the fields of higher education and technology. In this chapter, we explain how we have collected and analyzed information about the ways in which technology is currently managed in postsecondary educational institutions.

WHERE THE EVIDENCE COMES FROM

We have drawn on several different sources for this book.

A REVIEW OF RELEVANT LITERATURE

Both authors independently reviewed the literature on the management and governance of technology in universities and colleges. Important publications that have influenced the writing of this book are by Mintzberg (1994a, 1994b, 2009), the Australian Graduate School of Management (1996), APQC/SHEEO (1998), Epper and Bates, (2001), Coimbra Group of Universities (2002), Hanna (2003), OECD (2005), Bullen and Janes (2007), Katz (2008), Tierney and Hentschke (2007), Higgins and Prebble (2008), Christensen, Horn, and Johnson (2008), Zemsky (2009), McCarthy and Samors (2009), and Seaman (2009).

Web-Based Survey of Institutional Strategic Plans

Sangrà (2003) conducted a Web-based search and analysis of strategic planning documents available through the institutional Web sites at the time. He looked at a total of 16 universities worldwide (United States, eight; Spain, four; United Kingdom, two; Canada and Australia, one each).

Eleven Institutional Case Studies

Sangrà (2008) conducted five European case studies between 2004 and 2005. Bates, mainly drawing on other previously published studies, analyzed six cases, five from North America and one from Europe. The authors collected information across the studies over a period of 12 years, from 1998 to 2010, although most of the information was collected between 2002 and 2007. Thus we have information from some institutions that were just starting to integrate technology within the institution, and from others that were more mature in their technology applications. For some institutions, we have information that went from their first use of information and communications technology for teaching right through to full maturity.

Personal Work Experience

The authors worked for extensive periods in four of the case study institutions, where they were each actively engaged in policy and decision making about the use of technology for teaching. In addition, both authors have extensive experience as consultants, having worked in over 40 countries.

Altogether, information was collected from a total of 30 organizations (25 universities, two two-year colleges, and three postsecondary educational systems), of which 12 were in the United States, eight in Spain, five in Canada, two in the United Kingdom, one each in Australia, Portugal, and Italy. All organizations in the study were publicly financed. More details will be found in the following sections.

THE WEB-BASED SURVEY OF INSTITUTIONAL STRATEGIC PLANS FOR TECHNOLOGY

The starting point for the study was an analysis of publicly available institutional strategic plans that identified technology integration as an important strategic goal for the institution.

STRATEGIC GOALS FOR INFORMATION AND COMMUNICATIONS TECHNOLOGIES

Sangrà (2003) examined the Web-based strategic plans for technology integration in 16 universities worldwide. At the time of the survey, most institutions saw the integration of information and communications technologies as an essential component of becoming a twenty-first-century university. In other words, the main driver was modernization of the institution. This motivation expressed itself usually as a set of strategic goals for information and communications technologies. These goals can be classified as follows:

1. To improve the **technology infrastructure**, especially connectivity. This would mean ensuring adequate Internet bandwidth across the campus, wireless access, and technical support for all students, faculty, and staff.
2. To increase **accessibility** to technology for students, faculty, and staff. This might include establishing computer labs, online library access, or desktop machines for every faculty and staff member.
3. To improve **internal administrative processes** through the implementation of enterprise resource planning systems, such as financial systems, student information systems, and human resource management systems; and through accessible administrative Web services for students and faculty.
4. To improve internal and external **communication**, through e-mail, student portals, institutional Web sites for public relations, and contact with alumni.
5. To promote and facilitate **research**, through accessing and sharing large databases and high capacity computation, the

development of online professional networks, and the development of online "virtual" libraries.

6. To expand and improve **teaching and learning** through

- Using technology to support classroom teaching
- Development of blended or fully online learning courses/programs
- Access to digital resources, for example, enabling online access to library catalogues
- Design or purchase and installation of software to support teaching and learning, for example installing a learning management system
- Faculty development and training in the use of technology

Sangrà found that these goals were common across the 16 universities in the survey. At the same time, Sangrà found that the institutions differed in the priority or importance they gave to each of the goals, and that not all institutions had all these goals. Often there was no indication in the plans of how specific goals were to be implemented, or no evidence of successful implementation, as far as could be judged, such as by comparing plans with actual online courses listed on institutional Web sites. The study of course was limited not only to institutions that had written strategic plans for technology but which also had made them public through a Web-accessible publication.

How the Web-Based Survey Has Been Used

Sangrà used these six goals or areas of technology as the analytical framework or set of headings for his later in-depth study of technology integration in the five case studies. Bates also applied the same categorization to the six case studies he examined.

The Institutional Case Studies

Our main goal in these case studies is to identify how universities and colleges have integrated information and communications technologies into their activities under most of the six goals listed above, and what seemed to work and what did not in implementing strategies. Although for some of the cases we draw heavily on secondary sources, one or other of the authors was involved directly in each of the 11 case studies. The case studies combined analysis of documents, personal interviews with senior and mid-level administrators, focus groups with faculty and sometimes students, and statistical data collection (for example, number of different kinds of online courses, number of students enrolled in online courses).

Table 3.1 lists the institutions that we used directly as case studies.

There were three Tier-1 research universities (VT, UBC, UM), four comprehensive universities (UCF, UaC, UA, URV), two two-year colleges (SAIT, CB), and two open universities (UOC, UAb).

Table 3.1. Case Study Institutions

North America	Country	Europe	Country
Virginia Tech (VT)	United States		
University of British Columbia (UBC)	Canada		
		University of Milan (UNIMI)	Italy
University of Central Florida (UCF)	United States		
		University of A Coruña (UDC)	Spain
		University of Alicante (UA)	Spain
		University of Rovira i Virgili (URV)	Spain
Southern Alberta Institute of Technology (SAIT)	Canada		
Collège Boréal (CB)	Canada		
		Open University of Catalonia (UOC)	Spain
		Open University of Portugal (UAb)	Portugal

Summarizing the results from 11 individual case studies spanning more than 10 years is fraught with difficulties. The results are mainly qualitative, and there is a tendency in summarizing to focus on quantitative results that apply across all the institutions, thus missing the richness of interconnections between the various strategies, policies, actions, institutional contexts, and outcomes. Indeed, the whole of this book is an extrapolation from the case studies, the literature, and personal experiences. However, to give readers a better idea of the institutional contexts, we provide brief, thumbnail sketches of each of the 11 institutions.

Virginia Tech, United States

This case was derived from one of several studies conducted by the State Higher Education Executive Officers (SHEEO) and the American Productivity and Quality Centre (APQC) into best practices in supporting faculty use of technology in teaching (Epper & Bates, 2001). Although the SHEEO/APQC project was focused specifically on faculty development and training in technology, a considerable amount of data was collected in each of the studies about institutional strategies for technology integration.

Virginia Tech was just one of five institutions selected from over 100 as being a best-practice example in faculty development for teaching with technology. For this book, we drew heavily on a publication by Anne Moore (2001) about the SHEEO/APQC study. She is now associate vice president for Learning Technologies and director of Information Technology Initiatives at Virginia Tech.

Virginia Tech is a comprehensive land-grant, Tier-1 research university based at Blacksburg. At the time of the study (2000) it had 1,500 faculty and 25,000 students, and was ranked in the top 50 universities in the United States. Its technology planning can be traced to the early 1990s, when the state experienced a severe recession. Moore wrote (p. 80): "Charged with serving more students with fewer state resources, Virginia Tech decided to attempt to build institutional capacity using technology."

One outcome was the Math Emporium, a learning center for the study of mathematics. It serves over 7,000 students annually with over 20 math courses, using over 500 Apple computer workstations. Math staff are available 60 hours a week in the general computer area to help students enrolled in any of the courses offered through the Math Emporium. Another outcome was the CAVE, which allows faculty to create three-dimensional simulations and visualizations. Both initiatives were very successful and are still operating in 2010.

By 2010, Virginia Tech's Center for Innovation in Learning had provided over $3 million in grants to faculty since 1996 to support more than 120 strategic instructional projects. The Center for Innovation and Learning's project assessments show greater student and faculty interaction, equal or superior assessment performance, and more active learning in technology-supported teaching compared with standard lectures.

At the end of the first four-year cycle of faculty development, 96% of the faculty had attended workshops and seminars on using technology for teaching. The faculty established on a voluntary basis a cyberschool for faculty to share experience and assist one another in the use of learning technologies.

University of British Columbia, Canada

One of the authors was employed by the university as director of distance education and technology from 1995 to 2003, and the case study also draws heavily on a publication by Lamberson and Fleming (2008), and subsequent follow-up visits to the university. Michelle Lamberson is currently director, Centre for Teaching, Learning and Technology, where Kele Fleming also works.

The University of British Columbia (UBC) is one of Canada's major research universities, ranked in the top 50 universities worldwide. In 2008, there were approximately 50,000 full-time students, 45,000 on the main campus in Vancouver (36,600 undergraduate and 8,400 graduate) and 5,000 at the Okanagan campus in Kelowna, about 400 kilometers from Vancouver. In 2009, it had annual revenues of C$1.5 billion (US$1.4 billion), of which $800 million (53%) is from government sources, and $300 million (20%) from student tuition fees. The rest is from investments, sales, and services. Almost one-third ($500 million) is research funding. Out of a total of 13,622 staff, 4,669 (34%) are faculty, research, and associated.

In 1993 and 1994, the government of British Columbia withheld a total of 2.5% of operating grants for postsecondary institutions to create an innovation fund. UBC developed a set of proposals for innovation and received the full amount ($2.1 million) withheld from its budget. This was the start of a decade of developments in the use of information and communications technologies for teaching and learning, as well as in the development of Web-based administrative services.

WebCT, historically the most-used learning management system in postsecondary education, was developed at UBC, following a grant from the innovation fund in 1995. More than 25,000 students (50%) and 3,000 instructors (64%) were using WebCT Vista as part of their course experience by 2009. There were 283 fully online courses in 2009, with 8,400 enrollments equivalent to approximately 1,000 FTEs. Most undergraduate students taking fully online courses were taking just one or two, to complete their undergraduate studies, although several master's programs are also offered fully online. UBC also offers a unique distributed medical education program in collaboration with the Government of British Columbia, the University of Northern British Columbia (UNBC), the University of Victoria (UVic), and provincial regional health authorities. The program will almost double undergraduate class sizes over a period of 10 years at sites on Vancouver Island, the interior of the province, and in the lower mainland around Vancouver. The program depends heavily on a range of technologies for delivery.

University of Central Florida, United States

This was another study conducted by SHEEO and the APQC into best practices in supporting faculty use of technology in teaching, and the University of Central Florida (UCF) was one of the five selected best practices. The study was written by Joel Hartman and Barbara Truman-Davis (2001). Hartman is currently vice provost for Information Technologies and Resources at the University of Central Florida in Orlando, and Truman-Davis is the director of course development Web services.

The University of Central Florida is a metropolitan, state-funded university based in Orlando with 11 branch campuses in central Florida. At the time of the study (2000) it had 877 full-time and 293 part-time faculty, and 32,000 students. In 2000, its student population was expected to reach 48,000 by 2010 (it actually reached 53,000). The average student age was 26, and approximately 40% of the students were part-time, with less than 10% resident on campus.

The university has always been strongly associated with technology, being initially founded in the 1960s to service the space industry at nearby Cape Canaveral. It has been a rapidly growing institution since its foundation, and its plans for technology were partly influenced by the difficulty of building campuses fast enough within a heavily populated area to keep up with growth and demand. The 1996–2001 Strategic Plan referred strongly to the importance of IT in helping to achieve the university's goals.

UCF developed a unique online course about teaching online, available to all faculty. It also has a permanent research group (RITE: http://www.rite.ucf.edu/) that tracks and evaluates the use of technology at UCF. By 2010, UCF was offering four undergraduate degree completion programs, 12 graduate degree programs, and 12 graduate certificates, plus hundreds of courses every semester from most academic areas, through online distributed learning. In 2009, approximately 20% of all registrations were either fully online (17%) or had reduced seat team (3.3%). Another 20% of registrations were using WebCT to enhance conventional classroom teaching, making a total of approximately 40% of registrations in distributed learning programs in 2010. Over the years 2006–2009, fully online enrollments increased by 33%, while registrations in reduced class time courses remained steady.

The Open University of Catalonia (Universitat Oberta de Catalunya—UOC), Spain

Both authors have worked extensively at UOC. Sangrà was one of the first staff appointed in 1995 and is currently the academic director of the eLearn Centre at UOC. Bates was a part-time research chair in e-learning at UOC between 2001 and 2005. Sangrà developed the case study as part of his study "The

Integration of Information and Communication Technologies in the University: Models, Problems and Challenges" (2008).

UOC is a fully online distance university, with headquarters in Barcelona. Founded in 1995, it had 50,000 students in 2010. It is a Catalan university, partly funded by the regional government of Catalonia, with programs in the Catalan language (although Spanish and English versions are also often available). The university owes much of its existence and development to its first rector, Dr. Gabriel Ferraté, whose vision was for a virtual university based on the Internet, with an emphasis on lifelong learning. The university has a unique funding structure, with parts of its operations (for instance, publishing) being public-private partnerships.

Courses are developed and delivered primarily by subject experts contracted from other Catalan universities, with a small core of full-time faculty at UOC who manage and coordinate programs. UOC also has two research centers and programs, one focused on research on the information society (IN3) and the other on e-learning. Courses are delivered fully online, using primarily text-based asynchronous learning through the institution's own learning management system, called Virtual Campus. The teaching materials are specially designed for online learning, following the university's own pedagogical model based on asynchronous, cohort-based group learning that exploits the flexibility of the Internet. There are programs at the undergraduate and graduate level, including a distance PhD program on the information society, and one on e-learning still in development in 2010. Increasingly, courses are designed with the European market in mind (for instance, English versions of graduate programs).

The university has been very successful in terms of enrollments, providing Catalan-based higher education, mainly to working adults, using an innovative teaching model. It is still the only fully online, virtual university in the world partially funded by government. Its Virtual Campus, which serves as both an administrative and learning management system, has been sold to a number of universities in Latin America. UOC has won numerous European and distance education awards for its innovative teaching. It is an organization based on the three pillars of pedagogy, technology, and organization.

One concern, though, is that in its search to be innovative, there have been many organizational changes and a lack of consistency in policy. The devolved businesses have not been altogether successful. Because of their part-time status, contract faculty often do not receive sufficient training in teaching online. There is often resistance to both the constructivist teaching model and the use of technology from the contracted faculty. Finally, the growth of online learning from conventional universities is leading to increased competition for students. To address these problems, UOC has created an Innovation Office to support faculty in developing new approaches to teaching and learning, and the eLearn Centre, which as well as conducting research and innovation in online learning, also runs a professional development program for faculty focusing on e-learning.

The Open University of Portugal (Universidade Aberta—UAb)

The Open University of Portugal is a publicly funded open and distance teaching university founded in 1988. It had 9,000 students in 2008, approximately 200 full-time faculty, and 300 employees. Its headquarters are in Lisbon.

The university, open to anyone 21 or over who speaks Portuguese, has students in Portugal, in Angola and Mozambique in Africa, and in several other parts of the world. Part of its mission is to promote the Portuguese language and culture, in Portugal and abroad. The university has developed a network of local learning centers spread over the country that support the university's learning activities and promote lifelong learning.

Until 2006, UAb's programs were delivered using a combination of print-based materials, audio, and broadcast television, with 3,500 hours of AV production and 6,000 hours of television broadcasting produced in the university studios. However, by 2006, the Portuguese government was questioning its relevance. The government had recently appointed a new rector and he was given a clear mandate: make this university relevant for the twenty-first century, or it will no longer be funded. The aim of the rector and his team was to make the university a world leader in the use of technology for teaching, by meeting the highest standards of effective teaching and learning. As a result, the university embarked on a major reorganization. The primary activity was to move all of its courses online between 2006 and 2007, using a constructivist pedagogical model.

It was at this point that both the authors of this book were asked to join a small international advisory panel that would monitor what they were doing, and would provide advice as appropriate. Thus this is not quite the same as the majority of the other cases, where the focus was on collecting data specifically about the integration of technology within the institution through interviews and an analysis of statistical data and strategic plans and directions. However, we both learned some interesting lessons about the integration of technology by watching this major intervention unfold.

What was distinct about UAb's strategy was that the move to online delivery was accompanied by a radical shift in pedagogy, away from a more didactic style of teaching, with an emphasis on comprehension, memorization, and reproduction of correct or standardized answers for assessment, toward a more constructivist approach to learning, based on reflection, discussion, and critical thinking. The move to Internet delivery enabled asynchronous discussion and interaction on a continuous basis between not only students and instructors, but between students as well, thus overcoming a major weakness of print- and broadcast-based distance education.

The decision to use constructivist-based online delivery for all UAb programs, and to make the change over a period of no more than two years, was even more ambitious. This meant, in effect, redesigning UAb's entire offerings. The change was not to be optional but mandatory. The university achieved this transition reasonably successfully by the end of 2007. A key factor was a comprehensive and mandatory training program for all faculty in pedagogy, course design, and technological delivery.

Despite the overall success of the innovation, some challenges remain. First, the overall curriculum of UAb is still unbalanced. It has few practical science or technology courses and few courses or programs aimed at qualifying professionals in health, technology, or science. Second, there was some resistance from especially the mathematics department to a social constructivist approach to teaching. Third, the UAb experience demonstrated that a radical move to online teaching also has major implications for the administrative side of the university. However, the senior administrator at the time had other priorities than providing Web-based services to faculty and students. Finally, the most difficult challenge of going online for a large number of students was technology access, not only for African students, but also for Portuguese students of low income or in nonurban areas (Portugal has one of the lowest Internet access rates in Europe). One of the functions of the local learning centers is to improve technology access for students. Despite the remaining challenges, UAb provides a unique example of a radical and comprehensive effort to move all programs online, and in a very short time.

COLLÈGE BORÉAL, CANADA

This was a third institution included by SHEEO and the APQC in its study of best practices in supporting faculty use of technology in teaching, and Collège Boréal was also one of the five selected best practices. The study was written by Chantal Pollock and colleagues (2001).

Founded in 1995, Collège Boréal is a publicly funded, two-year community college based in Sudbury, Ontario, that serves 165,000 Francophone speakers across the very large, sparsely populated area of Northern Ontario. It has seven widely dispersed campuses. In 2001 it had approximately 1,500 full-time students, which had grown to 2,000 by 2010.

"Historically, few Franco-Ontarians pursued their studies at postsecondary level. Thus one of the challenges is to create a new culture within the Franco-Ontarian community regarding post-secondary education" (Pollock, Fasciano, Gervais-Guy, Gingras, Guy, & Hallee, 2001, p. 59). Collège Boréal took on the challenge of offering programs in French in seven communities "by implementing a number of strategies to bring about academic transformation, by encouraging faculty to move from traditional to nontraditional teaching" (Pollock Fasciano, Gervais-Guy, Gingras, Guy, & Hallee, p. 60).

In its first five years the college went through three waves of technology: video-conferencing; student and faculty use of laptops;

and online learning, mainly to support classroom teaching. In November 2009, the college was offering 111 points of service, 28 videoconferencing sites in 13 cities, a mobile learning center, and 21 fully online courses. However, as senior management changed over time, the goal of being a leader in technology-based teaching has become less pronounced, and the college has become more focused on campus-based teaching, although technology applications still remain extensive in the college.

The University of Alicante (Universitat Alacant), Spain

This case study was conducted by Sangrà (2008). The University of Alicante (UA) was founded in 1979. It is situated between the much older universities of Valencia and Murcia. In 2004, UA had 28,000 students. The Alicante province has traditionally been one of the most economically advanced in Spain with 25% of GDP. The university is located in a large scientific park and has strong connections with local businesses. The university also has a strong international focus.

The teaching is predominantly face-to-face, with a strong emphasis on hands-on activities, and teaching is closely linked to the needs of local employers. The university's main technology focus has been to develop Web-based services for administrative purposes, and to use technology to enhance classroom teaching. The university has developed its own in-house administrative and teaching support system, called Virtual Campus. There is also a program focused on fostering open source and open content at the university.

The university considers itself a leader in the use of information and communications technologies because of its Web activities for administration and because of its advanced infrastructure (wireless, and so on) for teachers and students, and because it is a young university with dynamic staff (compared to the nearby universities of Valencia and Murcia). All administrative staff use Virtual Campus, and 20% of faculty make full use of the platform for both administrative and teaching purposes. The university made a major effort to get faculty to use technology, including grants to encourage the use of technology in courses.

Strategy was driven mainly by the vision of the rector, but because there was no clear strategic plan, many in the institution did not feel directly involved or understand the vision. Despite the efforts of the university leadership, there was general faculty resistance to change, which was not helped by a lack of training in using technology, or by the lack of a learning technology support unit. There was no alternative model of teaching offered that tried to exploit fully the use of information and communications technology; the aim was to enhance traditional teaching methods. Indeed, distance education is not permitted by the university's statutes, except for noncredit, continuing education, despite a growing demand for distance courses. Finally, there was no evaluation strategy.

Southern Alberta Institute of Technology (SAIT), Canada

SAIT is a public two-year, campus-based postsecondary technical institution focused on business, computer technology, health and safety, trades, and vocational training, located in Calgary, Alberta. In 2004, there were just under 12,000 full time, on-campus students, and a total of 66,000 individual learners (part-time and full-time) enrolled in courses at SAIT.

SAIT receives grant funding from the province of Alberta, tuition fees from students, and funded contracts from business and industry. Its total annual budget was approximately C\$200 million in 2004. SAIT also receives substantial grants and endowments from industry, on an intermittent basis. For instance, a research chair in e-learning is partly funded from an endowment from Cisco Systems. Revenue generation is a major goal for deans.

SAIT is mainly campus based, using conventional classroom and lab-based teaching. There were just a few print-based distance courses in 2004. SAIT, though, wanted to position itself as a world leader among polytechnics; part of the strategy to accomplish this was to become a leader in the use of e-learning in polytechnics. A move to e-learning was seen as an opportunity for increased government funding for SAIT. Consequently SAIT hired one of the authors (Bates) as a part-time research chair in e-learning between May 2004 and September 2005, with a mandate to develop a strategic plan for e-learning for the institute. A report of the plan and the planning process was published by Bates (2007).

The strategic plan for e-learning was accepted by the executive team, but subject to additional funding becoming available. An implementation plan was also developed. Most of the 82 recommendations in the strategic plan for e-learning that did not involve additional expenditure were implemented between 2005 and 2008. SAIT has built a strong Centre for Instructional Technology and Development, with excellent staff to support e-learning. There is now a full-time research chair in e-learning. By 2009, there were 90 fully online courses and 73 blended courses, with a total of approximately 5,000 course registrations (500 FTEs). There was one degree, two diplomas, and 14 certificates available fully online.

In retrospect, the e-learning strategic plan was overambitious, requiring additional expenditure of $50 million over five years (5% of total operating budget per annum), which was not forthcoming from the provincial government. Targets and recommendations were not revised to take account of the lack of additional funding, and there was no clear budget strategy linked to the implementation of the plan. Thus, some core recommendations were not implemented due to lack of allocated funds. For instance, instructors still have a heavy teaching load of over 20 hours a week, which leaves very little time for the training in e-learning recommended in the plan. Finally, e-learning was still seen mainly as a supplement to classroom teaching. For instance, SAIT's Strategic Plan (2006, p. 14) stated that: "While e-Learning is part of SAIT's plan, it enhances learning and does not replace the traditional face-to-face experience."

UNIVERSITAT ROVIRA I VIRGILI, SPAIN

This is another of Sangrà's five case studies (2008). The university was created in 1991 from former campuses of the University of Barcelona in the cities of Tarragona and Reus. In 2004, it had 23,000 students and 1,000 faculty spread over five campuses.

The university strategic plans refer to a commitment to change and innovation. This is reflected in a move to learner-centered teaching, with a focus not just on contents but also on the skills and needs of learners (competency-based learning). The university stresses the importance of active and social, collaborative learning. There is an emphasis on quality assurance in the teaching process; faculty development and training are seen as the key to this change.

There was strong support from the institution's executive team in 2002 for "digitalizing" the university. Strong infrastructure was seen as the first stage of the plan, then access, then ensuring the capability of faculty, staff, and students in using the technology. Some fully online and hybrid courses were developed, but the main thrust was to use technology to support face-to-face teaching, through course Web sites that provide administrative information for students and some teaching resources and a collaborative learning space.

The university has a good national and international reputation in teaching and research and is seen as a leader among Spanish universities in the use of information and communications technologies. The infrastructure and administrative systems were completely changed; the teaching system in contrast incorporated technology but did not change its basic classroom-based model. Between 2002 and 2004, 49 innovation-in-teaching projects were funded involving 254 professors (25%). In the same period, the university went from 122 to 398 courses either fully or partly online. Thus many courses were digitalized, but always with the aim of improving face-to-face teaching, rather than hybrid or fully online, although there were in the end two online master's degrees, and a distance doctorate in educational technology offered jointly with three other universities.

There was no institution-wide standardization on a learning management system (at least three different systems were in use). The application of information and communications technologies varied considerably between departments. Ensuring consistency in technology applications across the university was a major challenge. Despite the rapid integration of technology into teaching and administration over the period of study, at the end the faculty still had not discovered new methods of teaching that fully exploited the potential of technology. The major use of the Internet was still for e-mail and to support research. Thus, the faculty had not transformed their teaching.

The University of A Coruña (Universidade de Coruña—UDC), Spain

This is another of Sangrà's case studies (2008). The University of A Coruña is located in Galicia, Northern Spain. It was founded in 1998. There was formerly a campus in the city of A Coruña that was part of the Universidad de Santiago de Compostela. UDC has 25,000 students, of which over half are studying sciences or technology, spread over two campuses in different cities.

The university's predominant teaching model is traditional classroom-based teaching. The university's aim was to install an advanced technology infrastructure and to develop blended learning through integrating information and communications technologies into the classroom. In 2004, the university created a project called INNOVATE with the aim of building Web sites for departments, a virtual library, the digital conversion of administrative processes, and developing an in-house learning management system.

Two years after the start of the INNOVATE project, 70 professors (just under 25%) had created digital materials with a great variety of applications and quality. Despite this, the technology infrastructure could not easily handle the expansion of information technology applications. The INNOVATE project turned out to be unsustainable financially or technically, and the learning management system did not meet faculty expectations. After just two years, the project was cancelled by an incoming administration.

The INNOVATE project was driven primarily by one senior manager who was not directly responsible for teaching. There was no overall plan for the use of information and communications technologies and the attempt to develop an in-house platform was a huge distraction from implementing online teaching. There was no training and no reward or incentives for the faculty to use technology, and no learning technology support unit was created.

THE UNIVERSITY OF MILAN (LA UNIVERSITA DEGLI STUDI DI MILANO), ITALY

This is the last of the Sangrà (2008) case studies. The University of Milan (UM) is a public, multidisciplinary teaching and research institution with nine faculties, 19 doctoral schools, and 92 specialization schools. The university has 65,000 students and 2,500 professors. According to the university Web site, its research is ranked among the best in Italy and Europe. It claims to be ranked first among universities in Italy, among the top 20 in Europe, and in the top 100 worldwide. Its annual budget in 2007 was 555 million euros (US$772 million).

Some background about the context in Italy is necessary to understand fully UM's strategy and actions regarding information and communications technologies. The Italian government in 2004 wanted to modernize what it called the "decadent" university system, and it saw information and communications technologies as being essential to this process. However, there was relatively low penetration of the Internet in Italy (37% of homes in 2004, and 45% by 2009). The predominant teaching model at the University of Milan was traditional classroom-based teaching combined in several faculties with practical work in laboratories.

The university's main strategy was to use information and communications technologies to improve the administration of the institution. The rector wanted to see it also be moved into other areas, to support research, teaching, the library, and so forth. "Everyone agrees with its use for administration; but there is no general consensus on its suitability for teaching." The university developed its own learning platform called Ariel, which is a course information system, a place to locate course materials, provides computer-based self-testing and can be used for fully online courses.

However, there was a very limited number of blended or online courses (less than 1,000 course enrollments) by 2005, and only one online program, in computer sciences. Only 10% of the faculty were using Ariel and there was a general rejection of distance teaching on principle by a large majority of the faculty.

There was no strategic plan for information and communications technologies, although there were many individual initiatives and a general direction that was "understood" due to the recognition of the importance of information and communications technologies for the efficient administration of the university. However, the digital student information system was still not working at the time of study (2005). Nevertheless, the senior administration believed that the university was on a par with leading North American universities in its use of technology.

CRITERIA FOR ASSESSING THE SUCCESS OR OTHERWISE OF TECHNOLOGY INTEGRATION

The main aim of the cases was to identify strategies, policies, and management approaches, which will be discussed in the subsequent chapters. However, sharp-eyed readers may have suspected an implicit ordering of the institutional case studies, from most to least successful. We have not done this ordering in a hard, quantitative way, and thus there is an inevitable subjectivity in this ordering. It would be unwise to place too much emphasis on whether one institution should be higher or lower than the next one. There are too many factors, and too many unknowns, for this to be a precise ordering. However, Virginia Tech, UBC, the University of Central Florida, and the Open University of Catalonia did seem to be the most advanced in successfully integrating technology within their institutions. How did we come to this conclusion?

We found ourselves using certain criteria to judge success or failure in the integration of technology, and we therefore should make these explicit. These criteria are in no particular order of priority; we believe that each one is equally important as a measure of technology integration. Also these criteria were derived after we had analyzed each case; they emerged as we looked at the similarities and differences between the institutions.

1. **Are there "champions" with power and influence in the institution who recognize the importance of technology for conducting the business of the institution?**

   A desire by the senior administration—or at least some key members of the senior administration—to integrate technology into the activities of the institution was common in all the case studies. Large and complex organizations, such as universities and colleges, depend increasingly on technology for the efficiency and effectiveness of at least some of their operations. The question becomes then not whether to use technology, but how best to use and integrate technology within postsecondary institutions, and whether there are powerful champions to drive this activity.

2. **Does the institution have an advanced, comprehensive technology infrastructure that enables all staff, students, and faculty to access computers, networks, software, and services as required?**

   This is a necessary condition for technology integration, but it was not a strong discriminator between the institutions in this study, because all the institutions had good technology infrastructure in place. However, for one or two institutions, this was the prime criterion used by the senior administration in assessing their status as technology leaders.

3. **Has the institution digitalized its administrative systems, and can staff, students, and faculty access administrative information and services easily over the Web?**

   Again, all the institutions had the digitization of administrative services as a high priority for technology integration. However, we begin to see some divergences between the case study institutions on this criterion, particularly regarding the provision of Web services, such as student portals, online admissions and registrations. Also there was a wide variation in the dates at which institutions reached this level of integration.

4. **Has the institution identified a clear, strategic rationale for the use of technology within the institution?**

   Why is technology being used? What benefits are perceived to be gained from using technology? How can this be measured—or put another way, how will it be known whether the intended benefits have been achieved? Some institutions were using technology for quite specific reasons, such as to increase access to the university's programs, to use technology to maintain quality with fewer resources, to improve the quality of teaching by moving to a more constructivist approach, and so on, while others were quite vague about their reasons, such as "to be a modern university" or to be seen as a leading university in using technology (without defining what this meant). We will argue elsewhere in the book that clearly defined and measurable goals are essential to justify the high cost of using technology.

5. **Has the institution identified additional financial resources or reallocated resources to support the integration of technology within the institution?**

   Information and communications technologies require substantial investment in both money and the time of faculty and staff, if they are to be successfully implemented and integrated within the institution. There were several examples in the case studies, particularly regarding the use of technology for teaching and learning, where no investment or additional resources were provided to support technology integration.

6. **What proportion of staff, students, and faculty are using technology and for which activities?**

   This is a somewhat obvious criterion, but one where data was sometimes lacking. Again, we saw wide variation in the extent to which technology had penetrated different institutions. At one end, there were some institutions where over 50% of the faculty were using technology in their teaching on a regular basis, and others where there was almost no use of technology for teaching. Some institutions had widened use beyond supporting classroom teaching, to new methods of program delivery. Some had almost no online distance education students while others had many (indeed in two cases, all students were online). In some cases, very few faculty were using a learning management system; in others almost all faculty were using an LMS in some way or other. Regrettably, a few institutions did not know the level of usage of technology, because no data were collected, analyzed, or published.

7. **How innovative is the use of technology, particularly for teaching?**

   One institution had completely redesigned its mathematics undergraduate program so that it was all available by computer. Another institution was using technology for a provincewide distributed undergraduate medical program.

In other institutions, the main use was for course information and loading PowerPoint or PDF files as backup to classroom teaching, which may be useful, but is not in our view an innovative use of the technology. Again, there was not always evaluative data about the success of innovative approaches, but at least where innovation occurred the institution was trying to exploit the potential of technology for teaching.

8. **What level of support and training is given to instructors to ensure good-quality teaching when using technology?**

We will discuss standards and best practice in more detail later in the book, but in some of the cases, instructors were woefully supported in using technology for teaching. We will argue that proper training for anyone planning to use technology for teaching is essential. We will also argue that instructors should have reasonably good access to instructional design and technical support.

9. **Are students learning better and getting better services as a result of technology integration?**

This is probably the most important question and the hardest to answer. Only one of the 11 institutions had made any attempt to measure better learning resulting from the use of technology, and one had attempted to answer the better services question. The real issue here is that there needs to be a much wider discussion about what constitutes better learning in a knowledge-based society, and how this can be measured. So in the end this question was not a good discriminator between institutions, because there was insufficient information or evidence from most of the cases.

INTERPRETING THE RANKINGS

Although the European campus–based universities generally ranked lower on technology integration, it would be wrong to generalize that European universities are behind those in North America from the information in our studies. Our North American sample was biased by the fact that three of the five cases had been identified before our study as best-practice institutions in faculty development and training for technology-based teaching. It is reasonable to assume, then, that they also probably excelled on some of the other indicators as well. If we had chosen different cases in either Europe or North America, the relative rankings between European and North American institutions might have been very different.

The main value of the rankings is that they enable us to compare the strategies between those institutions that we consider the most successful with those considered the least successful; in this way we hope to be able to identify success factors for technology integrations.

CONCLUSION

We have used a variety of sources in the analysis of strategies and activities that support the effective integration of technology in postsecondary educational institutions. As well as the formal case studies, we have drawn on the literature and particularly from our own experience in assisting with the planning and management of technology-based teaching in a comparatively large number of institutions around the world as well as those included in the case studies.

LIMITATIONS OF THE METHODOLOGY

Universities and colleges vary tremendously within a single state or province. There is even greater variation between institutions across countries, so any attempt at generalization or extrapolation from a small sample to the whole world of postsecondary education will be strictly limited.

At the same time, we were somewhat surprised to find considerable similarities in culture and methods of decision making between similar kinds of institutions in the different countries. There were more likely to be similarities, for instance, between comprehensive universities in different countries, than between a comprehensive university and a two-year college in the same state or province. Large universities in particular have very devolved decision-making structures that reflect the autonomy of faculty. Nevertheless, at least regarding the governance and management of technology, we shall see that in addition to differences there are common threads that seem to run across all postsecond-ary institutions.

However, we make no claims that we have hard, scientific evidence for our conclusions, nor that what we found will apply to all institutions. We also recognize that these findings will have varying degrees of resonance with different institutions. Even within an institution, the findings will apply more to certain periods of time in their development and integration of technol-ogy than to others. Nevertheless, we have covered a large enough sample of institutions to be comfortable in concluding that what we have found is likely to apply to many universities and colleges. With these disclaimers we can now look at the results of our studies.

CHAPTER FOUR

LEADERSHIP AND STRATEGY

The most successful strategies are visions, not plans.
—H. MINTZBERG, 1994b

Pushing the Envelope: Using Technology to Improve the Quality of Teaching

L'université de Vaud is one of the top 100 research universities in several world rankings. It has an excellent IT infrastructure; a young and energetic vice rector of technology with business experience who focuses technology development on the main "business" of the university, namely teaching and research; and an executive team that has a clear vision for the university built around excellence in teaching and research.

Since the 1980s it has had a rolling five-year plan for technology, linked to the university's overall strategic plan, which is updated every year. The university supports an open source learning management system (Sakai) that is widely used by faculty throughout the university, mainly but not exclusively to support classroom teaching. It also has an extensive range of online distance education programs, offered not only through continuing studies, mainly for noncredit courses, but also through several faculties, such as the school of business and the faculty of education, also using primarily Sakai. Several of these programs at the postgraduate level are offered internationally in English, particularly but not exclusively to students in other European countries. Online courses at an undergraduate level are generally restricted to courses in the final year as an alternative to the face-to-face courses.

However, the vice provost of academic affairs has called a meeting with the deans and the vice rector of technology, as a result of recent external reviews of four of the 12 academic departments (faculties) over the last two years (schools of business, health, social sciences, and science). Generally, the reviews were excellent, particularly regarding research, the academic credentials of staff offering the courses, and the overall content of the programs.

However, in each of the reviews questions were raised about the quality of the undergraduate experience. Because of recent cuts in government funding, classes were increasing in size, more contract instructors were being hired, and there was less interaction between students and research faculty than in previous years. Student evaluations had shown a slight but consistent deterioration over the last three years.

The vice provost of academic affairs was particularly concerned by comments from some nonacademic members (mainly from industry and government) of the review panels who had complained that while students had good content knowledge, they often lacked the skills needed for work, such as creative thinking, problem solving, and taking responsibility for their own professional development. In particular, one review had pointed out that whereas 20% of undergraduates from the program went on to research in universities or industry, 80% went straight into employment. It was felt that these students in particular were not really well prepared for life after university. Some of the research faculty had also been complaining recently that graduate students were also not as well prepared as in previous years.

As a result, the vice provost of academic affairs is proposing a radical overhaul of undergraduate education, in order to maintain and improve the overall standing of the university. In particular, she is recommending a reorganization of first- and second-year programs, with three primary focuses:

- Interdisciplinary, theme-based programs that would lead to more specialization in the final year
- Teaching designed around problem or inquiry-based learning, drawing not only on the research experience of faculty but

also on the latest research into teaching and learning in higher education to ensure deep rather than surface learning

- A heavy use of learning technologies in a controlled way to

  - Provide students with access to a wide range of online learning resources
  - Enable the development of independent learning skills and collaborative learning
  - Reduce time research faculty spent in large lecture classes
  - Free up faculty time for small group, face-to-face interaction and essential hands-on work in wet labs (which would be supported by online virtual labs, where appropriate)

Her main concern now is how to get buy-in and implementation for the change.

INTRODUCTION

Each of the case study institutions started with the overall intention of modernizing the institution through the application of technology to at least some of its core activities. However, as we saw in Chapter Three, there were major differences between the institutions in the extent and manner of technology integration. In this chapter we examine the role of leadership in driving technology integration, then look at how institutions went about strategic planning, and its value in integrating technology.

We find that although good leadership is essential, leadership alone will not result in technology integration. Support and acceptance from a wide range of stakeholders is necessary for success. We also find that successful planning requires the development of compelling visions and goals for the use of technology within institutions, and that in general the case study institutions were too conservative in their vision for the role of technology in teaching and learning.

LEADERSHIP

To quote Mintzberg (2009, p. 65): "More has been written about leadership than probably all other aspects of managing combined." (He is also pretty dismissive of most of this writing.)

DEFINING LEADERSHIP

Mintzberg (2009, pp. 65–66) argues that

> leadership tends to be used in two different senses. The first is with regard to position and the led: the leader is in charge, motivates and inspires, elicits shock and awe. . . . In the second sense, leadership is seen more broadly, often beyond formal authority: a leader is anyone who breaks new ground, sets direction that shows others the way.

Mintzberg argues that although leadership is important, it has to work alongside other factors. In particular, Mintzberg sees leadership as "one component of management—specifically about helping to engage people . . . to function more effectively."

We saw various styles of leadership but, generally, evidence from the case studies supported the model of leaders helping to engage people to function more effectively, rather than the model of the charismatic leader developing a vision and personally driving the organization toward the implementation of the vision.

CHARISMATIC LEADERSHIP

There were certainly the first kind of leaders in our study. In particular, the founding president of the Open University of Catalonia, Dr. Gabriel Ferraté, was a charismatic leader who created the university in his own vision: an institution of the Information Society for the Information Society. He was the driver behind the idea of a fully online university, focused on lifelong learners in Catalan society. Even all academic research at UOC is focused on the Information Society: research on e-government, e-business, and e-learning. It is also a very successful vision: at a time when enrollments at all universities in Spain were dropping (due to demographics), UOC was the only university continuing to increase its enrollments.

We saw similar leadership from the rector, Dr. Carlos Reis, and the vice rector, Innovation, Antonio Moreira Texeira, at the Open University of Portugal. The original focus on technology at Collège Boréal was also driven very much by the vision of its first president, Jean Watters. In several other institutions, such as UBC and Alicante, the president or rector was important in identifying or initiating a strategy for technology integration, but in these cases the task of developing detailed plans or activities was delegated to other senior administrators.

Collective Leadership

We also saw examples of the second kind of leadership. Although presidents and rectors played an important role in identifying and supporting technology integration as a strategic goal, in our cases successful integration always depended on support from the whole executive team. This was particularly noticeable at Virginia Tech, the University of Central Florida, and the Open University of Catalonia. A close working relationship between the CIO, the VP of administration, and the VP of academic affairs, seems to be a particularly important factor in successful leadership of technology integration.

In other cases, a CIO, vice rector, or provost may have been the driver of change, but without support from the rest of the executive team, technology integration, although not impossible, was usually much more difficult, and always suffered from lack of adequate financial resources. Also, we did find in at least two cases nominal commitment to technology integration by a whole executive team which quickly vanished when it came to finding the resources necessary for ensuring successful technology integration.

Leadership by Example

In nearly all the cases, there were individual champions of technology who acted as leaders by example. Sometimes this may have been a vice rector or dean; more often it would be an individual instructor who would have an almost religious zeal in pushing a particular technology.

Occasionally, individual leaders would help effect wider change. For instance, Murray Goldberg's development of WebCT in 1995–1996 at UBC led to rapid and widespread adoption of the software, not only at UBC but also globally. It was the right technology at the right time. At the same time, this development took place when the whole of UBC was engaged in a major push toward innovation to secure government funding. In this case, it is difficult to know which was the chicken and which was the egg.

However, the efforts of an individual instructor toward applying a particular technology to their teaching rarely leads to widespread adoption by their colleagues. Bates (2000) describes such developers as "Lone Rangers," free-spirited cowboys who like to operate outside the system. Indeed, Bates has argued that because of their dedication to making the technology work, and hence the time they devote to teaching with technology, Lone Rangers often discourage other instructors, who see the use of technology as extra work that takes time away from research and family and social life. The Lone Ranger is also a reflection of the culture of teaching in most universities and colleges; it is a private act between instructor and students. Sharing is not always wanted or encouraged by individual instructors. Also, we found that institutions were not good in supporting innovation in teaching that came from individual instructors. We will explore the reasons for this in the next section on strategic planning.

DECENTRALIZED LEADERSHIP

Because of the often decentralized organizational structure of universities, change may be driven within a particular academic department by the faculty themselves, almost independently of the rest of the university. For instance, at the University of Alicante, the faculty of arts was the major user of technology for teaching, whereas at the University of Rovira i Virgili, the school of chemical sciences and the faculty of educational sciences and psychology were the main users.

At UBC, the faculty of medicine is an interesting example of an academic division operating almost independently of the rest of the university. In the early 1990s, the faculty as a whole decided to move to a problem-based approach to teaching medicine in the undergraduate program. This required a complete redesign of the curriculum. Part of the redesign entailed moving much of the content on to the Web, providing essentially a large database of information that students could draw on (together with readings from textbooks) for helping to solve problems presented in class. Then in the early 2000s, the provincial government worked with the university to develop a distributed program delivery model for undergraduate medicine, in collaboration with two other universities and hospitals in other parts of the province. This involved adding video-conferencing, particularly for surgical and other medical demonstrations. These technology developments were all driven mainly by the dean and the faculty within medicine, although there was also support from the university's senior administration, a strong stimulus from government, and cooperation from other universities and hospitals.

LEADERSHIP BY TECHNOLOGY PROFESSIONALS

Finally, another group of potential leaders are the technology professionals. These may be the CIO and staff within the IT department, or the directors and staff in learning technology support units or distance education departments.

We saw in at least three universities (A Coruña, UOC, and Alicante) the development of strategy and activities mainly by central IT units that developed in-house administrative and teaching software (Virtual Campus projects). However, this was more the exception than the rule, and in at least two of the cases, this go-it-alone strategy was not altogether successful.

The trend instead is increasingly toward a more complex, cross-institutional management structure involving not only technology professionals but also the end users. Nevertheless, although the concept of technology innovation being driven by the IT professionals may be changing, their importance in decision making and management of technology of course remains. We will discuss further the changing role of IT professionals on the governance of technology in Chapter Nine.

A second and much newer group of technology professionals are those concerned with support for teaching and learning with technology. Institutions are increasingly creating not only central learning technology units, but even multiple learning technology support centers located within academic departments or faculties. These are staffed by people with training and experience specifically in the design and application of technologies for teaching and learning. Often such staff are highly qualified, sometimes with postgraduate degrees in educational technology or in both education and computer science.

However, despite their professionalism and knowledge, learning technology professionals (and both authors would count themselves in this group) are effectively weak leaders in driving change, because, not being tenured faculty or in most cases not reporting directly to a member of the executive team, they have a relatively low status in postsecondary educational institutions (we call them "disenfranchised experts"). They need to find and persuade more powerful champions of the need for change and of the ways in which technology might help, and work through these champions. Nevertheless, we shall see that learning technology professionals can and should play a greater leadership role in technology innovation and management than they do at present.

CONCLUSIONS ON LEADERSHIP AND TECHNOLOGY INTEGRATION

Leadership is certainly one critical factor in successful technology integration. However, the case studies show that in successful technology integration, more than just a charismatic president or rector, or a single champion of change, is needed. Successful technology integration requires a complex environment that supports change, with engagement from a number of key players, all working together and developing and sharing a common vision or set of goals for the use of technology.

In particular, there are dangers in charismatic leadership. When the leader leaves the institution, the vision and drive toward technology integration also leaves at the same time. The clearest example of this in the case studies was at Collège Boréal, although we have seen the same happen particularly in Latin American universities, such as the University of Guadalajara in Mexico, where whole administrations change following the election of a new rector, resulting often in promising developments being abandoned for new activities—out with the old and in with the new—irrespective of the merits of previous strategies.

Finally, leadership alone will not result in technology integration. Support and acceptance from a wide range of stakeholders is necessary for success, and this means putting in place a whole raft of activities that will facilitate technology integration. We examine next one of the most common of these activities, strategic planning.

Strategic Planning

The decision to integrate technology within an institution is clearly a strategic issue, as it implies substantial investment and, at least implicitly, significant change in basic operations. First we start by looking at the extent to which the 11 case study institutions embedded the decision to integrate technology within strategic plans or planning, then we will look more generally at the value of strategic planning for technology integration, and we end by making some suggestions and recommendations about the process of planning technology integration.

Strategic Planning in the Case Study Institutions

Not surprisingly, we found wide variation in the extent to which technology integration was considered within a strategic planning process, reflecting to a large extent the variation between post-secondary educational institutions in strategic planning generally. In eight of the 11 cases, there was a formal institutional planning process of some kind. In six cases (all considered to have the highest level of technology integration in our rankings), technology integration was highlighted within the overall institutional strategic plan. In some cases, as well as strategic directions for technology integration at the institutional planning level, there were also specific plans for e-learning (some might consider these substrategies or goals within the broader vision).

Interestingly, of the three cases with (in our view) the lowest level of technology integration, none had a formal strategic plan of any kind. In each of these cases, the drive toward technology integration came from a single senior executive, in two cases the rector, and in the other a vice rector. In those institutions without a strategic plan, this does not mean there was no strategy, but it was often necessary to search and read diverse and often dispersed documentation, or to talk to the champions, to identify the strategies.

Indeed, Bradmore and Smyrnios (2009) claim that strategic plans made available to the general public by the universities do not in reality reflect the true plans or concerns of the university leadership. They claim that it is common for universities to have three versions of strategic plans: a published, publicly available version that tends to avoid provocative issues; a more detailed version with relatively sensitive information, made available to staff on a need-to-know basis; and an even more sensitive and confidential plan that "might never be committed to paper, but that resides in the heads of the senior university administration" (2009).

One wonders then of the point of public strategic plans, if the senior administration has alternative agendas, and how the senior administration expects these alternative agendas to succeed without communicating them to their board, faculty, or staff. And indeed, in the case study institutions without a strategic plan that highlighted technology integration, communication to the whole organization of the importance of technology, and faculty acceptance of technology for teaching, were much more problematic than in the institutions with a public plan.

Strategic Goals and Directions

Most institutions' plans or public statements about technology integration reflected the recognition that technology was an essential component of a modern or twenty-first-century university, but within that broad rationale there were wide variations in the specificity and the scope of their goals. All the institutions recognized the importance of technology for managing or improving administrative services, such as institutional financial records, payroll, and student records and admissions. In many cases administrative services had already been digitalized well before the start of our investigations. For other institutions (for example, the University of Milan and the University of Alicante) digitizing administrative functions was still a major work in progress in the mid-2000s, and so this goal was the most important or pressing for them during the period of our case studies.

However, although there was almost universal acceptance of the importance of technology for administration, there was much wider variation between the case study institutions in the importance they attached to technology integration for teaching and learning. For instance, Virginia Tech's university plan and Academic Agenda (the part of the plan specifically related to teaching, learning, and research) for 1996–2001 identified goals such as

- Facilitating teaching in a distributed learning environment
- Facilitating the integration of technology in teaching, research, and outreach
- The creative, efficient, and effective use of resources while improving student learning

In its 2006–2012 plan, priority is given to "strengthening the university's commitment to distance and distributed eLearning and the use of advanced learning technologies by faculty and students within and outside the classroom."

The University of Central Florida saw blended and distance learning as essential for coping with rapid growth in student numbers. For both the open and distance teaching universities, online teaching was seen as essential—in one case as a matter of principle and in the other as a matter of survival. Other institutions had much vaguer goals in their strategic plans for technology integration, such as "to be a twenty-first-century institution" or "to be a world leader in e-learning in polytechnics."

Most saw a connection between the use of technology and quality improvements in teaching, but here there was a critical divide between those institutions where technology was seen as a means of merely "enhancing" what was believed to be already good-quality classroom-based teaching (the University of Milan,

SAIT, the University Rovira i Virgili, the University of A Coruña, and the University of Alicante), and those that saw technology as a means to innovate and improve on the classroom teaching model (Virginia Tech, UCF, and UBC).

In a couple of the cases, senior administrators stated privately that they saw technology as a means of introducing much-needed organizational and cultural changes within the institution (the hidden agenda). However, when these goals were not stated publicly, and concealed behind the curtain of technological innovation, there was sometimes confusion or resentment when technology initiatives had consequences for those unaware of the hidden agenda.

In one of the cases, the strategy was pure *Field of Dreams:* "Build it and they will come." The strategy was to ensure access to technology infrastructure for faculty, students, and administrators and to build a campuswide broadband network. It was then assumed that teachers and staff would find their own way to use the technology. Not surprisingly, perhaps, there was general disappointment with the results.

SETTING A VISION AND PRIORITIES

Some institutions took a middle road between developing a highly specific plan and just setting a direction and hoping everyone would follow. For instance, UBC set up a small committee (ACCULT—Academic Committee on the Creative Use of Learning Technology) that did not produce a detailed strategic plan with specific strategies, targets, and time lines, but aimed more at creating an environment that encouraged the innovative use of learning technologies. ACCULT recommended increased allocations to learning technology projects through an already existing teaching and learning enhancement fund, the establishment of learning technology support units within academic departments, more faculty development opportunities focused on learning technologies, and building communities of practice around teaching with technology.

There were two cases where the planning for e-learning was distinctly separate from the overall strategic planning process. At the Southern Alberta Institute of Technology, the plan for e-learning ran somewhat independently of the overall institutional planning process, in that it was completed just as the institutional planning process for the next five years was beginning. This caused problems later when the required funding for the e-learning plan was not made available, as it clashed with other priorities in the institutional plan.

Also, at the Open University of Portugal, there was a detailed plan for technology innovation for teaching and learning, but no overall plan for technology for the institution as a whole. Consequently, although the innovation plan for teaching was highly successful in its implementation, there was no budget for it, and administrative services were not digitalized at the same time, because the head of administration had other priorities (such as moving the whole institution to a new building). This highlights the importance of having the whole executive team—not just the president or the vice president of academic affairs—driving a strategic plan that includes technology integration.

The Time Element

It is also worth noting that the importance of technology integration within strategic plans within the same institution sometimes varied over time. Thus, for example, at UBC it was much more central in the strategic plan 2000–2010 than in the latest strategic plan for 2010–2020. Similarly at Collège Boréal, technology was less strongly highlighted in its plans in 2010 compared with the period when the college was being established in the 1990s. In 2004 Alicante did not have a plan for technology; in 2010 it does.

This may reflect a view that while technology continues to be important, technology integration matures and becomes more of an operational rather than a strategic issue. If so, we think this may be a mistake, as few institutions have yet to fundamentally change their operations to exploit fully the benefits of technology, particularly in the area of teaching and learning.

The challenge now is not so much integration as innovation and change in methods, to improve learning outcomes and to use resources more efficiently. Planning should be an ongoing, continuous process. This is particularly so for technology planning, as the technologies change so rapidly.

TECHNOLOGY AND TEACHING

Finally, some institutions had a much more limited view of the potential role of technology than others, particularly regarding teaching and learning. The faculty at one institution were generally hostile to the idea of using any technology for teaching, and the senior administration was not prepared to push them on this. In three others, the role of technology was limited strictly to supporting traditional classroom teaching. Indeed, one institution had statutes prohibiting distance learning. Not surprisingly, then, high technology penetration was found in those institutions, including campus-based institutions, where there was a much broader view of the possible role of technology for teaching that included the substitution of technology for classroom teaching (as in the Math Emporium in Virginia Tech, distributed learning at UCF, and distance learning at UBC).

Nevertheless none of the nine campus-based institutions in the case studies explicitly supported the goal of radically changing the predominant classroom teaching model. What we found particularly disappointing across nearly all the institutions (UCF was an exception) was the lack of recognition of the potential of hybrid learning, where courses are redesigned to exploit the benefits of both face-to-face and online teaching and learning, rather than merely adding technology to the classroom model. We think course and program redesign should be the next stretch for technology planning and integration.

We also noted some common features across all the campus-based institutions regarding the sequencing of strategic actions. In almost all cases, the first priority was to put in place adequate technological infrastructure with access for all faculty, staff, and students. The second priority was to digitalize administrative processes. The third priority was to use technology to support teaching and learning. (Technology to support research is an important fourth priority area, but we did not focus on this in our case studies.)

Although the first priority is not surprising (without adequate technology infrastructure, it is difficult to do anything with technology), on reflection it might seem curious that administrative processes take priority over teaching and learning. One of the authors attended a meeting (not at one of the case study institutions) where several tens of million of dollars were being requested for the purchase and implementation of an enterprise resource planning (ERP) system for financial and student services. The only way the money could be found was by raiding funds from the academic areas. The VP of administration commented that this was necessary, because the digitalization of administrative processes was "mission critical for the institution," to which the VP of academic affairs commented: "And teaching isn't?" Nevertheless the VP of administration won.

We think this can best be explained by the culture of post-secondary educational institutions. There is general acceptance that technology can be of great value to business processes, but there are still major reservations about the value of technology for teaching and learning. This came out particularly strongly in the University of Milan case study, but the same concerns were found among faculty and instructors in many of the other institutions.

FORMAL IMPLEMENTATION PLANS

Although goal setting is critical, implementation planning is also important. As Mintzberg (1994b, p. 112) puts it:

> An appropriate image for the planner might be the person left behind in a meeting, together with the chief executive, after everyone else has departed. All of the strategic decisions that were made are symbolically strewn about the table. The CEO turns to the planner and says, "There they all are; clean them up. Package them neatly so we can tell everyone about them and get things going."

Often in a university or college, the planner will be the associate vice president academic, the CIO, or the head of the learning technologies unit (or all three). Their job is to find the best ways to implement the strategic decisions.

Some institutions had a detailed plan for implementation. For instance, SAIT took the 82 recommendations from the strategic plan for e-learning, and developed a matrix identifying each of the actions needed to implement each recommendation, as well as a reporting time line that indicated when the recommendation had been implemented. By 2009, almost all the recommendations that did not have financial implications had been implemented; however, this left several of the key recommendations, such as release time for instructors to develop online materials and a program to support research and development of trades-based simulations, still to be implemented "when resources became available."

PLANNING AND RESOURCE ALLOCATION

Dalrymple (2007, pp. 14–16) notes:

> Strategic plans often fail to move beyond the planning phase
> . . . many institutions, while embracing the basic connection
> between the strategic plan and the budget, nevertheless fail to
> adequately coordinate the two. . . . The plan that is not connected
> directly to the budget process could become a disjointed effort
> with minimal success and no long-term gains.

In a study of the institutional management of e-learning in New Zealand tertiary education institutions (TEIs), Higgins and Prebble (2008) reported:

> Most TEIs, with even one foot in the e-learning water, will have a
> published strategy on e-learning. These strategies will vary
> enormously in scope and emphasis, depending on the nature of
> the enterprise and their aspirations. These are important and
> necessary documents that provide a focused strategic statement
> about this important area of development and activity. Anyone
> seeking to understand how the institution plans to develop and
> use online technology to support its teaching programme should
> find this the most coherent and informative planning document
> available.

> The problem with such documents is that, all too frequently, their
> themes and imperatives are not picked up and integrated with the
> other key strategic planning instruments of the institution. At
> worst, they are lofty statements of intent with few of the strategies,
> resources or processes required to put them into action. At best,
> they provide sound guidance and direction.

Institutional leaders with a serious commitment to e-learning should ensure that the strategic directions to be found in the e-learning strategy are strongly reflected and supported in the other strategic instruments of the organisation.

The failure to make hard decisions about reallocation of existing resources is a good example of unrealistic, wishful thinking about the use of technology for teaching and learning (compare this with the hard-nosed attitude to the use of technology for administrative purposes, described earlier). Too often technology for teaching is seen as a desirable nice-to-have rather than a core activity that needs to be funded adequately. There were several clear examples of this in the case studies. In particular, several institutions failed to identify and budget for the real cost of training faculty and instructors to use technology effectively. This was particularly true of those institutions that did not have a strategic plan, or did not integrate the planning of e-learning within the overall institutional plan. Because resource issues are so critical to technology integration, we will return to this again in Chapter Seven.

EVALUATING STRATEGIES

Finally, we were struck by the lack of evaluation of the strategies for technology integration. Some (for example, UCF, SAIT, and UBC) collected data on the different uses of WebCT, and others collected data on fully online enrollments. The University of Central Florida has a research team (RITE) that conducts studies on student satisfaction and participation in different kinds of online courses, and UOC also conducts regular surveys of student satisfaction concerning various elements of online teaching, such as learner support, quality of the materials, and so forth. UBC's Distance Education and Technology unit did research on online learning and the relative costs of online and face-to-face teaching (but was eventually told to stop doing this research, because it was not an academic unit). UOC more recently has developed a procedure for formal evaluation of innovation and research projects focused on online learning.

However, none of the institutions had a formal evaluation plan for measuring the overall impact or effectiveness of their use of technology or the success of their strategic directions, as far as we could tell. According to Dalrymple (2007), this is not unusual. In an extensive literature review, she found almost no reported formal evaluations of university strategic plans.

The Value of Strategic Planning for Technology Integration

A great deal has been written about strategic planning and its usefulness (see in particular Mintzberg, 1994a, 1994b; Birnbaum, 2000; Dalrymple, 2007). Planning and decision making are messy processes in any organization, driven as much by personalities, departmental priorities, empire building, and plain jealousies, as they are by logic, vision, the desire to improve services, or other lofty goals. Strategic planning has a bad reputation (particularly among academics). As Mintzberg (1994b, p. 108) puts it:

> The label "strategic planning" has been applied to all kinds of activities, such as going off to an informal retreat in the mountains to talk about strategy. But call that activity "planning," let conventional planners organize it, and watch how quickly the event becomes formalized (mission statements in the morning, assessment of corporate strengths and weaknesses in the afternoon, strategies carefully articulated by 5 PM).

Dalrymple (2007, p. 3) writes specifically about university strategic plans:

> Most institutions . . . ended up with a large report gathering dust on the shelf viewed as yet another management fad that created a lot of busy work.

Nevertheless, we do believe, from the experience of the case studies, that strategic *thinking*, and the construction and communication of that thinking through a somewhat formal planning process, does help greatly in getting technology well integrated within an institution. Mintzberg (1994b) makes the important distinction between strategic *thinking*, and strategic *programming*. He sees planning as "the articulation and elaboration of strategies or visions that already exist." What is critical is the development of the vision or strategy for technology. Because the ultimate implementers of strategy in a university or college, at least regarding teaching and learning, are the faculty or instructors, they need to be closely involved in the development of strategic thinking about the use of technology.

The process by which institutions arrived at this varied. In the case of UBC, the overall strategic plan for 2000–2010 (TREK 2000) originated much more as a vision statement from the president at the time, Martha Piper. TREK 2000 eventually stated that UBC would "fully integrate information technology with instruction in all areas." However, the planning or implementation, as far as teaching and learning was concerned, was delegated to the vice president of academic affairs and provost, who in turn delegated the aspects associated with technology use in teaching and learning to the associate vice president, academic affairs. He called together a small committee (ACCULT), which produced a report that was accepted and approved by both the university senate and the governing board.

However, although the report was important in legitimizing directions and budget allocations for technology, much more important was the educational process the ACCULT committee went through with faculty. The committee held all-day meetings for faculty in every department to brainstorm on creative uses of technology for teaching and learning. These visions were collected and incorporated in the final report, and formed the basis for a short video (http://media.elearning.ubc.ca/det/accult-T1.html). Thus the strategy process was as much an educational exploration of the possibilities of teaching with technology as it was a planning experience. The focus was on the thinking, not on elaborate plans for implementation or rigid goals.

At the Open University of Portugal, the decision was made by the rector to move all programs online and these would incorporate a constructivist model of learning. The vice provost of innovation developed a detailed plan setting out how this would be done. A key component was the training of all faculty on the use of technology-based constructivist teaching, and then it was left to the faculty, supported by instructional designers and Web programmers, to work out how best to do this within their own subject area. Generally, this worked well, although some faculty in science had strong reservations and objections to a constructivist model of teaching.

Bottom-Up or Top-Down Planning and Innovation?

Finally, we have often heard the view that you cannot plan for technology, particularly for innovative uses of technology. These will emerge from the ground up ("Let a thousand flowers bloom"). Mintzberg (1994b) talks about emerging strategies that come from those working within organizations. These emerging strategies do not always fit with the top-down strategy from the senior management.

For sure, in some of the institutions without a strategic plan, there were grassroots initiatives, or initiatives driven by an individual senior administrator. However, these were often isolated within a particular department. For instance, in at least three of the institutions without an institutional plan, IT or computer science departments developed in-house software systems under names such as Virtual Campus. Although in two cases the administrative applications were more successful, the teaching applications were considered failures by faculty, and hence did not become integrated. One has to sympathize here with the IT departments; in these cases they were trying to provide leadership within a strategic vacuum. Indeed a feature of technology initiatives within the institutions without a plan (and in one or two with a plan) was a focus on the technology itself, such as network infrastructure or building software for administrative activities, rather than on the actual integration of technology within administrative or teaching processes.

An alternative and more effective strategy is to deliberately encourage innovation by creating an environment that rewards risk taking and new initiatives. Several of the institutions (for instance, Virginia Tech and UBC) and some government agencies (for example, BCCampus) provide annual grants for innovative teaching projects that enable faculty or instructors to be released from one semester of teaching to redesign their teaching, create online digital materials, or to hire technical support. In others (for example, the University of Central Florida,

UBC, and UOC), support units with specialists in the application of technology to teaching were hired to work with faculty to develop new course designs. Show-and-tell workshops where instructors can share their experience with other instructors, or "whole program design," where a whole degree is completely redesigned, are stronger actions that can encourage the spread of innovation. In the latter case, though, this may require the allocation of extra resources or a new business model (as in the case of UBC's master's of educational technology). These actions though were not always sufficient on their own to enable the innovations that occurred to spread to other instructors or programs.

With the rapid changes in technology, and with the autonomy of faculty in universities, innovation in using technology for teaching will come from the bottom up. An important function of an ongoing strategic planning process is to identify innovations and emerging strategies for technology applications that have wider possibilities beyond the context of an individual instructor or course, and to build this knowledge or intelligence into future strategic directions. In successful strategic planning, both emergent and top-down strategies become integrated, enabling an organization to remain flexible and adaptable to changing circumstances.

In general, postsecondary educational institutions have not done this well, often leaving many promising innovative projects in isolation and unsupported. We believe that one reason for this is because institutional plans for universities and colleges rarely aim at radical change to the current teaching system, or at least rarely state this explicitly. As we have seen, the goal more often is to use technology to enhance or support the current teaching model. This could be called a "technology-lite" or "decaffeinated technology" policy. It results, though, in leaving the most interesting projects, in terms of changing the current teaching model, isolated and unsupported. In addition, universities and colleges would do well to look at the literature and experience of innovation strategies in other types of organization, and learn from these to incorporate strategies to encourage innovation in teaching, and to ensure the transferability and sustainability of innovative practices across the institution.

Integrating Institutional and Departmental Plans

Finally, there was a tendency in some of the case studies to see strategic planning for technology as a separate exercise from academic planning at a departmental level. We believe that it is essential to integrate planning for learning technologies with the plans for academic programs and departmental budgets.

Some institutions, however, had very rudimentary program planning processes at a departmental level, driven mainly by the availability or interests of individual faculty members. Thus, if someone went on sabbatical, a course would be suspended, or replaced by another depending on who was able to substitute. Programs may remain largely unchanged, except for minor adjustments such as adopting a new textbook, for many years or until a faculty member retires or dies.

Given, however, the rapid changes in knowledge bases, learning technologies, and the needs of learners and employers, nearly all academic departments or faculties should have at least a three-year rolling plan for programs that is revised annually (a program would be a degree, such as a bachelors of arts, or a first-year foundation program). This planning would not only include *what* is in the courses or program but also *how* it is to be taught.

Thus program planning would include decisions about

- Learning outcomes and teaching methods (lectures, seminars, discussion, problem-based learning)
- Content (the curriculum, textbooks, and readings, assessment questions)
- Student learning activities (such as project work, lab work, group work, and assessment activities)
- The role of technology (the role of a learning management system, online discussion forums, e-portfolios, Webcasting)
- The appropriate mix of face-to-face and online learning at different points in the program

Such planning would involve all faculty or instructors in the program, and learning technology support staff, so that there is coherence and a common understanding across the whole program.

Out of this planning process would come a clear set of requirements for hiring new or replacing retiring faculty (because new subject areas may not be covered), for technology support in teaching, and possibly for innovative approaches that could be shared beyond the program. This plan would be the justification for a budget request for the department or program for the coming year.

Finally, if the senior administration wishes to support more strongly the use of technology and innovative teaching processes, this should be linked to the budget process. Thus faculty might not be automatically replaced when they retire or leave in those departments that do not have a "good" academic plan, however defined and communicated to departments, whereas those departments showing a wish to innovate and develop may get priority for resources. Such a process would also be immensely helpful in setting priorities for the allocation of scarce learning technology staff.

Conclusions and Recommendations Regarding Strategic Planning

First, it is clear that technology integration is more likely to occur in those institutions that have a flexible institutional plan in which the strategic importance of technology is recognized. This is particularly important for ensuring that the financial implications of technology integration are understood and acted on, as well as for communicating the importance of technology integration to all key staff.

Second, and in our view, most important, successful planning requires the development of compelling visions and goals for the use of technology within institutions. Too often in the case studies, vision was limited to supporting current administrative processes and classroom teaching methods, rather than using technology to lever radical change directed at new and better learning outcomes, greater flexibility for students, and increased cost efficiencies that are measurable through a formal process of evaluation.

Third, integration and innovation are more likely to occur when there is a process to draw faculty and instructors into the visioning and strategic thinking around the role of technology for teaching and learning.

Fourth, for successful technology integration, an institutional strategy must be fully supported by all members of the executive team, and that support needs to be continued over a considerable period, including changes in executive teams. Some of the most successful institutions in integrating technology had consistent strategies and key people in senior administration in place for many years. Other less successful institutions in the case studies often suffered from a lack of shared vision at the executive level, or continual changes in directions or key personnel.

Fifth, technology planning should be an ongoing process. New developments in technology with profound implications for teaching, research, and administration, and pressures on institutions from changing economic and social contexts that could be addressed to some extent through the intelligent application of technology, are likely to continue well into the future. Thus the need for ongoing technology planning is not going to go away, and should remain a feature of future institutional planning.

Finally, once strategic direction is set for technology integration, a process needs to be put in place to create and maintain an environment that supports and encourages the integration of technology. Of particular importance is the need to link strategic directions for technology to an annual academic program planning and budgeting process in each faculty or academic department.

In Chapter Nine we make suggestions for how these recommendations could be implemented.

CONCLUSION

In this chapter we have examined two aspects of technology integration within the 11 case studies: leadership and strategic planning. We found that leadership, not surprisingly, was an important element in facilitating the integration of technology, but leadership works best when it guides and facilitates the wide range of people within the organization that are needed to implement technology applications successfully. Particularly important is a shared vision and commitment toward technology integration across the whole executive team, and especially between the chief academic, administrative, and technology officers.

Strategic planning is also important, but more important is strategic thinking about the way technology could transform the organization. This means focusing on

- The learning outcomes that are required in a knowledge-based society and how technology can help develop such outcomes
- Developing competencies in the use of information and communications technologies within specific areas of study
- More flexible delivery of programs to accommodate a more heterogeneous student body
- The redesign of courses and programs to integrate technology better
- Better services to students
- Greater efficiencies in both teaching and administration (namely, better outcomes at lower cost)

In some of the cases (for example, Virginia Tech, UCF, UBC, and the two open universities) we did find elements of this kind of strategic thinking (although it was never stated so comprehensively). In others, we found little evidence of this level of thinking, the emphasis instead being on improving business as usual.

Clearly, outside our limited range of case studies there will be other institutions (particularly the for-profits, such as Kaplan and Full Sail) where such radical strategic thinking exists, but nevertheless within our cases we were surprised by the overall caution in the thinking and particularly the hesitation to openly declare a more radical strategy for technology in teaching and learning, even though there were individual senior administrators who privately expressed such feelings. Several times we were told that faculty were not ready for this kind of change, and this is probably a correct observation.

In the next chapter we will look at some of the organizational initiatives taken within the case studies to facilitate the integration of technology.

CHAPTER FIVE

ORGANIZATIONAL STRUCTURES AND INITIATIVES TO SUPPORT TECHNOLOGY INTEGRATION

There is nothing more difficult to carry out, nor no more doubtful of success, nor more dangerous to handle, than to initiate a new order of things. For the reformer has enemies in all those who profit from the old order, and only lukewarm defenders in those who would profit by the new order, this lukewarmness arising from the fears of their adversaries, who have the laws in their favour; and partly from the incredulity of mankind, who do not truly believe in anything new until they have had actual experience of it.
—MACHIAVELLI, 1532, P. 22

Dr. Angela Dubrowski, Vice President of Academic Affairs and Provost, Eastern Seaboard State University

Dr. Dubrowski has been vice president of academic affairs for nearly nine months. Before that she was dean of the faculty of arts. She is a respected scholar specializing in modern American literature, with two highly acclaimed books to her name. She had also earned the respect of her colleagues as dean by successfully protecting the budget for the faculty of arts when faculties of arts and humanities in similar neighboring state universities had been cut drastically. She is decisive, communicates well with her colleagues, and works in a very collaborative manner with the deans and her colleagues on the executive team. Her priority over the last nine months has been the integration of a former community college into the state university, as a result of a statewide reorganization aimed at saving money. But today she is facing a different problem.

She is having lunch with Michael Blackstone, the VP of administration. The university's contract with a commercial learning management system company is coming up for renewal. The CIO, who reports to the VP of administration, has recommended renewal of the contract, at a cost of approximately $1.2 million a year. However, as usage increases, this cost will also increase. Up to now, the cost of licensing has been absorbed wholly within the Admin VP's budget as part of IT infrastructure. Now, however, Blackstone wants this budget to be split 50–50 with the provost. His argument is that this is mainly an academic cost, but he is also constrained by the fact that the new contract represents an increase of 40% over the previous contract, and he has no room to maneuver in his own budget to absorb this extra cost.

Dr. Dubrowski's problem is further compounded by a memo from 25 faculty in education, who had argued that the university should move to other forms of electronic delivery, such as Web 2.0 tools, to "improve learner-centered teaching and more constructivist ways of learning," and by a very unpleasant meeting with the dean of science and the head of the computer sciences department, who had strongly criticized the CIO's decision to renew the commercial contract. They had argued that the university should be using an open source platform, such as Moodle, which would be much cheaper and better for teaching.

Adding to Dr. Dubrowski's anxiety about this decision was the fact that she herself had not much experience in using technology in her own teaching, which was largely classroom based, although she had used the learning management system for students to access her list of recommended reading, curriculum information, and sample assignment questions. She privately dreaded the thought of having to move all her "stuff" to another system, and she sensed that many faculty would also have the same fear. She was also concerned about how to find another $600,000 a year from her own budget, which was already stretched to the limit. Furthermore, this issue is one she could really do without, as there were many academic issues to be resolved with the merging of departments across the two campuses.

In this context, and given the fact that she may need some financial support from the VP of administration for the merger, she decided to support his decision to renew the commercial contract, and would try to find "her" $600,000 from perhaps the modest increase in tuition fees that she was proposing for next year, which the VP of administration also supported. However, she knew she was going to have to face some unpleasant meetings with some deans and faculty as a result of her decision—and possibly from students too, given that tuition fees would have to go up. But at least Blackstone had the decency to pick up the tab for lunch.

Although leadership and strategic planning are essential for setting general directions for information and communications technologies, and particularly for developing strategic thinking, the successful integration of technology requires daily and continuous attention throughout the organization. In this chapter, we will examine some of the organizational models developed to support the integration of technology.

We shall see that there needs to be ongoing mechanisms in place for dealing with technology issues as they arise, and that a clear and coherent governance structure for technology is required in every institution, which should be a prime responsibility of the executive team.

TECHNOLOGY PROJECTS

In the case studies it was not uncommon for the executive team or a senior administrator to establish a specific project or set of activities as the main thrust of their strategic directions for technology. We define a project as an activity with a clear if limited goal, defined resources such as staff time, a person with clear responsibility for the project, and a deadline for completion.

INFRASTRUCTURE PROJECTS

Although technology infrastructure continuously requires investment, maintenance, and new activities, several institutions during the case studies made extra efforts to upgrade their technology infrastructure over a short period of time as part of their technology strategy. For instance, the University of Central Florida in 1995 provided all their students and staff with network access and e-mail accounts and in 1996 completed a campus networking project to connect all faculty and staff offices to the campus fiber optic backbone. Several institutions (for example, UBC and Alicante) made concentrated efforts to ensure that wireless access was available across the whole campus.

Special technology infrastructure projects require an extra burst of investment and activity. They are driven partly by strategic plans, partly by demand from faculty, administrative staff, or students, partly by the normal life cycle management (upgrades and replacement), and occasionally by the latest technology trends (such as electronic whiteboards, multiple screens in classrooms, or lecture capture). Thus technology infrastructure projects could be considered standard activities, as part of an overall strategy to support a range of technology applications on campus, a little extra boost to the normal operating costs of keeping infrastructure current and secure.

However, the priority for such special projects should be related to meeting functional objectives, such as more interactive student services, improved learning outcomes, or reducing operational costs, and thus should be determined as part of an integrated planning process, not just because they are the latest technology trend or even because of strong demand from one or two powerful pressure groups.

THE DEVELOPMENT OF SOFTWARE BY THE EUROPEAN INSTITUTIONS

In several of the case studies, the development of software for administrative purposes and to support teaching were major projects that constituted a large part of an institution's technology strategy. These projects raised a number of issues.

We saw in Chapter Two that many institutions have installed large and expensive commercial ERP systems, and that in recent years these have been augmented with Web services that allow faculty, staff, and students to interact directly with these systems. In the North American cases, commercial administrative systems were installed, and commercial learning management systems were used. However, every single European campus–based institution in our sample (A Coruña, Alicante, Rovira i Virgili, and Milan) embarked in the mid-2000s on a major in-house project to develop or adapt software for their administrative systems, and also to incorporate in these projects software to support teaching, rather than go with commercial or open source solutions. (We were not able to establish whether this was just a random occurrence in our four European examples, or whether this is typical of European universities—we suspect not.) UOC also developed its own in-house system, in the 1990s. WebCT was developed at UBC, but not as an institutional project, and was quickly sold to Blackboard three years later.

It should be noted that in most cases, the software to support teaching in the European campus–based universities was not a full-blown learning management system, but areas where instructors could load teaching materials, provide some computer-based testing, and interact with students through e-mail, to support their classroom-based teaching, although in some cases they were also eventually used for the occasional fully online course.

The results for the European institutions were at best mixed. In particular the software systems for supporting teaching were not successful. Alicante had the most successful project (Campus Virtual), for its flexibility and quality in administrative services, but there was more of a mixed reaction from faculty to the software for supporting teaching. At A Coruña, the INNOVATE project was cancelled after two years by a new, incoming administration, for several reasons, including slow take-up by faculty, overload on the technology infrastructure, and poor-quality digital learning materials. Milan struggled both with its student information system software and the fact that less than 10% of faculty were using Ariel, the software for supporting teaching. Rovira i Virgili ended up with at least three completely different software systems for teaching, one developed by their IT department, one by the faculty of computer sciences, and Moodle was used by those instructors who liked neither of the other two systems.

LMS WARS

The University of Rovira i Virgili, and indeed the other projects described previously, are good examples of a phenomenon that is not uncommon, which we call LMS "wars." These center around the choice of a learning management system. Should the institution decide to support a single LMS, or should faculty or departments be allowed to choose whatever LMS they prefer (or even build their own)?

There are several main reasons for settling on a common LMS that is used throughout the organization. One is operational cost. It is much cheaper to provide technical support for one rather than a multitude of technology platforms. It is also much easier to provide training for all users on a single platform than to have multiple (or sometimes no) training programs for multiple platforms. This applies also to students as well as instructors. If students take courses across different faculties or departments, it can be confusing to have to switch from one learning management system to another.

The most important reason, though, is that LMS wars slow down the speed at which technology becomes integrated within the institution. Too much time is spent on arguing over the often very small functional differences between systems and not enough in actually using the system for teaching and learning. We have seen some institutions take over two years to make a decision on their first LMS, thus inhibiting any use during that period.

There is relatively little functional difference between at least the commercial and open source systems, in terms of an instructor's choice of teaching. Some will argue that open source allows more flexibility, but others will argue that commercial systems are more stable. In practice, good course design (clear objectives, well-structured learning materials, good graphics) is likely to be more influential on learning outcomes than the choice of an LMS.

It makes much more sense to have one, well-tested system in place and fully supported by the institution, to make sure there is adequate training on the use of the system, and to implement the system as quickly as possible. Alternative learning management systems should be permitted only as a deliberate test if the institution is considering a switch to a new system. Indeed, it might make more sense, at least for smaller institutions, for a learning management system to be available on a state- or provincewide basis, enabling the sharing of technical support and maintenance costs across the institutions.

There are difficult decisions to be made, however, if an institution wants to change to a different LMS. One is the cost and uncertainty of moving all the course materials from the old to the new system, and the concern about technical glitches when the new system opens. This does require careful planning to be successful.

Developing new systems from scratch is a high-risk activity. It may have made sense when the field was open, as in the mid-1990s. Going up against well-established commercial or open software systems in the mid-2000s is another matter. Although designing a learning management system is not a major programming challenge, there are major costs for technical maintenance and upgrading, customer support, and marketing. Although hard data is difficult to come by, the full commercialization of WebCT probably requires an investment in the range of $10 to $20 million, and several million dollars annually to market, maintain, and upgrade the system. It is these back-end costs of learning management systems that hurt, and most universities or colleges are not equipped for running such a large-scale business.

LESSONS LEARNED ABOUT SOFTWARE CHOICES

One can only speculate on why all the European institutions in the case studies tried to develop in-house systems, rather than use off-the-shelf products. Despite its frequency in our cases, we do not think that in-house development is a particularly European approach; it was just the way the cases were chosen. Indeed, there are many institutions in the English-speaking world that have tried to develop their own administrative and teaching software systems.

One major reason, of course, is cost. Commercial systems are very expensive and it is tempting to avoid the costs by developing systems in-house, especially if there are professional computer software engineers available either as staff or faculty. The wish to develop a Spanish or Italian software solution (that is, language and culture) is almost certainly another reason (although a Spanish version of WebCT was available in 2000). The European institutions probably also thought of technology innovation in terms of new software products, rather than thinking of technology innovation as facilitating new and more effective processes. The in-house administrative projects were also in some cases, such as Alicante, successful. Once a great deal of investment and energy has gone into developing a successful in-house administrative system, it will be tempting to try to extend its use to supporting teaching.

However, the attempts to develop in-house *teaching* systems were not successful in any of the four European campus–based institutions. Because the strategy in all these universities was to use technology primarily to support classroom teaching, the design of the teaching spaces was often minimal (a place for faculty to post documents or create a Web page), there was often a lack of consultation with the end users, and as a result it was often difficult and time-consuming to use the teaching spaces, compared to off-the-shelf learning management systems. The restricted view of the role of technology for teaching at these universities also probably resulted in the low use of the online teaching spaces by faculty. Furthermore, it is one thing to design a software system; it is quite another to market it to internal users, to operate it effectively and reliably, and to maintain it as technology changes. Sustainability becomes a challenge.

In the European cases, the projects aimed at developing software to support teaching all consumed a great deal of time, money, and energy when there were off-the-shelf options (both commercial and open source) available. These institutions would have done better to direct their resources and energies to other activities, such as training faculty in the use of technology, and developing a basic pedagogical model to support the use of technology for teaching.

The case for using off-the-shelf administrative systems is less clear. Even when using off-the-shelf commercial systems, there is still scope for in-house development of Web-based tools that draw on the ERP databases. A few large commercial companies have a lock on ERP systems, with escalating costs and lack of flexibility and adaptation to educational needs. Thus the development of the Kuali consortium of universities to develop collaborative open source ERPs is interesting.

However, participating in such a consortium of large research universities is very different from trying to go it alone. Few postsecondary educational institutions have the resources and commercial experience to develop and maintain their own, unique ERP systems, without it being a great drain on resources and a constant battle to adapt and maintain the service as technology changes.

The value of learning management systems is that they provide a common framework for course design, they have direct links with administrative systems, and they are now familiar tools both for the IT support staff and for instructors, and open source solutions offer the potential for cost savings. However, there is an increasing number of other digital technology tools becoming available that challenge the dependence on learning management systems for teaching and learning. For these new Web 2.0 tools to be exploited, though, a major shift in course design and pedagogy is needed. Learning management systems still provide faculty with a comfort zone that enables them to manage technology within a familiar pedagogical and teaching framework.

CONCLUSIONS REGARDING PROJECTS TO SUPPORT TECHNOLOGY INTEGRATION

The main strategy for technology implementation in several institutions was the development a major project, often around the design or installation of administrative or teaching software.

Where these projects operated in isolation of a more general strategy for technology integration, or were the initiative of a single senior administrator, they were more likely to fail or at least to restrict the extent of technology integration within the institution. Projects worked best when they were part of a more general strategy for technology implementation that included training of instructors, and a focus on teaching and learning as well as technology infrastructure, administrative, or software developments.

Thus, while specific projects can be valuable, at the same time it is important to establish ongoing and permanent structures to support technology integration, and this will be the topic of the next section.

Committee Structures

Most of the institutions in the case studies had technology committees of one kind or another. Universities in particular are prone to establishing committees (we found extensive committee structures less prevalent in two-year colleges). The main reason is that in a collegial organization such as a university, faculty in particular need to participate fully in decision making.

However, with technology, there is another reason. There are many stakeholders involved in decision making about technology. Knowledge and expertise about technology and its applications are not spread evenly throughout the organization. A committee is a useful way to bring together people with different kinds of technological expertise and those who will be directly affected by technology decisions, policies, or investment. In the case studies, though, the membership, mandates, and permanence of technology committees varied considerably.

Standing or Temporary Committees?

Sometimes, a committee was permanent or met on a regular basis (a standing committee), some with university-wide membership, some with elected faculty members, and others with faculty members appointed by deans (or represented by the deans themselves). University-wide technology standing committees existed at UCF, Alicante, Milan, Rovira i Virgili, and SAIT, and were more prevalent in the smaller institutions (Milan was an exception).

Some large universities, such as UBC and Virginia Tech, tended to avoid such committees, because to ensure that all stakeholders were represented, the committees would become very large and unwieldy. Instead, there would be several smaller committees or groups, sometimes informal, that would meet on an as-needed basis ("working group" might be a better term for such committees). In these large universities, it was not uncommon for a faculty or academic department to have its own technology committee. A feature of several of the case study institutions was that committees came and went, depending on the stage of development (more likely to be active during a strategic planning process, less active when technology was off the agenda or when champions of change left or were replaced).

Committee Mandates

Mandates also varied considerably. In some institutions, the CIO established an advisory committee that focused mainly on network and IT support issues. In other institutions, there were committees that focused mainly on teaching and learning, reporting to the chief academic officer, either directly or through an associate vice president or vice rector. The University of Milan had a university-wide Network Technology Committee that focused mainly on technology infrastructure issues, whereas the University of Central Florida and SAIT had standing committees that focused on distributed learning or e-learning. Sometimes, institutions had both kinds of committees, usually with some cross-membership, but not always.

Occasionally, university-wide committees would be called for very specific purposes, such as the choice of a learning management system, or to advise on the design and operation of an in-house software system (UOC, Alicante, and Rovira i Virgili). Also at UBC, the CIO established an e-strategy group that aimed at integrating all aspects of technology policy and planning, mainly through an annual university-wide town hall meeting, and an online monthly e-strategy newsletter.

Committee Membership

Not surprisingly, membership of committees also varied considerably between institutions. University-wide technology committees usually had representatives from faculty, students, and technology support areas. Generally, if there was no committee formally established by the institutional leadership, committees tended to become informally constituted. At UBC, some faculties had established their own learning technology support units, and their directors formed a committee (the Faculty Alliance for Technology in Education) that would meet occasionally with the associate vice president of academic affairs to discuss learning technology issues. However, the danger of such informal committees is that they become exclusive, focusing on their special interests, and sometimes deliberately excluding members from other groups seen to be in competition for internal resources or support.

COMMON ISSUES AND STRATEGIES FOR TECHNOLOGY COMMITTEES

Given the heterogeneity of the institutions in the case studies, it is not surprising that there were large variations in the committee structures. Faculty often complain about there being too many committees, that committees are slow and clumsy and do not handle decision making well, and, most of all, they eat away at the precious research time of faculty. However, it became clear to us that committees have an important role in technology governance and integration, but also that there are common issues that need to be addressed and strategies that should be followed if technology is to be professionally managed and governed.

Generally, in the case studies, committees had no formal powers other than making recommendations or advising senior administrators. Nevertheless they provided an essential function of identifying issues and drawing together often initially incoherent or conflicting views into solid recommendations for action, providing support and legitimacy for decisions ultimately taken by the senior administration, and, perhaps of most importance, providing a means to disseminate a better understanding of sometimes complex and technical issues to all those likely to be affected by such decisions. The committee structure is also an important mechanism for enabling bottom-up innovations in technology to become better known and evaluated and, where appropriate, integrated within the strategic planning process. However, for this to happen, committees need to be plugged in to the strategic planning process and this was rarely the reality in the case studies.

Second, in nearly all the case study institutions, committees tended to be established in an ad hoc way, sometimes at the request of a senior administrator, and sometimes informally constituted to meet a pressing need. In several of the most successful institutions in integrating technology, the ad hoc system of committees worked effectively. Senior administrators used their committees well, and worked together as an executive team to coordinate and integrate decisions from different committees. It would be fair to say that despite the lack of formal organizational structures for technology decision making, these institutions muddled through quite well, mainly due to the collegiality and competence of the senior administrators and the faculty and staff in these institutions.

The status and power of committees to make decisions in almost all the case studies were often limited, yet they were often the most informed and knowledgeable sources for complex decision making. Sometimes there was confusion or lack of clarity around which decisions a committee was empowered to make, or who outside the committee could make contributions to the committee's decision-making process. In some cases, committees, once established, did not meet on a regular basis, and sometimes recommendations of committees were ignored or overturned by the senior administrator to whom they reported. Too often, key decisions about technology were made by senior administrators without the necessary knowledge and skills to make an informed decision, or committee recommendations were overturned by other factors (such as competing priorities) that were not well explained or communicated to the committees that had done the work.

Permanent Organizational Units

Although committees perform many useful functions, all the institutions found that they needed to put in place permanent operational units to support technology integration.

Diversity and Complexity

All the institutions in our case studies created relatively permanent units to support the use of technology. However, the type of organizations and their respective roles and functions varied enormously. Each institution adopted different terminology, different reporting relationships, and different roles for these organizational units.

Indeed, in some organizations the arrangements were surprisingly complex, with multiple units with seemingly overlapping responsibilities. As one of the interviewees said, "It's not logical; it's just developed this way. But it seems to work." In one case, an institution prided itself in having no organizational structure that could be written down. The founding rector of the Open University of Catalonia put it this way: "We have tried to implement a unique organizational model based on the idea of project teams and networking across academic and administrative divisions. Its aim is for a flat, networked, dynamic operational structure."

Thus trying to provide a simple categorization of organizational units is not possible. Nevertheless, if we focus on the *functions* that these various organizational units carried out, some clear patterns become apparent, although in our aim for clarity we do not wish to make a somewhat foggy landscape look clearer than it is.

Central IT Services

The one thing that all 11 case studies had in common was a central IT division. At a minimum, this was responsible for telecommunications and campus network infrastructure and services (for example, wireless, fiber optic networks, network servers, e-mail, and internal telephone systems). Most were also responsible for IT strategic planning, administrative software systems support, IT security, and the technical support, network access, and software maintenance of the institutional learning management system. Some were also responsible for research computing; classroom learning technologies, such as classroom computers for instructors, overhead projectors, electronic whiteboards, and lecture-room presentation consoles; audio and video-conferencing facilities; and multimedia production.

However, the further down this list of functions we get, the more likely that some of these services would be decentralized to academic and sometimes even administrative units, who would hire and manage their own IT staff. This was particularly true for the larger research universities. There are many reasons for this move toward decentralisation of IT services in the larger institutions:

- The computer requirements for different academic departments can vary considerably.
- New, low-cost technologies can be run with little specialist IT knowledge.
- End users are increasingly accustomed to making their own decisions about technology, such as choice of personal computers, mobile phones, software, and Internet provider.
- Academic autonomy makes it difficult to restrict technology choice and decisions by individual faculty members or academic departments.
- It is increasingly accepted that technology decisions are best made by those in the front line of applications who know what functions or service they need from technology.
- New services, such as SaaS (Software as a Service) that enable any end user or department to obtain a service on the Web without going through the institution's IT department (providing the user is willing to pay for the service).

Nevertheless, there are also compelling reasons for some IT functions to be managed centrally. We will discuss in more detail in the Governance of Technology section in this chapter the issue of centralization or decentralization of services, and also the role of the chief information officer, as these affect not just IT infrastructure and services, but go to the heart of the governance of technology.

LEARNING TECHNOLOGY SERVICES

Most institutions had a formally established learning technology unit that worked directly with faculty and instructors to help them with overall course design, the design of specific learning modules, the creation or preparation of digital learning materials, and sometimes training and professional development in the use of technology. Such a unit may also help with the design and delivery of distributed or fully online learning, if the institution was moving in this direction. In some cases, this unit might also be responsible for classroom technology, or the business management of the learning management system (for example, the setting up of spaces for a course, development of generic course templates, assigning passwords to faculty and students, and so forth).

Seven of the nine campus-based institutions (VT, UCF, UBC, SAIT, Alicante, URV, Milan) had at least one learning technology unit or department. In one large research university (UBC), as well as a central learning technology unit, there were also learning technology units within the larger faculties. There was one university (A Coruña) that, at least during our investigations, had no central learning technology unit as we have defined it (providing direct help to faculty with designing and applying technologies), although there is a center (CUFIE) that provides faculty development and training, and IT and equipment support. In one other case, a small college (Collège Boréal) later merged the functions of an initial learning technology unit with IT technical support for both students and instructors. In the case of the two open universities, educational technology support was an integral part of course design and development, but the organization of such staff varied from time to time, sometimes being outsourced to an affiliated company (Eurecamedia at UOC), sometimes distributed in the academic departments, and sometimes located in a central unit (UDF at UOC).

Learning technology units would usually be staffed with instructional designers or course developers with both educational and technical expertise, and media production staff such as Web developers or audio-visual media technicians. However, professionally qualified instructional designers or course developers with expertise in educational design were rarely employed by the European campus–based institutions.

As well as responding to the day-to-day demands or requirements of instructors, learning technology units would also explore, test, and evaluate new or emerging technologies, usually in collaboration with interested instructors. Sometimes the learning technology units could be quite large, with over 60 full-time staff (for example, at UBC), if they provided a central service for the whole institution. Other times, though, they would be quite small (two or three people maximum), particularly if they were located within an individual faculty or academic department.

A recurring situation in at least two of the case studies was the recruitment of instructional designers or Web developers on short-term contracts by individual faculty or departments, usually paid for from external grants for e-learning development, when there were more experienced or better qualified full-time staff in the central unit. Sometimes the central unit was already fully extended and could not accommodate at short notice, and sometimes, academics felt they could manage their own projects better by hiring their own staff. However, this leads to a high turnover of scarce staff, and a loss of learning from one project to another.

It was not unusual for full-time staff in learning technology units to have difficulties with classification by the human resources department, as learning technology staff did not have faculty status but often had high academic qualifications, such as doctorates or two master's (one in education and one in information technologies). In particular, there was a lack of a clear career path which made the implementation of progressive salary scales and internal promotion difficult if not impossible. In several institutions, learning technology staff, particularly instructional designers and Web designers, were employed only on short-term contracts. Some institutions therefore had a high turnover of scarce and highly skilled personnel in their learning technology units. Occasionally, senior learning technology staff might be given adjunct faculty status in the Faculty of Education (without additional payment), on a case-by-case basis.

Reporting lines for learning technology units also varied. In about half the cases, central learning technology units reported to the VP of academic affairs or education, but in the other half they would report to the CIO or VP of administration or a vice rector for innovation and new technologies; of course, the departmental learning technology units would report to the relevant dean or head of department.

In all cases, instructors were free to choose not to use the services of learning technology units, if they did not wish to. Frequently, in many of the institutions, instructors either were unaware of the services available from learning technology units, or believed that they could manage better without external assistance. As one instructional designer in a Canadian institution put it, "When I worked in industry as an instructional designer, I had much more power over the instructional design than I do in post-secondary education. Now, in order to work smoothly with faculty who are not professional educators, I have to put up with some of their bad design whims. Otherwise, they ignore me and do what they want anyhow."

FACULTY DEVELOPMENT AND TRAINING

We were able to identify in 10 of the 11 institutions professional development or training for faculty and instructors in the use of technology for teaching delivered through a clearly identified unit on a regular basis. One institution (Milan) offered no specific, regularly delivered training in the use of technology for teaching that we could identify, although no doubt there were workshops and seminars delivered on an occasional basis. Within the ten institutions that offered regular training, the quality, scope (in terms of the number of participants), and the unit delivering training varied considerably.

Virginia Tech, the University of Central Florida, and the Open Universities of Portugal and Catalunya had systematic policies and strategies to ensure that all faculty and instructors using technology had training in the use of technology for teaching. In the other institutions, faculty development and training was on a purely voluntary basis and, as a result, the number of participants was often relatively small (figures ranged from 1 to 10% of faculty per annum receiving training in teaching with technology).

In the majority of the campus-based institutions with identified training, there were two completely separate units, one for general faculty development in classroom teaching, whereas training in teaching with technology would be handled by a different unit (usually the learning technologies unit). This might seem curious, but there are reasons for this. Faculty development is seen as a professional activity over which the faculty member has control. This may take the form of attendance at conferences or sabbaticals to keep up to date, or to improve their academic knowledge, and possibly, if they feel they need it, workshops or seminars to improve their teaching. Teaching development is often experience-based, drawing on "star" instructors as examples, and faculty development offices may be headed or staffed by star faculty released from regular teaching duties. In some cases, but by no means all, faculty development staff will have had some additional training or qualifications in teaching and learning, or may have taken time during a sabbatical to bone up on research in teaching. The focus, of course, in many faculty development offices is on the improvement of regular, face-to-face classroom teaching.

As a result, the introduction of technology for teaching can present challenges for the traditional faculty development office. Staff have no training or experience in this area, and indeed some are very suspicious of technology, fearing that it will weaken the close relationship between students and faculty that is often a core focus of their work. It is not so surprising, then, that in our sample of institutions, the task of training in technology was usually given to the specialist learning technology unit, sometimes, as at UBC, working with the faculty development office, other times, working quite independently of it.

We believe that faculty training in the use of technology is essential for the full integration of technology within the institution. It raises the skill set required of instructors. We will therefore discuss in much more detail the design and provision of faculty training in Chapter Eight.

Distance or Distributed Learning

Of the nine campus-based institutions, five institutions (Virginia Tech, the University of Central Florida, UBC, SAIT, and Collège Boréal) had staff responsible for the management and support of online distance education courses. In most cases, the learning technology units offered marketing, support, and administrative staff to support distance education courses, and provided funding to buy-out faculty to work on the courses, although at UBC, several faculties also managed their own distance courses.

Conclusions from the Analysis of Organizational Units to Support Technology Integration

The need for mainline information technology infrastructure and services within universities and colleges is now well established, although it is not an area without its challenges, particularly regarding changes in technology, the location of services, and governance issues, which we will discuss shortly. The emergence of technologies that directly influence teaching and learning, however, is more recent, and it has taken institutions some time to work out the full organizational implications. To manage and support the use of learning technologies, new organizational units have had to be created, and new categories of staff hired.

Furthermore, learning technologies straddle both technology and academic areas, blurring to some extent the lines of responsibility for management. The relationship of learning technology units with other parts of the university, such as central IT services, academic departments, and faculty development offices, has had to be worked out. In many institutions all of this is still work in progress, so it is not surprising that we found overlap and duplication, sometimes unclear or competing lines of responsibility, and excessive or unrealistic demands on learning technology units and IT infrastructure. At the same time, it needs to be noted that increased use of technology has led to a rapid increase in staffing outside the traditional academic departments. This has cost implications that will be addressed further in Chapter Seven.

Most institutions have been muddling their way through regarding organizational structures to support technology integration. Some have done this better than others, and in any dynamic organization, such organizational structures need to be flexible. What matters is not so much neat organizational charts, but a clear picture of responsibilities and authority for decision making about technology. In other words, institutions should have a clear governance structure for technology.

GOVERNANCE OF TECHNOLOGY

Because technology is now so pervasive, influencing teaching, research, and administration, the executive team needs a strategy for ensuring that all the people necessary for effective decision making are involved in the process, and that there are clear lines of communication and responsibility for decision making. Thus one way for the executive team to provide leadership in technology is through the development of a strong technology governance process.

A further complicating factor is the increasing demand for legal compliance with privacy laws, the need for security of data, and accountability. For instance, to protect the privacy of personal information and the security of information infrastructure investments, the auditor-general of the province of Alberta (Government of Alberta, 2008) recommended that

> the Department of Advanced Education and Technology give guidance to post-secondary institutions on using an IT control framework to develop control processes that are well-designed, efficient and effective.

In a complex organization such as a research university, this is no mean challenge. For example, a focus just on security would close down all IT activities (maximum security); security needs to be balanced against the strategic or business objectives for the use of information technology. Thus, if a professor wants his students to do a project in a virtual world such as Second Life, what protections would there be to ensure that student data is secure, that students are not harassed (as the space is public), and so on, especially as the virtual world software may well be on a server in a country with different privacy laws? Some institutions have indeed banned the use of Web 2.0 technologies that operate on servers outside the control of the institution. Others have preferred to educate faculty in the risks, and how to reduce risk. Who should decide such policies and how should they be enforced? These are the kinds of question a technology governance structure would deal with.

DEFINING GOVERNANCE

The governance of information and communications technology is basically the means by which decisions are made about technology, and who makes them. There are many definitions of ICT governance, but we prefer that of Standards Australia (2005):

> The system by which the current and future use of ICT is directed and controlled. It involves evaluating and directing the plans for

the use of ICT to support the organisation and monitoring this use to achieve plans. It includes the strategy and policies for using ICT within an organisation.

Standards Australia claims that their standard

is applicable to all organizations, including public and private companies, government entities, and not-for-profit organizations. The standard is applicable to organizations of all sizes from the smallest to the largest, regardless of the extent of their use of ICT.

The Wikipedia entry on IT governance (http://en. wikipedia.org/wiki/Information_technology_governance, accessed 16 February, 2010) states:

The traditional involvement of board-level executives in IT issues was to defer all key decisions to the company's IT professionals. IT governance implies a system in which all stakeholders, including the board, internal customers, and in particular departments such as finance, have the necessary input into the decision making process. This prevents IT [departments] from independently making and later being held solely responsible for poor decisions. It also prevents critical users from later finding that the system does not behave or perform as expected.

THE DIFFUSION OF TECHNOLOGY MANAGEMENT

In earlier chapters, we have argued that information and communications technologies are not just merely useful tools but are integral components of all core activities of a modern university. Therefore the traditional model of decision making, as depicted in the Wikipedia entry, of leaving it to the techies is not going to work in organizations where everyone is affected by decisions about technology.

Davis (2008, p. 118) writes:

IT is playing an increasingly important role in research and education, compelling institutional IT to become more deeply involved with individual academic units . . . while simultaneously regulatory and security requirements escalate rapidly and accountability broadens . . . the sheer complexity of technology development is increasing and technology requirements continue to change. But our longstanding IT deployment practices are also breaking down. . . . The centralized versus decentralized approach no longer aligns well with the programmatic objectives and regulatory requirements of the university.

Thus we see two conflicting pressures on technology management. The first is the need for university-wide strategies regarding internal networking, connections to the external world, and regulatory and security management (a centripetal force). At the same time, the application of technology is becoming increasingly end user driven. This means that decisions are now being made by administrative staff, faculty, and instructors, and increasingly, even by students and learners themselves, about what technologies they will use for doing business (a centrifugal force). Often, however, even local decision making requires consultation, technical support, and advice from central IT services or specialists.

This immensely complicates the management of technology, which is why Davis sees the either/or thinking in centralized versus decentralized arguments now becoming irrelevant. A model of governance is needed that enables both the needs of the institution as a whole and the needs of the many end users to be accommodated. The role of IT professionals in providing leadership in technology management and innovation remains critical, but increasingly this role is being shared with end users, such as faculty and administrators.

LINE MANAGEMENT

For this reason, the governance of technology cannot be left to line management under the sole responsibility of the director of central IT services. The growing recognition of this is reflected in our case studies. The differences between the cases in the reporting lines and level of seniority of the head of centralized IT services is worth noting, and especially how this has changed over time.

In some institutions, the chief information officer or vice president information systems reported directly to the president (for example, at Virginia Tech). At UBC, the associate vice president of information technology (and head of central IT services), was moved in 1996 from reporting to the VP of administration to reporting to the VP academic, because IT was seen as critical to future academic developments. Following an external review of central IT services at UBC in 2009, the job was split in two. A new position, chief information officer, was created, reporting to the VP of administrative services and responsible for operational issues. The associate vice president of information systems became vice provost of information technology (still reporting to the VP academic), with a mandate to identify and apply innovations in information technology that will enhance core academic functions in research, teaching, and student engagement. In other words, responsibility for IT operations and innovation in IT academic applications were split. In other institutions, such as SAIT and UOC, the head of central IT services reported to the VP of administration or chief financial officer.

Probably less important than specific lines of reporting is an understanding that technology decisions are increasingly diffused throughout the organization, that nevertheless there are central services that are needed, that there needs to be IT specialist input to decision making, and that someone or some group needs to be thinking holistically and institution-wide about technology developments and their implications for institutional strategy and operations. This mitigates against a silo approach based on a hierarchical line management system.

Mapping Responsibilities

With technology applications rapidly expanding throughout an organization, and more and more people being drawn into decision making, it becomes increasingly important to have clear policies and lines of responsibility in place. At the same time, the very dynamic nature of technology developments requires a governance structure that is flexible and adaptable.

We have seen that many of the case study institutions set up a committee structure to manage technology governance. We also found confusion over roles and responsibilities for decision making, with overlapping committee structures, or committees covering technical infrastructure but not learning technologies, recommendations by committees often ignored or not implemented by the senior administration, and issues allowed to drift until a crisis arose. Although reporting lines and committee structures are important aspects of governance, even more important is a coherent overall structure that ensures that technology issues are identified, addressed, and properly managed, and in particular that there are not gaps in governance. We did not identify in any of the institutions a formal institution-wide governance structure for decision making on technology, at least not one that was written down and communicated throughout the institution, although some institutions had partial governance structures.

To avoid this situation, a clear and coherent governance structure for technology is required in every institution. Although this will be a continually evolving structure, it needs to be codified in some way, with responsibilities clearly defined against the committees or individuals responsible for implementation and compliance. Education about issues will be more useful than a long list of bureaucratic rules and procedures, but someone needs to be responsible for ensuring that the education takes place, that the people who need the education receive it, and, where policies are needed, that they are clear, well communicated, and enforced when necessary. The design, definition, implementation, communication, and maintenance of such a governance structure should be a prime responsibility of the executive team, although the day-to-day management and recording of the governance structure may be the line responsibility of the CIO's office.

Although it was not intended for this purpose, Lamberson and Fleming (2008) provide an example of something that could be easily developed into a partial governance structure (partial in that it focuses on governance of e-learning) at UBC. It includes

- An organizational chart showing the various operational units engaged in e-learning and the reporting lines
- A framework describing the systems (such as course and program support) and services (such as instructional and learning design) that support teaching and learning with technology
- A table setting out the relationships between technology services, target audiences, goals, and methods of

communication in the life cycle of technology implementation

- A diagram depicting the mission-critical pilot and emerging technologies for e-learning

This would provide a good basis for developing a governance framework. Also needed, though, would be

- A link to strategic objectives or directions for technology as set out in the academic plan
- Identification of individuals or groups (committees) responsible for policies and actions in each of the defined areas of activity
- Means of measuring performance in the achievement of objectives
- Strategies for risk management
- A review to ensure that there were not gaps or omissions (for instance, security issues arising from the use of e-learning are not explicitly described at this stage in the Lamberson and Fleming paper)

Stacey (2010) provides another framework around which a governance structure could be organized. He presents a macro view of educational technology with all of the major structural components shown together as a comprehensive and complementary suite of technologies. In particular he focuses on

- What technologies learners bring within their personal learning environments
- What the institution might provide (such as learning management and student information systems)
- What might be provided on a state- or provincewide basis (such as student admission systems or statewide software licenses)
- What might be provided through cloud computing (such as e-mail systems)

Although, again, the paper was not written for this purpose, it enables an organization to identify where lines of responsibility for the governance of different technologies may (or should) lie.

In most cases, the information needed for a governance structure will be readily available but scattered all over the institution; the main task would be pulling it together, evaluating it, and keeping it current. A well-defined governance structure ensures accountability, identifies and closes gaps and addresses weaknesses, and provides an institution-wide reference point for information and issues resolution regarding the management of technology. We provide some suggestions of what this might look like in Chapter Nine.

CONCLUSION

Although flexibility and adaptability are important, it is not enough to rely on purely ad hoc arrangements for identifying, discussing, recommending, and deciding on technology issues. Single projects that are not embedded in a wider strategy for technology are unlikely to be effective or successful. There needs to be ongoing mechanisms in place for dealing with technology issues as they arise; and arise they will as the technology and the external environment continues to change.

The scope and range of technology applications has widened considerably with the applications of technology to teaching and learning. This has three key implications:

- A need for systematic and comprehensive training of instructors in teaching
- A need for professionally staffed units to support the use of learning technologies
- A clear governance structure for technology that involves all key stakeholders, and includes teaching, research, and administrative applications as well as technology infrastructure

Thus, a clear and coherent governance structure for technology is required in every institution. The design, definition, implementation, maintenance, and communication of such a structure should be a prime responsibility of the executive team. However, we did not encounter in any of the institutions a formal governance structure for decision making on technology, at least not one that was written down and communicated throughout the institution.

Too often, instead, we found confusion over roles and responsibilities for decision making, with overlapping committee structures, or committees covering technical infrastructure but not learning technologies, recommendations by committees often ignored or not implemented by the senior administration, and issues allowed to drift until a crisis arose.

This study indicates that the time has come for institutions to closely examine their organizational structure to see if duplication of technology services can be avoided, or whether there are large gaps in technology management. One major limitation is the industrial-style organizational structure of universities and colleges, and in particular the silos of academic, administrative, and technological support units. Technology management requires more flexible and more efficient organizational arrangements. Another limitation is the lack of training of instructors, so that large numbers of support staff are needed for technology to be used effectively in teaching. Finally, we need to examine whether academic freedom and autonomy is really challenged by a more disciplined approach to the allocation and efficient use of resources that aims to avoid unnecessary duplication.

CHAPTER SIX

QUALITY ASSURANCE

I have the same feeling about quality assurance processes as Goebbels had for culture: whenever I hear the words I reach for my gun.
—INSTRUCTOR IN A CASE STUDY INSTITUTION

Meet George, VP Education, Cornbelt Community College

Dr. George Carter has been in the post for three months. He has a problem. About five years ago, the college started putting in a lecture capture system, which suddenly rapidly expanded across nearly all departments. At the same time, several academic departments started enrolling fully online students, mainly using the lecture capture system, and specially hired adjuncts to deliver the online programs. The college executive team had seen this strategy as a great success, as the online enrollments had rapidly grown by about 40% over the last three years. Now over one-third of all enrollments were distance students. Furthermore, because online students paid a higher tuition fee, and the college made a handsome profit on the online courses, they were a source of essential revenues to the college at a time when the state was cutting its operating budget.

However, a graduate student at the nearby state university had just completed a study for her dissertation that compared completion rates between students taking courses on campus with students taking the same courses online at the college. She found that male,

Hispanic, and low-performing students fared worse in the online courses. The study was reported on the local TV station, and picked up around the country. George was particularly disturbed by an e-mail the college president had received from a distinguished scholar at a major university, who accused the college of criminal negligence in failing to follow best standards and practice in the design of online courses, and of "gouging" online students. All this had been discussed at a recent meeting with the college board of governors. A statement had been drafted by the director of communications, but George had asked for and been given a mandate to "clean up the mess."

One challenge he faces is that there is nothing in the college's strategic plan about online learning, and no strategy or priorities for it. The main decisions in the past about online learning had been made by the individual deans and faculty, working with the director of IT services, who was the champion for the lecture capture strategy. George now had to think about the best way to go about tackling this problem.

Note: This scenario is based on a study done by the U.S. National Bureau of Economic Research: see Figlio, Rush, and Yin, 2010.

In this chapter, we examine processes or procedures implemented by the case study institutions to ensure quality in the use of technology for teaching and to evaluate their strategies for technology integration. There is convincing evidence that technology-based teaching succeeds best when courses are redesigned to exploit the benefits of technology, using well-established quality assurance methods. To our surprise, though, we found that none of the case study institutions had a formal, systematic, and comprehensive strategy to evaluate its use of technology for teaching across the institution.

QUALITY ASSURANCE PROCESSES

This is one area where we found considerable differences internationally in the way institutions approached quality, the main differences being between the system in the United States and in the other countries.

Institutional and Program Accreditation

The U.S. Department of Education's Network for Education Information (2009) states:

> Quality assurance takes several forms in the U.S. education system. The approval of institutions and programs is generally undertaken by state agencies and accrediting agencies, with the latter also responsible for the establishment and maintenance of academic and administrative standards. Professional and academic disciplinary associations also play a role in influencing and assessing quality.

There are 74 private and state-based accrediting agencies that provide oversight of member institutions, of which 16 regional accrediting agencies are regarded as the most selective. Recognition from an accrediting body is not a requirement to operate legally, although institutions that are not accredited cannot participate in federal student aid programs. Most postsecondary institutions do seek formal accreditation, but standards vary considerably between different accrediting agencies. In addition to accrediting institutions, the accreditation agencies also review program proposals from institutions.

In Canada, universities are accredited by provincial governments. Most provincial governments have established degree quality assurance boards (the name varies from province to province) which approve applications for new degrees. Provincial governments also usually have a board that regulates privately funded postsecondary institutions. These boards aim at ensuring the quality, reliability, and standards of postsecondary qualifications. Similar arrangements exist for public community or two-year colleges. There are some similarities in Spain, although generally it is the national government that accredits public universities and programs. Sometimes the degree quality assurance boards have struggled with programs with a high level of online delivery, and have established specific questions or standards for online programs. In other words, the hurdle of approval for fully online programs is often higher.

In most public universities and colleges in Canada and Europe, before programs are submitted to state or provincial degree approval boards, they go through a similar internal approval process, first at an academic department level, then at a senate or institution-wide academic committee level. Again, faculty serving on these committees often give programs that are being offered online special and sometimes negative scrutiny. For most Canadian and European universities, the internal and external program approval processes are the main form of quality assurance, although the government-appointed degree quality assurance boards also provide important oversight.

QUALITY ASSURANCE MODELS

Several guidelines, best practices, or quality management criteria have been created and applied to online program assessment independently of the formal accreditation agencies and degree quality assurance boards in North America. The Sloan Quality Framework and Five Pillars (Moore, 2005), the Middle States Higher Education Commission's Guidelines for the Evaluation of Electronically Offered Degree and Certificate Programs (2002), and the Canadian Recommended e-Learning Guidelines (Barker, 2002) are just three examples. The e-Learning Maturity Model sets out common practices or ways of creating e-learning resources and learning environments that are "accepted, useful and able to be described in a way that others can adopt them and improve their own e-learning capabilities" (Marshall, 2006). All these guidelines and procedures have been derived from the experience of previously successful online programs, best practices in teaching and learning, and research and evaluation of e-learning.

In recent years, European and Australian universities and some North American two-year colleges have introduced a number of quality management approaches that originate from the corporate sector. These have been increasingly applied to online learning programming. One of the more common models applied is from the European Foundation for Quality Management (EFQM), a comprehensive, holistic approach aimed at continuous improvement in the management of an organization. (In Japan, it is called the Kaizen model.) The Six Sigma and Quality Circles are two other models close to the EFQM approach. ISO 9000 is a family of standards for quality management systems, maintained by the International Organization for Standardization. (It was in reference to the application of the ISO 9000 standard that the instructor made the quotation at the beginning of this chapter, feeling that it was bureaucratic, time-consuming, and totally inappropriate for online courses in a two-year community college.) Other benchmarking projects in Europe applied to online learning or e-learning are Quality on the Line and BENVIC. Germany has a federal office, ZFU, for the accreditation of distance learning, and some associations, such as the British Learning Association and the International Board of Standards for Training, Performance and Instruction (IBSTPI), provide quality marking or certificates, mainly for corporate e-learning, but also sometimes for vocational and educational programs in colleges.

Following a number of research and development projects on the use of ICTs for education and training, funded primarily by the European Commission, the European Foundation for Quality of e-Learning (EFQUEL) was established. EFQUEL has created UNIQUe, a quality certificate that recognizes excellence in the use of information and communications technologies for teaching and learning in universities and colleges. Other approaches adopted from the corporate sector sometimes used to ensure quality in online learning are the balanced scorecard method, which would look at a range of different performance measures for e-learning, and benchmarking an institution's practices against other leading e-learning practitioners. Wikipedia states that

> benchmarking e-learning is now seen in the UK as a key enabler of change in universities—some 40 universities and university-level colleges, around one quarter of all relevant UK institutions, are now starting work on this, with a further 12 having recently completed a pilot exercise. (Retrieved 4 June 2010 at http://en.wikipedia.org/wiki/Benchmarking_e-learning)

However, the main form of quality assurance in Europe and Canada still remains with the government regulated degree quality assurance boards (such as the Catalan Agency for Quality in Higher Education).

EVALUATION AND RESEARCH
IN LEARNING TECHNOLOGIES

Quality assurance processes aim to ensure quality in programs before they are offered, but there is no guarantee that the program will turn out as expected. Evaluation and research provide a means to check on the actual quality, after courses or programs have been offered.

Many institutions have an internal program review process that kicks in after a program has been running for some time. Usually this will consist of an internal evaluation report by the department offering the program, followed by a review of the internal committee's report by external assessors from other institutions. The use of technology could be one element reviewed. The main purpose is to improve or update the program, although sometimes program reviews can, in exceptional circumstances, lead to the closure of the program. Program reviews may occur automatically, for instance every five years, or may be instigated at the discretion of the institution's senior administration.

Many institutions now have standard student feedback questionnaires that are administered at the end of a course or program. The use is mainly formative, to provide information to instructors about the student response to their teaching, although sometimes this information is used to help decide about the rehiring of contract or adjunct faculty. The data from such surveys is often considered in program reviews.

Because the collection of such data across all courses is a major operation involving computer analysis of data and the production of many reports, it has sometimes been a struggle to modify the student questionnaires to include questions about teaching with technology. However, even when data about the use of technology is collected, the information is rarely used to assess the success or otherwise of technology for teaching across the institution. (One major barrier to doing this cross-course comparison is student privacy. Ethics committees are often reluctant to give access to student grade data for comparative research purposes; permission may be required of every student in each class being analyzed, even though only aggregate data is being analyzed. In any case, there is often not the staffing or funds to do this kind of analysis properly.)

Many universities have institutional research units but their focus tends to be on providing data to meet accountability requirements (such as enrollment statistics, average class sizes, financial reporting), but rarely includes an assessment of technology use and effectiveness. Sometimes, usually on the initiative of a faculty member or staff in a learning technology or distance education support unit, small research projects are conducted on e-learning. In a very small number of cases, research into e-learning is conducted within faculties of education, but here the focus tends to be on a particular academic's research interests. In other words, these initiatives are not focused specifically on evaluating the institution's strategies for technology integration, or on the institution's overall use of technology for teaching.

There are reports in the research literature of many attempts to compare the effectiveness of face-to-face teaching and e-learning. Generally, when the research is carefully done, and there are sufficient similarities in conditions other than the mode of teaching, online learning compares well with face-to-face teaching. For instance, at UBC, students are often able to choose whether to take a third or fourth year undergraduate course face-to-face or online at a distance. Often each version of the course will have the same instructor, and in all cases, students take the same examinations and assessments. The director of distance education and technology at UBC reported that students received comparable grades in most of the online courses, although completion rates were slightly lower (around 85% compared with 90%) on average for online courses.

The U.S. Department of Education commissioned a meta-study of the literature comparing face-to-face, hybrid, and fully online courses (Means, Toyama, Murphy, & Bakia, 2009). The report stated:

> A systematic search of the research literature from 1996 through July 2008 identified more than a thousand empirical studies of online learning. Analysts screened these studies to find those that (a) contrasted an online to a face-to-face condition, (b) measured student learning outcomes, (c) used a rigorous research design,

and (d) provided adequate information to calculate an effect size. As a result of this screening, 51 independent effects were identified that could be subjected to meta-analysis. The meta-analysis found that, on average, students in online learning conditions performed better than those receiving face-to-face instruction.

This is but one of a long line of research reports going back to 1977 (Schramm, 1977) comparing teaching with various forms of media with teaching face-to-face, which all usually end up with a result of "no significant difference." Other "classic" meta-analyses are by Clark, 1983; Kozma, 1994; and Russell, 1999. However, such research results are often interpreted wrongly.

The first mistake is to assume that because there are no significant differences, online teaching (or face-to-face teaching) is always just as good (or better) than the other, and therefore it does not matter which mode is used. This is not so. As Schramm pointed out as long ago as 1977, what influences the results are the conditions in which each of the teaching modes best flourishes. Because so many different conditions can vary (the quality of the instructor, the context or the motivation of the student, the quality of the teaching, and so on) the results are statistically insignificant in meta-analyses because the different conditions cancel each other out across a large number of studies. In other words, there are often greater variations within a mode of teaching than there are between modes of teaching. Thus the "no significant difference" is often an artifact of the research design. By trying to keep all the conditions exactly the same, we often remove the conditions under which one mode or the other best flourishes.

This may seem abstract, but one of the conditions uniquely associated with online teaching is flexibility. If we have a face-to-face class that includes a mix of full-time and part-time students, and we have the same mix in an online course, then the average learning results may be the same across the two modes. However, if all the students were part-time students in each of the conditions, the results are likely to be very different, with online students doing much better because of the increased flexibility. Similarly, full-time students straight out of high school may do better in a face-to-face mode (everything else being equal, which they never are).

Because the context of teaching varies so much it is important that research on technology-based teaching be context-based, which means that generalization from one situation to another is not always possible, which makes meta-analyses particularly difficult to interpret. This makes it even more important for each institution to conduct its own research and evaluation of technology-based teaching, to identify the conditions where it works best.

METHOD OF COURSE DEVELOPMENT AND DELIVERY

One of the biggest factors affecting the quality of technology-based teaching is the method of designing, developing, and delivering a course. Bates (2000) identified four main methods (Lone Rangers, boutique, collaborative, and project management), and we add a fifth (open content) which could be used together with the other four or as a distinct method on its own. There are many different ways in which a course can be developed and delivered. The choice of model will depend on the scale and complexity of the course, and the centrality of the use of technology.

Lone Rangers

By far the most common model of course development is what Bates (2000) calls the Lone Ranger approach (after the old Hollywood cowboy films and subsequent television series). Instructors work on their own or with the help of a small grant from the university that provides for funding of a part-time graduate student and some equipment or software.

This Lone Ranger model fits well with the autonomy of the faculty member in higher education. Furthermore, Lone Rangers are essential for getting innovation started, for demonstrating the potential of technology for teaching, and for ensuring that technology is used when there is no systematic support from the institution. Usually Lone Rangers are dedicated teachers who put a great deal of time and effort into experimenting with technology for teaching.

However, there are considerable limitations of the Lone Ranger approach to the use of technology. The main problems are workload and quality. For an instructor to work alone or even with a graduate assistant, the Lone Ranger has to deal with all the activities associated with the use of technology, as well as with choosing and organizing content and student interaction. Consequently, the Lone Ranger model usually results in a great deal more work for the instructor, compared with a regular face-to-face class.

Furthermore, quality in teaching with technology requires expertise not just in content, but also in course or program planning, instructional design, media production, online moderating, student support, and course or program evaluation and maintenance. Particularly for tenured faculty with research responsibilities, for adjunct faculty hired on a contract basis, or for full-time instructors in colleges with no previous teaching background, it is very difficult to become experts or even experienced in all these areas without substantial additional training.

Boutique Course Development

Hartman and Truman-Davis (2001) describe the boutique approach. A professor approaches an instructional support unit for professional assistance on an individual, one-on-one basis from an instructional designer or technology support person. As Hartman and Truman-Davis explain, this is a satisfying experience for both instructor and support person and works well when there are relatively few instructors needing help.

However, the model starts to become unsustainable as demand increases, because of the resources needed. It causes particular difficulties for the instructional support unit or person, as there is no obvious way to determine priorities between multiple requests for help, and there is no boundary around the support commitment. Furthermore, because the instructor usually initiates the process, the wrong kind of assistance may be requested. For instance, the request may be limited to purely technical assistance, when what may be required is a different approach to course design for the technology to be used effectively. Nevertheless, the boutique model can be useful in helping individual professors to get started in using technology in a systematic and professional way.

Collegial Materials Development

Another model that is becoming more popular is the collegial materials development model. In this model, several academics work collaboratively, to develop online or multimedia educational materials. They may be from the same department or from other departments in the same institution, but teaching common subjects, such as statistics, or they may be subject experts from different institutions in the same discipline. By working collaboratively they can share ideas, jointly develop or share materials, and provide critical feedback to each other.

Collegial materials development may or may not use a project management approach, and may or may not develop or use open content materials (see below). The professors engaged may have no more than a graduate student to help, may have a Web programmer, or may have an instructional designer to help, or any combination. In collegial materials development, each participant in the project is free to decide which materials to include in their own courses, and which to share with other colleagues. Often the material is made public as open content. Another feature of collegial materials development is that rarely is a whole course produced. The focus is usually on developing materials that other instructors and students may find useful to use within their own courses.

However, at some stage, even collegial development approaches are likely to get to a point where there is a need for more formal management of the process, some form of evaluation or peer review of the materials, and the need for professional design and graphics.

Project Management

Project management is common in creative media areas, especially where the project is complex, such as film and television production, advertising, video and computer games design, and in many building, engineering, and information technology–based projects. There are many models and approaches to project management. What they all have in common is that project development and delivery involve a team of individuals each contributing different skills, and the process is managed by a team leader or project manager.

What defines project management is the process. It has a defined set of resources, usually determined at the outset of the project, a timeline, and a clear deliverable, in that it is clear what the project has to achieve and it is obvious when it is completed. In the case of teaching with technology, a deliverable may be development of a DVD; the development of learning objects; the design of a departmental Web site; a computerized simulation or animation; or the design, development, and delivery of a whole online course or program. The resources may be cash, but more often the key resource will be the time of the instructors, which under project management would be clearly defined (for instance, a set number of days for design and development of learning materials, and another set number of hours or days for the actual teaching or delivery of the course).

There are several advantages to the project management model. The main one is quality control. With a team of professionals working together, the quality is likely to be higher.

A Web programmer and graphic designer will get material up on a Web site or learning management system more quickly and more effectively than an untrained instructor. A video producer will understand the potential and limitations of video, and the most effective way to design and produce video materials. An instructional designer can help with program planning, to ensure that the technology is properly exploited and integrated within courses.

The second advantage is cost control. All the other methods have no set boundaries around the time that instructors and support staff will spend on a project. With project management, the design of the course is built around the set times agreed on by the different members of the team. In particular, a good instructional designer can help design the course so that the instructor's workload is kept to a minimum, without limiting the instructor's control over content or teaching method.

The main disadvantage of project management is that faculty or instructors see it as bureaucratic or reducing their academic autonomy (especially since meeting deadlines is a critical element of project management). Other priorities, such as research deadlines, often intrude. The other disadvantage is the additional costs of hiring instructional designers and Web programmers, although these need to be set against the hidden costs of instructors working without help.

Open Content

As more learning materials of high quality become available digitally over the Internet, the costs of developing digital materials from scratch can be dramatically reduced. The design can range from the instructor choosing and incorporating open content into his or her own design to building a whole course around the concept of students seeking and integrating open content into the course, with the instructor acting as a guide and facilitator. Note that an open content approach can be used in conjunction with any of the other four course development methods.

Which Approach?

The decision whether to adopt a Lone Ranger, boutique, collegial materials development, project management, or an open content approach depends on a number of factors. The most critical are the size, complexity, and originality of a project, and the resources available. Thus a teacher thinking of adding PowerPoint presentations to her classroom teaching will not need project management for this, although she may well benefit from some advice from a graphics designer. This would be a boutique approach.

However, if a whole course is to be delivered online and at a distance, or if a hybrid course is to be developed, or if a large lecture class is to be completely redesigned, then project management becomes essential. Generally, the more important the role of technology becomes in a course, the more important it becomes to use a full project management approach. Thus, in terms of Figure 2.1 in Chapter Two, the more an instructor or course moves along the continuum toward fully online learning, the more likely that the instructor will need increased levels of help. In particular, courses designed from scratch as hybrid courses will particularly benefit from a project management approach.

Also, the level of intervention will depend on the experience and training of instructors. Instructors themselves become more skilled in using technology with increased exposure to project management and the skills of instructional and media designers, or with systematic training.

QUALITY ASSURANCE IN THE CASE STUDIES
QUALITY ASSURANCE MODELS

Interestingly, of the three institutions rated with the highest level of technology integration, none used any of the formal quality assurance processes (other than the standard internal and external program approval processes, and program reviews). Virginia Tech, UBC, and the University of Central Florida instead relied heavily on highly qualified technology support staff, best practices established over a long period of time in using technology for teaching, and extensive faculty development and training in the use of technology, to ensure quality in their e-learning programs.

The Open University of Catalonia received the gold label of the EFQM Excellence Model; and Southern Alberta Institute of Technology, for its curriculum development process, and the University of A Coruña for processes in some of its academic departments, both received ISO 9000 accreditation. However, these were not directly linked to e-learning activities. The Open University of Portugal has put in place an extensive quality assurance process for its online courses.

At the University of Alicante, the DIT Commission monitored and evaluated developments in the Campus Virtual, which attempted to integrate information and communications technologies into teaching and learning activities, on a course-by-course basis. However, there was no institution-wide attempt at aggregating or comparing the data for an institution-wide evaluation of Campus Virtual, although the Commission did find four main barriers to technology integration:

- Lack of adequate resources set aside for the innovation
- Faculty resistance to change
- Failure to develop new models of teaching that exploited the use of technology
- Lack of systematic evaluation of the project

Most institutions relied heavily on student feedback questionnaires to provide formative evaluation for individual courses.

Although these questionnaires provide indications of student dissatisfaction, however, they do not usually provide information on exactly what needs fixing, especially where technology is used in a blended mode.

RESEARCH INTO E-LEARNING

Several of the sample institutions had set up small units to do research on learning technologies (University of Central Florida, UBC, SAIT, the Open Universities of Portugal and Catalonia). Both SAIT and UOC established research chairs in e-learning, and UOC eventually established an e-learning research center.

The research varied from institution to institution. Some was more like development, such as testing new technologies (for example, Alicante, A Coruña, Rovira i Virgili). Other research was focused on utilization of the learning management system. In several of the cases, research focused on measures of student satisfaction, or on developing tools for student evaluation of online teaching (for example, University of Central Florida).

At UBC the distance education department established a research group, MAPLE, which conducted general research into the planning and management of e-learning for five years, until the senior administration told it to close down, as the distance education unit was not considered to be an academic department (despite its success in attracting major research grants).

METHODS OF COURSE PRODUCTION

The Lone Ranger model was the primary model at the Universities of Milan, A Coruña, Rovira i Virgili, and Alicante in the case studies, and was the model in many departments in some of the other case studies. We suspect that this model is still the most prevalent in many other institutions.

The boutique model was most apparent in the case studies at Collège Boréal and at those institutions that had decentralized learning technology support to the faculties and departments, such as UBC. Again, we believe this to be a common model in many universities and colleges.

The Faculty of Pharmaceutical Sciences at the University of British Columbia provided an example of collegial materials development. Three professors who each started as Lone Rangers began to work together, with the help of a Web programmer hired by the department. This resulted in consistency of design and terminology, sharing of interactive techniques such as online test software, and development of video demonstrations of equipment that would commonly be used in more than one course.

The University of Central Florida, the Distance Education and Technology unit at UBC, SAIT, and the two Open Universities all used a project management approach to course design.

Project management has been used for many years in education for course development and delivery. However, it has tended to be restricted to distance teaching, either on dedicated distance teaching universities such as the Open University in the United Kingdom, or to distance teaching programs in dual mode institutions such as Penn State University or UBC. Nevertheless, as the use of technology in regular campus-based teaching becomes more complex, project management will become increasingly important as a means of controlling workload and quality (see Chapter Seven for more discussion of this issue).

SUMMARY

Most institutions in the case studies were still finding their way toward ensuring quality in technology-based teaching. In most cases, a great deal was left to the individual instructor.

Some of the institutions had implemented a formal quality assurance process, but most relied mainly on the traditional program review process, with perhaps some extra vigilance regarding the online courses. None of the institutions in our sample had a formal, systematic, and comprehensive evaluation strategy for its use of technology for teaching and learning. There was in all the cases a lack of any systematic attempt to evaluate the overall success or otherwise of technology integration strategies. Objectives, when stated, were not framed in such a way that they could easily be evaluated, and institutions lacked the means by which to assess properly the success or otherwise of the use or integration of technology.

However, several institutions were moving tentatively toward a project management model, and many institutions had recognized the importance of professional support in the form of technical help and, to a lesser extent, the value of instructional designers in ensuring quality.

How Useful Is Quality Assurance?

One reason for the heavy emphasis on quality assurance is that e-learning is still under a cloud of suspicion in many institutions. Faculty often are suspicious of or hostile to using technology for teaching (although over time the fear factor seems to be diminishing). Thus even more rigorous forms of quality assurance are demanded than for face-to-face teaching.

However, many of the quality assurance models focus on the management of e-learning processes, more than on what actually happens within teaching and learning with technology. At its worst, quality management can end up with many boxes on a questionnaire being checked, in that the management processes are all in place, without in fact investigating whether students are really learning more or better as a result of using technology. Consequently, faculty often groan when quality assurance procedures are being proposed. It seems to add yet more bureaucracy without catching the essence of what teaching and learning are about.

We have another worry about quality assurance processes, in that they can act as a brake on innovation. By definition, they are predicated on past best practices using older technology such as learning management systems or asynchronous online learning. However, when a new technology comes along, or when instructors start to think differently about how existing technology can be used, by definition it is unlikely to reflect current best practice, especially if the quality assurance process does not look at the relationship between processes and learning outcomes.

Nevertheless, quality assurance methods are valuable for agencies concerned about rogue, private providers, or institutions using e-learning to cut corners or reduce costs without maintaining standards (for instance, by hiring untrained adjuncts, and giving them an unacceptably high student-teacher ratio to manage). They can be useful for providing instructors new to teaching with technology, or struggling with its use, with models of best practice to follow. However, at the end of the day, the best guarantees of quality in e-learning are

- Well-qualified subject experts also well trained in both teaching methods and the use of technology for teaching
- Highly qualified and professional learning technology support staff
- Adequate resources, including appropriate instructor-student ratios
- Appropriate methods of working (teamwork, project management)
- Systematic evaluation leading to continuous improvement

CONCLUSION

First there were distinct differences in the formal process of accreditation of institutions and programs between, on the one hand, institutions in the United States, and on the other, institutions in Canada and Europe. However, the national differences were not so significant in the context of quality assurance of teaching with technology.

Generally, most institutions in the case studies depended heavily on conventional formal degree quality assurance processes (both internally and at a state or provincial level) to ensure that teaching with technology met the necessary standards. Fully online programs often received particular scrutiny.

There is convincing evidence that online students do just as well if not better than students in face-to-face courses, but more important, the results depend on the conditions in which students are studying. All modes of delivery will suffer from badly designed teaching or inadequate resources.

One important condition affecting the quality of technology-based teaching is the method of designing, developing, and delivering a course. The greater the role of technology, the more important it is to move to a project management model, involving instructional and media designers as well as subject experts.

Although most institutions had in place methods to assess the quality of individual courses or programs, none of the case study institutions had a formal, systematic, and comprehensive strategy to evaluate its use of technology for teaching across the institution. Given the level of investment in this area, it is hard to justify the lack of formal evaluation.

Quality assurance processes developed specifically for online learning were not used in the case study institutions with the highest degree of technology integration. The online or e-learning QA processes focus mainly on management processes and not on specific learning outcomes associated with the use of technology.

Nevertheless, quality assurance is important, not just for online learning, but for all forms of teaching, and especially for rooting out poor teaching methods as well as unprofessional, unscrupulous, or unethical institutional practices in technology-based teaching (as highlighted in the scenario at the beginning of this chapter). Quality assurance can take several forms, though, that will include

- Traditional pre- and post-program reviews
- Benchmarking against other institutions
- Setting and measuring standards for e-learning (for a comprehensive selection, see "e-learning quality assurance standards, organizations and research" at http://www.tonybates.ca/2010/08/15/e-learning-quality-assurance-standards-organizations-and-research/)
- Ensuring that adequate resources are available for meeting quality assurance standards
- Hiring professional instructional designers and Web programmers to work with faculty
- Systematic training of faculty
- Project management
- Formal evaluation of objectives and outcomes for learning technology based on goals set in institutional or departmental plans

Best practice institutions are likely to use a combination of these methods. A key factor in quality assurance is ensuring that there are adequate resources for the task in hand. The next chapter examines the management of resources for technology-based teaching.

CHAPTER SEVEN

RESOURCES, MONEY, AND DECISION MAKING

*On our campus only some of the increase in on-line
courses can be linked to formal plans. The rest has come
about in an unplanned, organic manner. Both have
serious implications for resources*
—BRINKMAN AND MORGAN, 2010, P. 9

Dr. Shari Sandhu, Associate Professor, Faculty of Medicine

Dr. Sandhu is an associate professor in the Department of Occupational Therapy in a research university in Canada. Her students are mainly qualified and experienced nurses wishing to specialize in occupational therapy and rehabilitation. Dr. Sandhu is one of the country's leading researchers in the field, and also one of a team teaching graduate courses in this area.

The majority of her students are working, and come mainly from the urban area around the university, even though this is the only graduate program offered in the province. Two years ago, she approached Jim Flower, deputy director of distance education, of the university's Center for Teaching, Learning, and Technology, with an idea to put one of her courses fully online, as she had already developed a number of online resources to support her classroom teaching. He provided her with an instructional designer from the center, and they worked together to develop her first online course.

The problem now is that the course has been too successful. She is having to turn students away, and students are asking for more online courses. She is meeting with Jim Flower to see if he can provide some more resources to enable her to offer another online course, and help her open more sections for the existing course. He has a more radical suggestion: why not put the whole program online? This would enable the program to reach a much wider range of students.

Her immediate reaction is that this is a bad idea. She doesn't think the department is ready for such a move. Also, she is worried about the extra work, which would affect her research. But Jim has a plan. He suggests that she start first with adding one more fully online course, but with a view to gradually moving the whole program online in the form of a full master's degree. His center will provide initial funding to cover part of her salary for one year, while she works on the proposal for a whole online program, and develops her second online course. This would enable the department to hire an adjunct to cover her classroom teaching.

Also, if she can persuade the department to move in this direction, the center will help her develop a business plan that will enable the whole program to be self-funding. This would enable the campus program to continue, while adding a new fully online program that would be offered across the country.

To avoid financial risk to the department, the center will provide a loan. This would cover the initial hiring of an additional tenured faculty member to help Dr. Sandhu develop the program, plus the other resources needed, such as staff from the center, and the extra costs of administrative services, such as student admission and registration. The loan would eventually be repaid from tuition fees. Dr. Sandhu's research time and teaching load will remain the same, but her teaching time would be focused entirely on online teaching and helping to develop the program. The business plan though includes funding for a program manager, to take the administrative load off Dr. Sandhu's shoulders.

To reduce risk, the program would develop two courses per year, with the option to cancel further courses if demand is less or costs higher than expected. The first five courses would lead to a postgraduate certificate, to test demand and for the department to assess the quality of the program. If successful, an additional three courses would be added, plus a research-based dissertation, to constitute a full master's degree in rehabilitation science. The full program would enable two additional tenured faculty to be hired (although in practice, much of the teaching would be done by existing staff, with the new tenured staff covering the face-to-face teaching).

The loan would total a maximum of C$150,000, as revenues from the first courses would start to flow within 12 months, with the loan to be repaid in full over seven years. The tuition fee will be set at a rate the market can bear, but it must cover the costs of the program, or the program will not go ahead. The university, not the department, will assume the risk, if enrollments and costs do not meet expectations. The center has already negotiated with the provost and the university treasurer to use unspent revenues that are usually invested in short-term Treasury bonds, to help with the funding of such innovative programs, subject to a full business plan being approved by the academic department, the provost, and the university treasurer. The loans are to be repaid with the same interest yielded by Treasury bonds.

Jim Flower is confident in the estimation of costs for the program, as he has been tracking the costs of online courses for some years, and the center uses a strong project management model to control costs. After lengthy negotiations with the head of department, the dean of medicine, the dean of graduate studies, and several lively faculty meetings, the deal is done. Strong support from the provost is a critical factor.

Six years later, the program graduates its first 30 master's students, with enrollments totaling approximately 300 students across the program (students can take up to five years to graduate). More than one-third of the students are from out of province. This compares with 30 students per year in the classroom program, nearly all from the immediate urban area. The loan has been fully repaid and the program is totally self-funding, including contributions to university overheads.

Note: This scenario is based on an amalgam of the master in rehab science and the master of educational technology, both offered fully online at UBC. The characters in the scenario are fictional, but the academics who drove these programs through at UBC were Sue Stanton in occupational therapy and Jim Gaskell in education, assisted by Jeff Miller from distance education and technology.

Introduction

In this chapter, we explore how institutions have attempted to identify and find the resources needed to support technology-based teaching. We also examine the costs of e-learning, and finally make some suggestions about how decision making in this area might be improved.

We wish to make clear from the beginning that this is a difficult topic. Decision making about money in universities and colleges is very much like sex in Victorian England: nearly everyone is doing it; no one wants to talk about it in public; and some people don't seem to get better at it as they get older. As well as a lack of transparency, there are profound technical and cultural reasons why this is a difficult topic. There is surprisingly little research not only on the costs of using technology in universities and colleges but also into how those resources are found and allocated. Finally, we did not attempt in the case studies to collect extensive data on technology costs and or determine in detail how resources were allocated to support the use of technology, partly because we knew this information would be difficult or impossible to access. How universities and colleges make decisions about resource allocation is a topic that needs much more research.

Nevertheless, it was clear from the case studies that there is in general a lack of understanding or knowledge about the costs of technology-based teaching. This is hampered by budget models that are based more on controlling departmental expenditures than on measuring the costs of different activities. In this chapter we are able to identify the main drivers of cost, and also provide a methodology for identifying costs. Finally we indicate that unintended consequences can arise when there is no clear strategy for identifying how the costs of using technology for teaching will be paid for.

Experience from the Case Studies
Kick-Starting Technology Integration

In the case studies, Virginia Tech, UBC, Collège Boréal, SAIT, and UOC were all able to find substantial funds (more than $1 million) at some stage to kick-start the integration of technology for teaching and learning. SAIT received some large endowments from industry, one of which it used to establish and equip a central e-learning center, and another to create a research chair in e-learning. In other cases, such as the universities of Alicante and A Coruña, vice provosts were able to find much smaller amounts of money for specific projects, such as the development of administrative and teaching software. However, these funds were often not sufficient to sustain these projects over an ongoing period.

Special funding proved to be very helpful, even necessary, to kick-start or rapidly expand applications of technology to teaching. It also sent a clear message to faculty and instructors about the institution's priorities. However, evidence from the case studies suggest that substantial funds (in the order of millions of dollars) need to be found if they are to have a lasting effect.

SUSTAINABILITY AND REALLOCATION OF FUNDING

Although special funding is valuable, eventually administrative and teaching applications of technology need to be funded on an ongoing, sustainable basis, which means embedding the costs of technology within regular operating budgets. Both Virginia Tech and UBC had earmarked internal funds on an annual basis to support innovation in teaching and learning, to which individual faculty or departments could apply. However, other funds need to go to central IT services, learning technology units, and faculty development offices, as well as funds located within academic department or faculty budgets for technology support. As there is usually little flexibility in operating budgets, this usually requires some form of reallocation; in other words, taking resources away from one set of activities to pay for or to support technology-based teaching.

In at least two cases (the Open University of Portugal and SAIT) we know there was no allocation of extra resources even though major strategic changes were desired. At the Open University of Portugal, resources and staff previously allocated to print-based and broadcast production were used instead to train instructors and to get online courses developed. This was a clear example of the substitution of one set of activities for another.

In SAIT's case, the e-learning strategic plan recommended substantial extra funding (several million dollars per year) for hiring more instructors, instructor training, and increasing staff in the Centre for Instructional Development, the Library, and IT Services. The SAIT executive decided that these allocations would be made "when resources become available," so at present SAIT still operates roughly on the basis of its previous budget allocations, which is one reason why there has been only slow expansion of e-learning in the institution.

In general in the case studies, once operating funds were allocated to academic departments, it was extremely difficult to track exactly how funds were applied. In particular, it was difficult to track in what ways money and resources were allocated to different kinds of teaching activities within a department, such as to courses using blended learning, hybrid courses with reduced classroom time, or fully online distance education courses. Indeed few institutions in the case studies tracked even the number of courses and enrollments using e-learning, either overall, or in its different forms (the University of Central Florida was an exception).

Some institutions, such as UBC, Alicante, and Rovira i Virgili, analyzed data from their learning management systems, which can provide a crude indication of whether and how an instructor and students in a course are using the LMS, such as the volume of content and the number of student comments in discussion forums, but it is difficult to turn such data into clear reports that identify specific types of e-learning. Institutions with a separate distance education department, such as UBC and SAIT, were able to track the volume of online distance courses and student enrollments, as did, of course, the two open universities in the study. However, with the exception of UBC, no institution in the case studies attempted to measure the direct costs of teaching with technology, and at UBC, this was done only for fully online courses offered through the distance education and technology unit.

We did not investigate how most of the institutions in the case studies managed the process of funding technology support within academic departments or central units through the budget allocation process. However, in those institutions with the highest technology integration, substantial funding had clearly been found on an ongoing basis to support learning technology units.

For nearly all the case studies, however, it was a mystery to us how funds were reallocated to enable a move to technology-based teaching on a sustainable basis, or what sacrifices or cuts (if any) were made in other budget areas to accommodate this. Indeed, it was clear that some senior administrators were also in the same position. It was not unusual to hear comments such as: "I don't know where the money's coming from, but it's something that we have to do." We think the assumption often made was that instructors would replace existing activities with technology-based activities, but because the main goal in all the campus-based institutions was to enhance and not replace the traditional classroom model, this was unlikely, hence instructors' complaints of the extra workload associated with technology-based teaching.

Our fear is that in some cases, the integration of technology has been paid for unintentionally by larger classes, by heavier workloads for instructors, by a move to the use of lower-paid adjunct faculty, by slowing down the updating or development of new programs, or by any combination of these actions. If these unintended outcomes are to be avoided, a deliberate strategy needs to be developed for identifying new revenue sources (for instance, increased enrollments due to more flexible delivery), or areas or activities from where funds will be reallocated, or activities replaced. With the level of resources now being committed to technology-based teaching, institutions will need to track much more carefully both the costs and the benefits of using technology for teaching. We discuss below ways in which this could be done.

METHODOLOGICAL ISSUES IN ASSESSING THE TRUE COST OF E-LEARNING

Costs will depend on a wide range of factors. Laurillard (2007) provides a comprehensive review of research into the costs and benefits of technology-based teaching in higher education. She noted that "all the researchers in the field are agreed on the importance of understanding the costs and benefits of technology innovation, and on the difficulty of doing it."

The research to date clearly indicates the importance of context ("it all depends") and the difficulty of generalizing between institutions on this matter. Also, most of the research into costs fails to take into account organizational culture, which affects the whole attitude and approach of university and college administrators toward cost analysis. So, although it is important to be aware of the research, what institutions need to do is to put in place operational procedures for tracking costs, and for using that data for both strategic and day-to-day decision making. Our aim here is not to provide a comprehensive review of the research, but to offer an introduction to the methodological issues, and to suggest some ways in which costs can be tracked and analyzed to facilitate decision making about the use of technology for teaching. We begin by discussing some issues around organizational culture.

Lack of Transparency

Wellman (2010, p. 31) comments that

> relatively few institutions incorporate data on costs into internal decision-making about budgets, which continue to be primarily incremental and revenue based rather than spending based . . . they have yet to connect the dots between spending and other aspects of institutional performance.

In other words, it is easier to increase tuition fees when state funding is cut than to look at being more cost-efficient (and hence keep tuition fees down). Indeed, if universities *did* become more efficient they would be likely to lose even more government grant. Revenues per student are one of the critical factors used in world university rankings and hence there is pressure on universities to keep revenues up rather than reduce costs. Yet Wellman (2010) writes: "The assumption that money is related to quality is so deep-seated that there are remarkably few analyses about whether it is true." Indeed, she quoted a study that found no correlation between revenues and degree productivity (Kelly & Jones, 2005), and another (Gansemer-Topf, Saunders, Schuh, & Shelley, 2004) that found that "total resource availability is less relevant than how institutions use the resources they have."

There is often a lack of transparency in decisions about the allocation of money and resources in all organizations, because it is not just a technical but also a political process, in the sense of having to satisfy a number of competing institutional priorities and stakeholders' interests. Also, as a proportion of total resources, actual money to facilitate change is often extremely limited in even large universities, because so much of any operational budget is committed to ongoing activities that have to be funded off the top, such as salaries and benefits for permanent employees, maintenance of buildings, support for the IT infrastructure, and so forth. If this money is suddenly or arbitrarily removed, disaster almost certainly follows.

Brinkman and Morgan (2010, p. 10) argue, however, that

> an institution that relies on an entirely incremental approach, i.e. the new budget is the prior version plus a proportional share of any new money, will have a tough time steering the budget allocation process.

But even the suggestion of gradual variations of regular operating funds, such as a reduction in salary costs or positions within an academic department where enrollments are dropping, will meet huge resistance and extensive lobbying from the interested parties, and may not be possible for contractual reasons. As a result, those with apparent control over funds often have to resort to what may appear devious or opaque maneuvering if they wish to find resources to initiate or support any major changes within the organization.

To avoid this problem, Brinkman and Morgan suggest that institutions need to assemble strategic resources over time, such as accumulating reserve funds under central control for strategic purposes. Thus sometimes a president or a VP of academic affairs or administration will have a secret pot of money that can be used for executive-level projects or priorities.

Because technology, especially in the teaching and learning area, is a relatively new item of expenditure, it may not even have a specified budget line. Indeed, it is often not a separate activity, if one thinks of training to use technology as an integral part of the teaching budget, but also a real technology cost. Thus subtle reallocation of resources to technology activities are made without being easily detected in formal statements of budget or operating costs. Although this is often necessary to facilitate change, it makes tracking of costs by activities much more difficult.

Thus much of the data about allocation of resources to different types of teaching is locked within individual institution's budgeting processes but has rarely been analyzed on a cross-institutional, statistical basis to identify average costs, and, more important, to identify the factors that drive costs in each of these contexts. A lack of transparency in identifying the true costs of technology integration is not dishonest or even unethical, but a practical outcome of the reality of managing complex organizations. Nevertheless, it does create problems when reasonable questions are asked, such as how much it will cost to move to e-learning, or what will be the return on investment.

What Counts as a Cost?

This seemingly philosophical question is an important one in reality. Unfortunately, there is no general agreement or methodology on what counts as a cost regarding technology integration. To take an obvious example, how do you cost out a professor's time, and especially the time she spends using technology for teaching?

Instructors often argue that online learning is more work (and it is if technology is merely added on to classroom teaching, and not used to replace other activities). How does one cost out this extra work? Indeed, *should* one cost it out? After all, the university pays the professor's salary; if the professor chooses to spend more time preparing for her teaching, it costs the university nothing more. The cost shows itself in other ways, though, such as a reduction in research activity or less family or social life. At some point, these hidden costs become unacceptable to the instructor, and technology becomes rejected. Thus we believe that these hidden costs too should be identified, not just the university's salary costs, and methods should be used that avoid such hidden costs, as far as possible.

Financial Records

Although in universities and colleges, money is allocated to academic departments, and academic departments do teaching and research, it is difficult to cost out the separate activities involved in teaching, such as the cost of a program, a lecture versus a lab class, or the cost of a face-to-face course versus an online course, because these cut across accounting lines such as salaries and expenses. However, if we want an accurate basis of the cost of technology-based teaching, we need to relate it to activities such as hybrid or online learning.

Department-Driven Financial Records

Most university and college accounting is department and expenditure driven, rather than activity and revenue driven. Although there are exceptions, generally, all income, such as government grants, student tuition fees, and any profits from campus operations such as car parking or business development, goes into a central pot which is then reallocated to organizational units, such as a faculty, school, or academic department. Quite often in this form of accounting, funds are reallocated first to overheads or general expenditures, then what remains to academic faculties or departments through the VP of academic affairs or provost, and then the academic faculties or departments will allocate resources (mainly faculty or instructors) to programs or courses. Thus a faculty, school, or department will be allocated funds from which faculty and academic administrative salaries and expenses are paid (the bulk of the funding), and from which technology equipment such as computers for faculty or computer labs for students may be paid, depending on the degree of decentralization.

We have already noted that this funding is often historical and perpetuating in nature; that is, the same as the previous year, plus or minus a few percentage points to reflect changing overall financial conditions or relatively minor changes in activities. Usually funds are allocated from the beginning of the financial year and the account holder such as a dean must not exceed those funds by the end of the year (although they usually have freedom to move funds around within the overall budget for their department). The main accounting activity is to track expenditures and reconcile them to allocated funds.

This model works well when an organization is stable and activities in a new financial year will be very much similar to activities in previous years. It is also a common means of financial operation for other public or government agencies. However, it locks up funding in existing activities, leaves little elbow room for new initiatives, and provides no incentives to reduce costs other than in those years where overall funding is cut or financial mismanagement has occurred. It creates major problems when new activities, such as an increase in the use of technology for teaching, need to be funded.

Activity-Based Accounting

In activity-based accounting, activities generate revenues or grants and drive expenditures. In this model, if applied to a university, revenues directly associated with an academic program, such as tuition fees and government grant per FTE, would go directly to the program. For instance, instead of allocating money to an academic department, it would be allocated directly to a program, such as a baccalaureate degree, and would cover all the costs associated with that activity. It might not seem much of a difference to allocate money to a bachelor of arts program as distinct from the Faculty of Arts, but in reality the difference is profound. With activity-based accounting it is the program director who controls the budget and pays from that budget all the costs associated with the program, including administrative costs and overheads.

Very few public or state universities operate this way, except in ancillary or nonacademic areas, and sometimes for full cost-recovery programs, such as MBAs or in continuing education. It is also very difficult in practice to separate activity costs in post-secondary education (for instance, research and teaching). However, activity-based costing is often practiced in businesses, especially those with different product lines or services. The main advantage of activity-based costing is that being program- or project-based, funding starts and ends with the program, and thus enables a much more flexible approach to bringing in new programs, closing old ones, and doing things differently from one program to another.

Another advantage of activity-based costing is that it increases pressure to keep overheads down, because the overhead services are being paid directly out of program funding. In some activity-based funding projects, program directors are free to shop around for the best services they need, going outside the organization if necessary. It also facilitates unbundling of activities, such as course design, course development, and course delivery. However, activity-based costing has another advantage from our perspective. It enables the cost of the technology component to be much more easily identified and tracked.

OVERHEADS

Another difficulty in costing the influence of technology is the way overheads are treated in universities and colleges. Overheads are the costs that may be necessary for the running of a university or college, but which are not direct teaching (or research) costs. These might include the president's office, maintenance of buildings and grounds, administrative departments such as finance, the registry and student services, heating and lighting, marketing and public relations, and myriad other activities.

Which costs are counted as an overhead, and how they are treated, varies from institution to institution, and even within the same institution. For instance, continuing studies and full cost-recovery programs may be charged a hefty overhead, whereas mainline undergraduate programs or academic departments may pay or be charged no overheads. Sometimes information technology infrastructure, such as networks and servers, telephone services, and technical support, are treated as general overheads; sometimes they are treated as direct costs and have to be paid for out of faculty or department budgets.

In a large research university, however overheads are handled, general or central nonteaching costs constitute a very large proportion of the operating budget. For instance, only about half the operating budget at UBC is spent directly on academic departments, and Wellman, Desrochers, Lenihan, Kirshstein, Hurlburt, and Honegger (2009) has shown that in recent years, although tuition fees have increased in the United States, these increases have not gone mainly to the teaching areas but to cover the shortfall in government funding which had previously been used to cover many of the overhead or nonteaching costs.

What happens, though, when programs start being delivered online is that this changes (or should change) assumptions and policies about what constitutes an overhead cost. For instance, students studying fully online do not usually use the campus. Should the costs of a fully online program be exempt a proportion for building maintenance and heating and lighting (and maybe include a higher proportion for IT networks and infrastructure)? Again, the main point here is that if overheads constitute almost half the costs of an institution's operating budget, they cannot be ignored when costing different activities with different effects on overheads. In particular, we need to ask to what extent could overheads be reduced and hence efficiencies gained by moving a proportion of teaching to online learning? There is plenty of scope.

Having discussed just a few of the methodological challenges in costing technology-based teaching, we will look now at a method for costing a fully online program.

A BUSINESS MODEL FOR AN ONLINE LEARNING PROGRAM

DEVELOPING SUSTAINABLE BUSINESS MODELS FOR QUALITY E-LEARNING

For-profit online universities, such as the University of Phoenix, Capella, Full Sail, and Kaplan, have developed sustainable business models for their online programs that leverage the use of technology, and as a result have attracted a growing share of the online market in the United States, particularly in the more lucrative lifelong learning area, where working students can and will pay full fee for programs that have direct benefit for employment and career development. This is also an important market for public and private nonprofit universities, where there is growing demand from working adults for access to the latest research and new practices. If public universities are to meet this challenge, they will need to develop sustainable business models for online credit programs that are not only competitive in quality but also provide value for money.

We provide an example of such a program from one of our case studies, the University of British Columbia, where one of the authors worked extensively on the development of this business model. Also the scenario at the beginning of this chapter is partly based on this program.

Table 7.1 is an example adapted from the business model for UBC's fully online master in educational technology, first offered

Table 7.1. A Business Model for an Online Program

	Year 1	Year 2	Year 3	Year 7	Totals (over Seven Years)
	$$	$$	$$	$$	$$
Development					
Program Coordination ($90,000 base salary)	22,500	45,900	45,900	46,359	300,000
Program Coordinator Benefits (23% of base salary)	5,175	10,557	10,557	10,663	69,000
Subject Expert ($7,500 per course: 12.5 days work)	30,000	30,000	15,000	0	
Academic Reviewer	2,800	2,800	1,400	0	
Instructional Designer ($270/day: 12 days per course)	12,960	12,960	6,480	0	
Web Programmer ($180/day: 9 days per course)	6,480	6,480	3,240	0	
Graphic Designer ($270/day: 5 days per course)	5,400	5,400	2,700	0	
Library Resources	4,000	4,000	4,000	0	
Copyright Fees	4,000	4,000	2,000	0	
Multimedia Production	20,000	20,000	40,000	5,000	
Marketing and Advertising	20,000	5,000	5,000	6,000	
Subtotal Development	**133,315**	**147,097**	**136,277**	**68,022**	**370,000**
Program Planning and Development					
10% of Development and Delivery Costs		21,047	27,522	57,225	317,000
Maintenance of Courses					
Subject Expert (1 credit = $2,500 per course)			10,000	30,000	

(continued on next page)

TABLE 7.1. *Continued*

	Year 1	Year 2	Year 3	Year 7	Totals (over Seven Years)
Project Manager/Instructional Designer ($270/day)			3,240	9,720	
Web Programmer ($180/day)			2,160	6,480	
Graphic Designer ($270/day)			1,080	3,240	
Library Tutor ($1,000 per course offering)		4,000	8,000	12,000	
Payment to Graduate Studies (50% of admission fees)		3,216	3,216	3,216	
Subtotal Maintenance	**0**	**7,216**	**27,696**	**64,656**	**267,000**
Course Development Costs	133,315	147,097	136,277	68,022	
Maintenance Costs	0	7,216	27,696	64,656	
Overheads					
Faculty of Education (30% of Rows 5, 7, 8, 23)	16,590	23,610	21,690	22,908	
DET (30% of Rows 9, 10, 11, 14, 15, 24, 25, 26)	19,452	14,952	19,170	7,332	
Total Development Costs	**169,357**	**192,875**	**204,833**	**162,917**	
Delivery Costs					
Program Admission	7,500	15,000	15,000	15,000	
Faculty Tutor ($7,500 per course)	15,000	30,000	60,000	90,000	
Tutors ($220 per student x 20 students per course)	8,800	17,600	35,200	52,800	
Printed Course Materials ($15 per student)	1,200	2,400	4,800	7,200	

Student Administration	4,824	11,520	23,040	34,560	
Faculty of Education Administration	3,015	7,200	14,400	21,600	
OHST	1,332	3,181	6,362	9,542	
Total Delivery Costs	**41,671**	**86,901**	**158,802**	**230,702**	**1,019,000**
Program Administration and Overheads					880,000
Subtotal—Development and Delivery Costs	211,028	279,776	363,635	393,620	
Total Development and Delivery Costs	**211,028**	**279,823**	**391,156**	**450,844**	**2,853,000**
Revenues					
Student Fees	83,750	200,000	400,000	600,000	2,983,750
Admission Fees	3,015	6,030	6,030	6,030	39,195
Total Revenues	**86,765**	**206,030**	**406,030**	**606,030**	**3,023,000**
Annual Cash Deficit/Surplus	(134,263)	(100,793)	8,874	155,186	170,000
Loan Required	134,263	100,793	0	0	235,056
Interest Paid	(8,660)	(15,720)	16,734	0	79,150
Cumulated Balance (profit/loss)	**(142,923)**	**(259,435)**	**(267,296)**	**62,146**	**236,260**
Assumptions					
Number of Courses Under Development	4	4	2	0	0
Number of Courses Being Maintained	0	0	4	12	12
Number of Courses Offered	2	4	8	12	12
Students Admitted/Year	67	67	67	67	402

(continued on next page)

TABLE 7.1. *Continued*

	Year 1	Year 2	Year 3	Year 7	Totals (over Seven Years)
Number of Course Enrollments	80	160	320	480	2,387
Estimated Enrollment per Course:	40				
Breakeven Fee per Course	$1,091				
Suggested Fee per Course	$1,250				
OHST (7.5% on $265 per student)	$20				
Graduate Studies Admission Fees	$90				
DET Student Admin/Student	$72				
Faculty of Education Student Admin/Student	$45				
Interest Rate	6.45%				

Notes: 1. These are projections, not actual costs, but the program paid back all the loan by year 6.

2. One notable omission is licensing costs for the learning management system. UBC was not required to pay licensing fees for its online learning management system for this project. In general, though, this cost should be included as a significant expenditure.

3. OHST is a "tax" on all programs that goes into the university's Teaching and Learning Enhancement Fund, which is used to fund innovative teaching projects.

4. The financial goal was full cost recovery, not profit. Any "profit" is invested back into course maintenance and new courses.

5. This model is for a fully online program. A different model with similar cost headings could be developed for hybrid and technology-enhanced face-to-face courses and programs, thus enabling comparison of costs, for different numbers of course enrollments.

6. Items in italics have been included under program administration and overheads. Subtotals for development, maintenance, and delivery exclude these figures.

in 2003. The business model projected revenues and expenditures over a nine-year period. (For simplicity, data for years 4–6, and years 8–9, have been omitted from Table 7.1.)

The program is not fully complete until year five, when all 12 courses are available and the student enrollment target is reached. The program was designed to pay back all loans and recover all costs by year seven (which it did). An ongoing maintenance activity ensured that courses were kept up to date so they would not have to be withdrawn and completely redesigned after a few years. Any projected profits after seven years ($400,000 plus per annum) would be invested back into new course activity. Thus the business model has built-in financial sustainability, if cost and revenue targets are met, as they were overall.

An activity-based business model such as this also provides a wealth of information about the cost structure of a fully online program. Table 7.2 provides a summary.

In teaching with technology, the separate activities can be described as follows:

- *Planning* includes deciding on the content coverage and course structure, the method of teaching, what technologies to use, and above all working the program proposal through all the stakeholders for formal approval. In this case, planning included the development of a new business model, and persuading the faculties of education and graduate studies, as well as administrative departments whose services would be

TABLE 7.2. SUMMARY OF BUSINESS PLAN BY ACTIVITY,
OVER SEVEN YEARS

Activity	Cost (Seven Years)	Percentage
Planning	$317,000	11
Program administration and overheads	$880,000	31
Development	$370,000	13
Maintenance	$267,000	9
Delivery	$1,019,000	36
Total	**$2,853,000**	**100**

used, about the viability of such a model. Often planning costs are "sunk" or just ignored, but they are very real, involving a great deal of time from a large number of people. In our example, a rough guess of the planning costs was made, but instead of putting all these costs into the first year (requiring a much larger loan and hence higher interest charges), they were paid back throughout the life of the program. Planning constituted just over $300,000, or 11%, of the total cost of this program over seven years.

- *Program administration.* A major cost (included under development in the business plan, but extracted for the graph under its own heading), is the program coordinator, an academic responsible for the management of the program, but who did not contribute directly to the development and delivery of courses. Nevertheless, this turned out to be a critical role, as the program coordinator was the one who had to find the academic staff to teach on the program, who oversaw the financial aspects, and was ultimately accountable for the program. Program administration constituted 13% of the overall costs ($369,000) over seven years.

- *Overheads* are those costs not directly associated with the planning, development, maintenance, or delivery of courses, but which are still necessary for the program to function. The business model was based on identifying as exactly as possible all the direct costs, such as admissions and the library, and including these costs, with direct payments from revenues to the relevant departments, to keep general overheads down to a minimum. This involved a great deal of negotiation with the provost's office, and because the senior administration was strongly supportive of the initiative, the allocation of overheads for general university overheads was very small, and probably underestimated, although the faculty of education and distance education did include general overheads for their administration. General overheads constituted about 18% of the overall cost over seven years ($511,000).

- *Development* includes the design of the courses, including choice of technologies and teaching approach; creating materials for use by students, such as a loading a learning management system and creating graphics and video clips. This involves instructors working with learning technology staff. In this program, students could take 10 courses from a total of 12. In years one and two, four new courses a year were designed, and in years three and four, two more new courses a year were developed. Excluding indirect costs or overheads, each course cost averaged approximately $21,000 to develop. After that, programs were regularly maintained and updated. Development constituted 13% of the costs of this program ($370,000) by year seven, but it will be seen that the main development costs were incurred early in the program (years one to four).

- *Maintenance* includes changes to materials in subsequent offerings of the course, such as adding or removing online readings, new assessments, or examination questions; improving the clarity of the online teaching materials; and replacing parts of a course with new or better content. Maintenance changes are based mainly on feedback from students and teaching staff. In this program, maintenance constituted 9% of the total cost of the program by year seven ($267,000, slightly more than $5,400 per course per year, over seven years), and was based on spending roughly 25% of a course's development costs each year after the first year of the course, so that the whole course could be renewed over a period of five years if necessary.

- *Delivery* constitutes the online teaching of the program, with online support from instructors, and student assessment/marking. Again, delivery costs will vary considerably with the design of the course. These programs depended largely on a learning management system and online discussion forums, with both individual and group assignments, in the form of projects, essays, and later, e-portfolios. The class enrollments were expected to average about 40 per class, divided into two sections of 20 with two instructors, one a full faculty member and one an adjunct under the supervision of the faculty member. Delivery costs constituted 36% of the cost of the program over seven years ($1,019,000).

TABLE 7.3. COSTS OF INSTRUCTORS ($)

	Development	Maintenance	Delivery
Tenured faculty	90,000	115,000	450,000
Adjunct faculty	0	0	264,000
Total	**90,000**	**115,000**	**714,000**
Total costs of each activity	370,000	267,000	1,019,000
Instructors as a percentage of expenditure on each activity	24%	31%	70%

It should also be noted that instructor time constituted a relatively small proportion of the costs. Table 7.3 summarizes the costs of tenured and adjunct faculty, over seven years (this excludes the program coordinator, who was a tenured faculty member, but not an instructor in the program).

Instructional design, Web programmers, and multimedia production accounted for the majority of course development costs. There was much discussion over the appropriate rate to be charged for tenured faculty. The dean's office finally settled on a figure of $7,500 per course, for 12.5 days' work, for both development and delivery. This rate is equivalent to $600 a day for a tenured professor, which based on 220 working days, equates to a faculty salary, including benefits, of $132,000 a year. Faculty working on the program had permanent employment status. Adjunct faculty were paid $220 per student (roughly $4,000–$4,400 per course, depending on enrollments), and were on yearly contracts, for the equivalent of 12.5 days' work per course, equivalent to $70,000–$77,000 annual salary.

The Relationship Between Revenue and Expenditure over Time for an Online Program

Figure 7.1 shows the relationship between revenues and expenditures over a seven-year period.

In the first years, there is a large deficit, due to the costs of planning and development (in this chart we have moved all plan-

FIGURE 7.1. PROJECTED REVENUES AND EXPENDITURES FOR
AN ONLINE MASTER'S PROGRAM

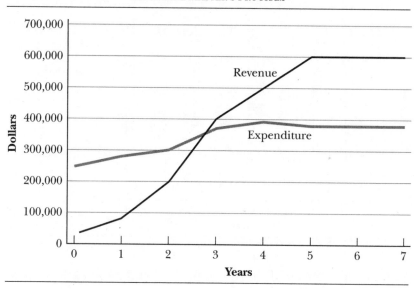

ning costs to the front, which is where they were incurred). By year three, revenues are slightly exceeding expenditure, but four more years are needed before the investment is fully recovered (including loan and interest repayments). From year seven, a large "profit" is technically possible, but it is likely that this would be invested in new course development to keep the program up to date. In fact, by careful management (for example, by paying back the planning costs when revenues were flowing) and borrowing the money at the end of the financial year, the actual amount borrowed from the university for the program was quite small (under $200,000). The graph indicates, though, the importance of having funds to invest up front for innovative programming.

Breakdown of Expenditures over Time
In traditional classroom teaching, the planning of the course, the preparation of teaching, the delivery of the course, and student assessment are all done by the same person. When we start using technology for teaching, however, these different functions

Figure 7.2. Breakdown of Different Kinds of Expenditure over Time

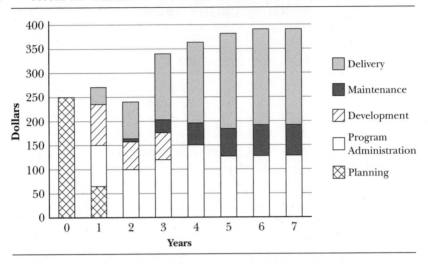

become disaggregated, and other professionals besides the instructor become involved (this can also happen with large face-to-face classes, of course, with the use of parallel sections run by teaching assistants). Also, the costs also shift over time between different activities, as illustrated in Figure 7.1. In our example, we provide a breakdown of costs between activities over seven years. However, an analysis at different times would show a different ratio of costs, with course development higher in the early years, and delivery higher in the later years (see Figure 7.2).

Revenues

Because this was a totally new program, requiring additional faculty, it was designed as fully cost recoverable. The program was designed specifically for working students, so that they could take individual courses, or five courses for a postgraduate certificate, then take another five courses for the master's (trading in their certificate to do this). Students were allowed up to five years to complete the master's program, and were able to pay per course (a major change from the policy of charging for a full year for a master's program, irrespective of the number of courses a student takes in that year). The fee was set at $1,250 per three-credit course, totaling $12,500 for the full master's degree. The fee was determined partly by an examination of fees for similar programs elsewhere (what the market will bear), and partly in order to meet the estimated cost of the program, plus a risk factor of about 15% over the breakeven cost, in case enrollments were less or costs higher than expected.

Although this particular program was designed to recover all costs through tuition fees, the business model would also work for base or grant-funded programs or courses, such as undergraduate programs. Instead of all costs coming from tuition fees, revenues would include an allocation of grant money to the program reflecting the average grant per full-time equivalent student, plus any student tuition fees that would normally be charged.

COSTS OF FACULTY AND LEARNING TECHNOLOGY SUPPORT STAFF

Research (for example, Bates, 2005) has shown that the instructor's concerns about the impact of technology on teaching load is a critical factor that influences adoption.

Setting Workload for the Online Courses

In the business model, set times were assigned to academic and instructional design staff for course development, maintenance, and delivery, as shown in Table 7.4.

Also note that if student enrollments for a course in this graduate program exceed 20, an adjunct faculty member would be hired to open up a second section. (For undergraduate online courses at UBC, the number triggering an extra adjunct is usually

TABLE 7.4. WORK ESTIMATES FOR VARIOUS ACTIVITIES FOR AN ONLINE COURSE

	Course Development	Course Maintenance	Course Delivery
Tenured faculty	12.5*	4.0	12.5
Instructional designer	12.0	2.5	0
Web/multimedia designer	7.0	4.0	0

*Days per course per year.

30.) In other words, once the course is developed, extra students can be added, so long as the tuition fees cover the additional cost of an adjunct faculty, which they more than do in this case, at $1,250 a student. (Even for grant-subsidized online undergraduate courses at UBC, the cost of adjuncts is more than covered by the much lower student tuition fees.) This is where the economies of scale for online courses really begin to show.

Calculating Faculty Workloads

How were these allocations of time decided? The short answer is on experience. Using "light" project management methods, a learning management system, and a team approach, the distance education and technology department had a rough idea of how much time it takes to develop, maintain, and deliver good-quality online courses, based on an already existing curriculum. The aim, though, was also to make sure the teaching load for a fully online course is no more than that of a face-to-face course for a tenured professor.

In the online program, the actual amount a tenured faculty member has to work in the program varies from year to year, depending on the stage of development of the program. In year one, the course would be developed (12.5 days), but not offered or maintained. In year two, it would be offered for the first time, involving 12.5 days' delivery, but as a new course it would require no or very little maintenance time. In subsequent years it would require four days' maintenance time and 12.5 days for delivery, for a total of 16.5 hours per year. Of course, it never works out that neatly, but these are general guidelines that can be set.

In traditional classroom teaching, the usual way of assigning faculty or instructor time is through the credit system. A class with three hours of classroom time per week over 13 weeks is a three-credit class, with students needing, for example, 120 credits (or the equivalent of 40 three-credit courses) for a four-year bachelor's program. A tenured faculty member in a large research university may have a teaching load of four three-credit courses, teaching two courses a semester over two semesters.

However, classroom time does not include either the time students spend studying outside of the class (such as reading and doing assignments for assessment), or the time that instructors spend on course planning, lesson preparation, student help (such as office hours), and, in what can be a particularly heavy load for many instructors, grading and student feedback. The only way to assess accurately the time spent teaching this way would be for instructors to keep accurate logs of their activities, and for students to do the same. Then one gets into the issue of whether instructors spend too much or too little time on out-of-class teaching activities, because there are no standards for this. However, the larger the class the more the workload is likely to increase, for grading alone, unless additional help is provided, or some form of automation (such as computerized testing) is used.

Another way to look at this problem is to calculate the number of hours or days available to instructors for teaching. For instance, in a research university the standard may be 40% of the professor's time for teaching, 40% for research or consultancies, and 20% for administration and public service. If weekends and holidays are then subtracted, we can calculate the amount of time available for teaching.

Table 7.5 provides a simple example. If we assume 104 days for weekends, and 12 days for statutory holidays, and 30 days for annual holidays for a senior professor, we end up with a total of roughly 220 working days, which leaves 88 days for teaching, 88 days for research, and 44 days for administrative and public service duties.

With a teaching load of four courses, the professor has 22 days on average to spend on each course per year, so the UBC online

TABLE 7.5. BREAKDOWN OF ACTIVITIES FOR A SENIOR PROFESSOR DURING ONE YEAR WITH A TEACHING LOAD OF FOUR THREE-CREDIT COURSES PER ANNUM

Activity	Days
Teaching	88
Research	88
Administration/service	44
Weekends/holidays/vacation	145
Total	365

model is actually *less* time demanding. The difference is made up by the time spent by less expensive learning technology support staff (although faculty, of course, may choose or feel they must spend more time than allocated). The critical factor here is the design of the course, which aims to shift the work from the instructor to the students working online. The course is deliberately designed to fit the time available for the instructor (and the learning technology support staff, whose time also has to be managed).

The model can be adapted to courses with different requirements. For instance, if there is no existing curriculum, or animations need to be developed, more time would need to be allocated (in the case of new curriculum development) to the instructors and instructional designer, and (in the case of large amounts of animation) to the learning technology support staff, and probably the instructor as well. Thus major changes in curriculum or the use of higher-cost media would mean that resources would need to be found over and above the standard model. In a similar way, the model could be adapted to hybrid courses.

The Importance of Good Course Design in Controlling Costs

Good course design in the preparation of learning materials can reduce the amount of interaction needed between instructor and students (for instance by reducing the number of times students ask questions for clarification, and using computer-marked assignments), but in many cases the main goal of the teaching is to provide high-quality interaction between instructor and students. Nevertheless, through the design of independent learning activities, the use of peer-to-peer interaction in study groups, the use of adjuncts or teaching assistants in well-defined ways, and careful planning of the time and nature of the senior research professor's interaction with study groups, high-quality interaction can be maintained even within large online classes. Course design is therefore the key to improving cost-effectiveness in technology-based teaching and learning.

Identifying or setting standards for instructional workload is important if we wish to look at the effect of increasing the use of technology for teaching. It also provides a framework for controlling the costs of technology-based teaching. Different institutions may have different assumptions about teaching load, but basically the goal should be that using technology for teaching should not take more time than current face-to-face teaching activities; indeed, if possible, it should reduce teaching workload, or allow for more interaction with students, for more research time, or for other clearly identified benefits. However, instructors constantly complain that technology increases their teaching load. This will occur, though, only when technology is added on to the existing activities of instructors, rather than being used to replace some traditional instructor-led activities, such as regular weekly lectures.

Calculating Revenues, Costs, and the Number of Students

Business models are not fixed, but dynamic. The figures provided for UBC are really a snapshot in time, before the program was developed. Over time, the model would be adapted to reality, such as faculty requiring more time for development or delivery, different enrollment patterns from those anticipated, and other changing features. Thus none of the costs or assumptions is fixed in time.

However, a constant of any business plan for technology-based teaching is the relationship between program costs, student fees (or costs per FTE for base-funded programs), and the number of course enrollments (one student is likely to take several courses at a time; it is the total of course enrollments that matter, not the number of students, in this model). If we know any two of these factors, the third can be calculated. This can be expressed as follows:

1. *Revenues* must be equal to or more than the total costs of the program divided by the number of course enrollments. If the target is to break even in year seven, the total revenues should equal the total expenditures over seven years. In our example, in year seven, expenditures are targeted at $2,853,000 and course enrollments at 2,387. $2,853,000/2,387 = $1,195 over seven years; at $1,250 per course, the tuition fee is $55 above the breakeven fee, plus other revenues from admission fees ($39,000). When calculations are made over nine years, the figures are as follows: $3,571,366/3,347 = $1,067, a 15% margin,

plus revenues from admission fees. $1,250 was considered the maximum tuition fee that could be charged.

2. Total *costs* must equal or not exceed revenues multiplied by the number of student enrollments ($1,250 × 2,387 = $2,984,000). Total costs over seven years are $2,853,136. Thus marketing must focus on getting 2,387 course enrollments over seven years, that is, roughly 480 new course enrollments per year when all 12 courses are available. Given that students must take a minimum of two courses per year, it was estimated that a target of 67 new students per year was the minimum that needed to be recruited to reach the course enrollment target. Because the programs were online, marketing could be worldwide.

3. *Student course enrollments* must equal or exceed total costs divided by the fee ($2,984,000/$1,250 = 2,387). Since both the level of the tuition fee and the number of enrollments have limits, it was important for the program to keep overall costs below $3 million by year seven. This forced a careful examination of costs and especially overheads.

It can be seen that a business plan is an iterative process. As more facts, such as enrollments, become clear, adjustments will need to be made. Indeed, a business plan only comes to a close when a program is wound down.

This analysis also indicates the importance of looking at a business plan over a considerable length of time. The program looks more risky at seven years than at nine years (which is five years after the program is fully implemented). Putting all the costs in the business plan, including overheads and planning costs that were spent before the program began, provides a cushion if enrollments do not meet their target as quickly as planned. It should be remembered that this program started gradually, testing the market at each stage, and the program paid back the loan in year six, and is still running successfully eight years after starting. In the end, though, there is always an element of risk in launching a new program, whether online or not. However, a business plan allows risks to be identified and to some extent quantified and managed. More important, it provides a way to identify and manage the costs of technology-based teaching, even for base-funded programs.

CONCLUSION

This chapter is more of a call to action than a report on best practices in the financial management of technology resources. We summarize here our main conclusions.

1. KNOW WHAT IS BEING DONE

Given the increasing investment in technology, decision makers at all levels within the institution should understand the costs of using technology for teaching. In particular, we need to better understand how instructors use their time in teaching, and how this affects costs. Technology can enable research professors to use their limited teaching time much more effectively. For this to happen, though, methods of course development and delivery, and the organization and reporting of financial data, must be changed.

None of the institutions in the case studies measured the effects of technology investment, especially on teaching and learning. We are not referring here to the more difficult area of learning outcomes (although that is important) but to much simpler measures, such as the way technology is being used for teaching (for instance, how many courses were blended, hybrid, or distance, and the trend over the years). Collecting this kind of data in a consistent and comprehensive manner is essential for understanding the effects of investing in technology. One way to do this would be to build this kind of reporting into the annual program planning process (for instance, what kind of courses were offered this year, and how this will change for next year).

2. CHANGE IS NEEDED IN HOW COSTS ARE TRACKED

We have argued the need to move to activity-based costing to be able to track accurately the costs of various types of courses. Because most financial data are now in computerized databases, this can be done by combining the traditional department-based financial reporting system with additional breakdowns by activity, using business intelligence tools. The challenge is to ensure that financial data is initially collected and stored in such a way as to make activity-based costing possible. This needs more research and development, but it is going to be essential for the cost-effective management of all forms of teaching, as the use of technology for teaching expands.

3. BE CLEAR ON HOW TECHNOLOGY-BASED TEACHING WILL BE PAID FOR

Although we did not attempt to collect this information, we suspect that most institutions do not have clear strategies about how technology-based teaching will be funded on a day-to-day operational basis. One reason for this is that costs are not tracked by activity; thus, it is difficult to measure the effects (positive or negative) of subtle and not always apparent shifts in funding and activities.

What is often not measured are the losses or unintended consequences of transferring increasing amounts of resources to technology-supported teaching. We are not arguing that this should not be done, but it becomes critical to be clear about what will be given up or replaced as a result. We recommend that investment in technology is linked to strategies and procedures that replace rather than add to existing practice, and that there is a deliberate strategy to identify where savings can be made to cover the additional costs of technology investment and application.

Standards for overall time spent teaching that are consistent between all types of course delivery is one way to control costs or increase productivity, recognizing, however, that the distribution of time between different teaching activities within the standard overall time will vary by the type of course and the extent of technology use. Another way to control costs and increase benefits is to use open content, instructional designers, Web support staff, and project management, to free up instructor time for more interaction with students. A third way is the redesign of large lecture courses, as developed by the National Center for Academic Transformation (see Twigg, 1999).

4. LINK COSTS TO BENEFITS

Decisions about the allocation of resources need to be linked to the benefits and losses that result. Laurillard (2007) notes that

> Inevitably, most costing studies have focused mainly on the difficulty of costing, avoiding the difficulty of measuring benefit. However, an adequate cost-benefit analysis should bring the two together at the detailed level of the nature of the innovation.

We have already commented on the tendency to see technology as enhancing the traditional classroom model, rather than as being used for innovative changes in the design and delivery of courses. Whatever the goals for teaching, they need to be clearly identified, measured, and related to costs.

5. DEVELOP BUSINESS PLANS FOR TECHNOLOGY-BASED PROGRAMS—AND TRADITIONAL PROGRAMS

Business plans use activity-based costing to estimate the costs of moving to technology-based learning. Business plans enable costs and risks to be identified and calculated, and provide a basis for tracking and comparing costs for different program designs, such as blended, hybrid, and fully online learning.

In conclusion, this area is very much a work in progress. We have suggested one methodology that has been tried and found useful for tracking costs. There are other methods that could also be used. What is clear, though, is that more research and more strategic thinking about the relationship between the costs, benefits, and possible unintended consequences of increasing technology-based teaching activities are needed.

Finally, we noted at the beginning of this chapter that organizational culture strongly influences the way resources are managed. In the next chapter, we explore more generally the influence of organizational culture on technology management.

CHAPTER EIGHT

BARRIERS TO CHANGE AND TWO WAYS TO REMOVE THEM

*The changes we are looking at now are millennial
changes because they require learning completely new
classes of skills. And, these changes must replace a system
in place for centuries.*
—TRENT BATSON, 2010

INTRODUCTION

If by chance this book should fall into the hands of someone with little experience of postsecondary education, they will be perplexed by the need for this book. Some of our recommendations (for instance the importance of strategic planning, for technology integration to be included in that planning, and the need for instructors to be trained in the use of technology) seem obvious, and thus the question arises, why does this not happen already in all institutions? Many commentators, particularly in North America, have been calling for more and better use of technology, and greater change in the public sector institutions (see, for instance, Kamenetz, 2010; Tapscott & Williams, 2010). What these calls for action fail to do is explain why these changes have not happened, if they are so obvious. We have the same obligation to explain. This means addressing the issue of organizational culture.

Schein (2005) defines organizational culture as "a pattern of shared basic assumptions that the group learned as it solved its problems that has worked well enough to be considered valid and is passed on to new members as the correct way to perceive, think, and feel in relation to those problems." Because organizational culture has developed to protect the core mission of an organization (and, as Schein notes, has proved to work in the past), suggested changes that undermine any of the "shared basic assumptions" are seen as highly threatening.

Universities in particular are recognized as having very strong "shared assumptions," and are notorious for changing relatively slowly. However, for organizations to adapt and thrive in rapidly changing environments, their organizational culture too will need to change, at least in some respects. We are arguing here that technology will not achieve its full potential unless there are some changes in organizational culture. In this chapter we also argue that the best way to bring about the necessary changes in organizational culture that will still protect and even strengthen the core mission of postsecondary education is through better training of its core staff, not so much in technology, but in teaching and management.

Systemic Barriers to Change

Batson (2010) puts forward a whole set of arguments as to "why it is taking so long for higher education faculty to adapt to the myriad opportunities made available by information technology and Web 2.0 interfaces and functionalities":

- Most college and university classrooms are designed for lectures.
- Students come to college expecting lectures; new methods are challenging to students as well as faculty so faculty are assessed by students on old models of teaching.
- Existing written syllabi or curriculum templates for courses reflect traditional methods of teaching.
- Faculty review processes do not favor or even recognize, in most cases, innovation with technology.

He might have added that the system favors excellence in research over teaching, and that there is no mandatory training for faculty in even classroom teaching, never mind teaching with technology.

Our answer to why change is not happening more rapidly is both simple and complex at the same time. It's simple, because it can be summed up in two words: organizational culture. It's complex, partly because organizational culture is complex. It's also complex because the organizational culture will have to change if technology is to be successfully integrated, but the core mission needs to stay the same (otherwise they will no longer be universities or colleges). However, the organizational culture has grown up to protect that mission. So the trick is to change the organizational culture enough to implement necessary changes in the way universities and colleges operate, without throwing the baby out with the bath water, namely, without losing some of the core values that protect the mission, such as academic freedom.

WHAT IS ORGANIZATIONAL CULTURE AND WHY IS IT IMPORTANT?

Our aim in this section is to examine the relationship among organizational culture, the mission of universities and colleges, and technology management.

THE MISSION OF UNIVERSITIES AND COLLEGES

We believe that universities and, just as important, community, technical, and vocational colleges are desperately needed in the twenty-first century. We need excellent centers that generate, collect, preserve, and disseminate knowledge that is or has been rigorously validated and tested. We need to create and sustain expertise, especially in a world where technology enables anyone not only to have an opinion on anything, but also to disseminate such opinions all over the world in an instant. We need institutions that develop learners who can differentiate between creationism and science, who can ask where the data comes from, who can challenge emotional or sloppy thinking, just as much as we will continue to need doctors, scientists, engineers, social workers, skilled tradesmen, and all the other professionals that can draw from a well-substantiated knowledge base to enable the world to run better. And these institutions should be fiercely independent of short-term business interests, political expediency, and special interest groups. So, in our view, the mission of at least the publicly funded university and college does not need to change. Indeed, we would like it to become more effective.

Nevertheless, *how* that mission is delivered must and will change, if independent, publicly funded educational institutions are to survive; such change in turn is dependent on modifying substantially the existing dominant organizational culture, if technology is to become a critical component of the necessary changes.

WHAT IS ORGANIZATIONAL CULTURE IN POSTSECONDARY EDUCATION?

Typical aspects of university culture are views on academic freedom, the optimum conditions for academic work, what makes a good scholar, how students should be taught, the way decisions should be made and who should be involved, and the role of senior administrators, both as seen by themselves and by other members of the academic community.

One of the strongest differences we found between the institutions in our case studies was their organizational culture. The culture of campus-based universities was very different from that of the open universities and the two colleges in our case studies. The management style of the campus-based universities was less hierarchical and decision making was more diffuse and often difficult to pin down. The colleges tended to have more policies, which were more strictly enforced, and much greater top-down management. Most universities were content to cede intellectual ownership of teaching materials to faculty, whereas in the colleges (and the open universities), the institution owned the teaching materials and this was written into the collective agreement with the unions. The differences are driven mainly by the variation in employment conditions between tenured research professors and contract instructors, but also by differences in mission, the types of students, and desired learning outcomes between universities and two-year colleges. Our following comments on organizational culture apply more specifically to research universities; nevertheless there are also different elements in the organizational culture of community colleges (and the open universities) that act as barriers to change.

TEACHING AND ORGANIZATIONAL CULTURE

We were surprised by the level of complacency about the quality of teaching in most institutions. Although faculty often complained about workload, too-large classes, and a generally deteriorating teaching situation, they themselves tended to rank their own teaching highly. We have seen that most of the institutions saw technology as enhancing (rather than improving) what was considered already "good" teaching. From our point of view this is almost delusional.

Christensen Hughes and Mighty (2010) have reviewed the research on teaching and learning in higher education. In their book, one of the contributors, Chris Knapper, writes (2010, pp. 229–230):

> There is increasing empirical evidence from a variety of international settings that prevailing teaching practices in higher education do not encourage the sort of learning that contemporary society demands. . . . Teaching remains largely didactic, assessment of student work is often trivial, and curricula are more likely to emphasize content coverage than acquisition of lifelong and life-wide skills. . . .
>
> [However] there is an impressive body of evidence on how teaching methods and curriculum design affect deep, autonomous and reflective learning. Yet most faculty are largely ignorant of this scholarship, and instructional practices are dominated by tradition rather than research evidence.

This is an excellent example of how the assumptions and beliefs embedded in organizational culture affect behavior. Faculty that place the highest value on scholarship and research are able to ignore these values when it comes to their own practice of teaching. We shall see, though, that without a more professional approach to the training of faculty in teaching and learning, technology is unlikely to be used to its full potential.

How Organizational Culture Operates

During a meeting at one of the case study institutions to determine what strategies could be used to increase the innovative use of technology in teaching, and drawing on the experience at both Virginia Tech and the University of Central Florida in training in the use of technology for teaching, one of the authors suggested that the university might want to change the way it trained graduate students, and include within the PhD program a requirement to take some courses on educational theory and practice. This was immediately rejected, because it would create problems in recruiting the best research students. "If they had to take time away from their research, they would go to another university which did not have this requirement." In other words, this is not a solution that can be addressed by one institution in isolation; it is a systemic problem. Although a problem was recognized, it could not be touched.

Another comment during the same conversation is even more revealing. An alternative suggestion was that the university require all faculty who have applied for tenure to have some formal qualification in teaching, or proof of quality teaching, as well as research, as a condition for tenure. This too was rejected, for a similar reason: that it would inhibit the institution's ability to attract the best research faculty. "Even though it would be in the best interests of the students?" commented the author. "You don't understand," was the reply. "The primary stakeholder here is the faculty member. If we don't get the best research professors, we won't attract the best students, and the reputation of the university will suffer." We are not arguing that the senior administrator was wrong; he was merely making clear the priorities within the organizational culture.

It should be noted that conditions for the appointment, tenure, and promotion of faculty in universities are not imposed by senior management, but by faculty themselves. Senior professors sit on tenure and promotion committees and make and then apply the rules for tenure appointments and promotion. Thus senior faculty members are in control of the main institutional reward system and it is used ruthlessly to protect the dominant organizational culture. This is one of the last guild systems by which a trade or profession protects itself from outside influences.

However, as long as research is king, and as long as there is competition between institutions for the best research faculty, there is little likelihood of universities requiring faculty to be qualified in teaching, even though teaching is always given lip service in the conditions for appointment, tenure, and promotion. Giving as much attention to a faculty member's teaching performance as to their research record for tenure and promotion will require a transformation in organizational culture and behavior. However, this is unlikely to happen if left to faculty themselves. As a result, students and the public suffer: students, because they are not getting better quality teaching; and the public, because teaching is less effective than it could be, and hence costly.

ORGANIZATIONAL CULTURE AND MANAGEMENT

Senior administrators too are often faculty. Thus the usual term for a vice president of academic affairs or a dean (at least in North American universities) is not "manager" or "executive" but "senior administrator"; they are there to "serve" the main stakeholders in the university (and faculty in particular), not to "manage" things. The feeling is that they are first among equals, and only for a limited time (most terms are five years or less). The terminology is important. The idea of service rather than command and control is nice, and certainly a good one for a public institution. Unfortunately, though, the word "administrator" is a less than accurate term to describe the function of senior decision makers in organizations with billion-dollar budgets facing great challenges, both externally and internally. Such institutions need senior decision makers with a high level of managerial and executive skills. Continuity in strategy is also important, and this is less likely to happen when senior managers are constantly changing.

However, the whole concept of management is much more resisted in universities than the colleges. (As an aside, we found that in colleges, decision making was often *too* hierarchical and rigid, with not enough consultation with instructors or students.) Faculty often complain about the increasing prevalence of a disease called "managerialism," which is materialistic and driven by the bottom line. Managerialism restricts the idealism and freedom of faculty, and above all impinges on their autonomy. As such, much of this book will be seen by some university faculty as a direct attack on academic freedom, although it is not. Academic freedom is the ability to comment and publish without fear of being fired, and being able to choose areas of research, methods of research, and topics and methods of teaching, and being able to publish freely.

However, academic freedom is often mistakenly equated with academic autonomy. And even academic freedom—as with all other freedoms—is not absolute. Academic freedom should not be used as an excuse for tenured professors to do whatever they like (and avoid doing things they don't like—such as refusing to teach undergraduates). Faculty are expected to teach, do research, and assist with the administration and management of the institution. We just ask that they do it professionally, but some of the things we are proposing under the heading of "professional management" will run counter to much of the prevailing organizational culture in many universities. Our hope is that we can persuade faculty and administrators to change because this will enable the mission of universities and colleges to be better implemented, not because we wish to deny the freedom to research or teach freely.

Myths in Organizational Culture

One way in which organizational culture is strengthened is through myths or stories that embody the cultural values of an organization. There are several myths that strongly influence faculty views about teaching and learning. Particularly powerful is the Socratic myth as described by Plato in his *Dialogues*. This is the myth of the inspired teacher sitting under the shadow of a tree with a small coterie of devoted students. This is the ideal often held by teachers in higher education. (It is worth noting, though, that Socrates, as described by Plato, was highly manipulative and selective in his argumentation, and hence far removed from modern concepts of learner-centered teaching and constructivism. He also argued that true knowledge could not be achieved through media such as writing and reading, but only through oral communication, so the distrust of technology as a medium for teaching is at least 2,000 years old.)

From this myth stems the desire for small classes, and the value of close personal interaction with students, and the oral tradition of teaching and learning. Also implicit in this model is the unity of knowledge and teaching; if you have the knowledge, you know how to teach it (through dialogue). Thus there is no need for university professors with PhDs to be trained in teaching, although they may be able, like all professionals, to pick up some tips from their equally brilliant colleagues.

We fully accept the value of discussion and interaction between teacher and students. However, the context for higher education in today's world is very different from the Socratic myth. We have much larger classes, there has been a great deal of research on how best to teach, and our students are not the privileged sons of Greek aristocrats.

One way to challenge myths is through education. We believe that technology adds new levels of complexity and requires new knowledge and skill sets, and that this is as true for academic teaching as it is for other professions. It is very difficult if not impossible for instructors to innovate or teach differently from the historical or mythical model if they have no understanding of possible alternative ways to teach, based on theory and research.

We argue, therefore, that if technology is to be used successfully for teaching and learning, instructors need to be properly trained. Similarly, if technology is to be managed properly, senior administrators also will need some form of training or preparation. Note again the importance of organizational culture in the terminology. Generally universities do not do training in teaching; it is described under the rubric of "faculty development." However, we are recommending compulsory training, and deliberately use those words.

TRAINING IN TECHNOLOGY AND TEACHING

How did our case study institutions prepare their instructors for teaching with technology? Why is training important for using technology for teaching? What are the cultural barriers to more training? We examine these issues in the following section.

EXPERIENCE FROM THE CASE STUDIES

We begin by examining how the institutions in our case studies tackled the issue of preparing faculty and administrators regarding technology integration. All the 11 institutions in our case studies provided some form of training for faculty and instructors in the use of technology for teaching. However, the form and extent of the training varied considerably.

Methods of Training

Except for the open universities, almost all institutions treated training in the use of technology for teaching as a professional development activity, thus making it the responsibility of individual faculty members to decide whether to participate in formal training opportunities. However, it was particularly difficult to identify actual practice in faculty development and training for the use of technology in teaching in the case studies, as sometimes academic departments would organize their own professional development activities, such as lunch time seminars, which may or may not include topics related to using technology for teaching. Sometimes institutions such as UBC would organize open days, with poster sessions about projects using technology for teaching, with perhaps up to 200 faculty drifting through during the two or three hours the exhibition was open. Individual faculty would sometimes attend conferences on teaching within their discipline and in this way almost accidentally hear of how technology was being applied in their subject discipline by another professor.

Some institutions were highly innovative in their efforts to get faculty to training sessions. In the 1990s, Virginia Tech would provide faculty with new computers every three years, but to get their new computer, faculty had to come to a half-day subject area workshop and show how they might use the computer for teaching their subject. Eventually, Virginia Tech managed to get the majority of faculty (96%) to participate in two-, three-, or four-day instructional development workshops each year, through its Faculty Development Institute.

At the University of Central Florida, the Course Development and Web Services unit developed an eight-week "blended" faculty development program (IDL6543) to prepare faculty to develop and deliver interactive learning environments online, while at the same time providing each faculty member taking the program with an instructional designer as a consultant. UCF also provided a needs assessment to gauge the level of the instructor's technical skills. There is a strong expectation at UCF that all faculty aiming to teach online will take the IDL6543 course, which is still running in 2010. UBC offers an online training module for instructors teaching online, including guidance on online presence and the facilitation of online discussion forums.

Several of the institutions, such as SAIT and UBC, would run one- or two-day face-to-face workshops on teaching with new technologies, or related topics, such as describing how Web 2.0 tools could be used for teaching. These again were usually held in the summer sessions, and were entirely voluntary. They usually involved innovative teachers demonstrating their use of the technology.

Both the University of British Columbia and the Open University of Catalonia have developed fully online master's programs in educational technology and e-learning, respectively. Indeed, learners can take individual courses within the UBC master (paying a single course tuition fee), or five courses for a certificate, and add another five courses to get the masters. Interestingly, though, the majority of students taking the UBC master courses are not university or college faculty, but instructional designers, corporate trainers, schoolteachers, and so on.

Training in some institutions (mainly the European campus–based institutions) was limited to how to use the administrative or learning management systems from a purely technological perspective (how to log on, what functions the software provided, navigation, and so forth). In other cases, training consisted of both technological and educational design issues.

The Extent of Training

Even more striking was the variation in the extent of training. Two institutions (Virginia Tech and the Open University of Portugal) managed to give almost all faculty some training in technology-based teaching. The University of Central Florida and the Open

University of Catalonia were two other institutions that trained a high proportion of full-time faculty in using technology for teaching, although the Open University of Catalonia had problems getting professors hired on contract from other conventional universities to participate.

In most of the other institutions, though, there was no regular training program in the use of learning technologies (or in even other forms of professional development) for *all* faculty. Workshops were organized on an occasional or ad hoc basis, usually after exams in the summer. In all cases except the open universities, training was voluntary; faculty or instructors could opt out if necessary, and many did. As a result, in most of the cases, the majority of instructors had little or no training in using technology for teaching.

In at least seven of the nine campus-based institutions, it was reported that many faculty were hostile or negative toward using technology for teaching. Without adequate training, this is not surprising. As Hartman and Truman-Davis (2001, p. 48) note:

> Many faculty development programs use workshops, guest speakers, or walk-in consultation. These offerings are relevant and useful, but often do not lead to the cultural change required to achieve a transformative integration of technology into teaching and learning.

Adjunct Faculty and Community College Instructors

Over the last fifteen years there has been a major increase in the number and proportion of adjunct faculty working on short-term contracts for lower wages than tenured professors in universities. This is because public funding has not matched the increase in student numbers, because any additional funds have often been diverted to nonteaching activities (see Wellman, Desrochers, Lenihan, Kirshstein, Hurlburt, & Honegger, 2009), and because senior research professors have opted to teach less to concentrate on research, and when they do teach they tend to teach graduate rather than undergraduate students. As a result, universities have hired extra "adjunct" instructors on part-time contracts to teach undergraduate courses in particular. This has been possible because the universities have been turning out far more PhDs than there are tenured jobs or other forms of employment for doctoral graduates. There is therefore a glut of people whose qualifications are similar to those already tenured, but who are obliged to work for less pay and poorer conditions if they wish to teach in postsecondary education.

However, because adjunct faculty are paid on contract (and may be unionized in many institutions), they are paid according to the number of hours they teach. They are not paid for any time spent training, and institutions are not keen anyway on paying adjunct faculty to be trained, because being on short-term contracts they are free to take that training to another institution. The main reason why they are not trained, though, is because they have had the same graduate education as tenured faculty (so are generally almost as well qualified academically), and the institution is looking to adjuncts as a way of saving money; paying them for training would be an additional cost.

The situation is somewhat similar for community college instructors, even though they may have more security of employment than adjunct instructors in universities. Many college instructors have been hired because of their work experience, such as in the trades, accountancy, or health areas. Prior to recruitment to a college, they are not usually trained as teachers. In some provinces and states, there may be a province- or state-wide instructor development diploma for instructors, which instructors are expected to take, and these may have a section or component on the use of technology for teaching. However, community college instructors often have a heavy teaching load (over 20 hours classroom time a week, plus lesson preparation and grading), so the only realistic time for additional in-service training is usually over the summer. The tradition, though, is for most instructors to disappear on leave once the exams are over in April or May.

In short, if the bulk of teaching now in our universities and colleges is being done by underpaid, undertrained, and overworked instructors, there is a serious problem that needs to be addressed. It would be far better (and much cheaper) in our view to provide training *before* instructors and faculty are hired for full-time or adjunct positions.

THE NEED FOR SYSTEMATIC TRAINING IN TEACHING

Few case study institutions provided systematic training in teaching with technology (or indeed any form of teaching) for *all* faculty. However, formal training is essential for all instructors. It is not just a question of learning how to use a learning management or lecture capture system. The use of technology needs to be combined with an understanding of how students learn, how skills and competencies are developed, how knowledge is represented through different media and then processed, and how learners use different senses for learning. It means examining different approaches to learning, such as the construction of knowledge compared with a transmissive model of teaching, and how technology best works with either approach. Above all, it means linking the use of technology to the specific requirements of a particular knowledge domain or subject area.

RESEARCH OVER TEACHING

The issue here is not technology, but how poorly teachers in post-secondary education are trained to teach. Most tenured faculty positions in universities require a PhD, but a PhD is training in research, not teaching. Tierney and Hentschke (2007, p. 135) comment that

> individuals who are to become future faculty members are trained and socialized in graduate schools at research universities. At these institutions, graduate students learn and internalize the academic values of their professors, which generally give prominence to research rather than teaching.

Teaching undergraduates was traditionally the main focus of university education until the last fifty years. Tierney and Hentschke claim that "research did not become important in any systematic way until the late nineteenth century, and even then only for a minority of faculty." For parents, students, and governments, teaching undergraduates is still the more prevalent focus, but doing research is accorded greater respect by faculty themselves and by the institutions they work for. (For instance, in the Times Higher Education Supplement's World Rankings for universities, teaching counts for less than 30% of each institution's score, and half of the teaching ranking is based on the proportion of PhDs who are on the teaching staff—and who are not trained in teaching.)

When university education was limited to an elite few students, where faculty had a close, one-on-one relationship with students, it was possible to manage quite effectively without formal training in teaching. That is not the case today. Faculty are challenged by large classes and heterogeneous students who learn in a variety of ways, with different skills and abilities. The emphasis is changing from knowledge as content to knowledge as process. Teaching methods need to be chosen that will develop the skills and competencies needed in a knowledge-base society, and on top of all this, constantly changing technology requires instructors to have analytical frameworks to help choose and use technologies appropriately for teaching (see Bates, 2005).

Of course, a deep understanding of a subject area helps make an outstanding teacher, and a relatively few faculty are outstanding natural teachers. Others learn to be good teachers the hard way, by trial and error (with students suffering the errors). However, it is one of the few professions where you are not required to be trained in one of your main areas of work. Indeed, academics are often highly suspicious or skeptical of educational theory or pedagogy. It is ironic, however, that faculty who pride themselves in being up to date in research in their subject domain are often willfully ignorant of research into teaching and learning, and how it could be applied to their everyday activities.

WHAT DO INSTRUCTORS NEED TO KNOW ABOUT TEACHING WITH TECHNOLOGY?

In this section we examine what should be in the training for instructors.

Initial, Pre-Service Training

Any training program is a balance between the minimum that a learner needs to know to operate effectively and the time available for training. A full one-year master program will obviously cover much more ground than an eight-week part-time program. Also, there are bound to be different views on what instructors need to know to teach well in postsecondary education, but there is also likely to be a great deal of agreement. Initial training does not have to be perfect and satisfy all requirements, because we see professional development as a continuous process.

We will concentrate here on what we consider the minimum that an instructor needs to know to teach effectively in postsecondary education (given that they already have a good knowledge base in the subject area):

- *Epistemology:* understanding different kinds of knowledge, for instance, the difference between objectivism (often reflected in the teaching of science and engineering) and the social construction of knowledge; a discussion of the nature of networked knowledge. Recognizing differences in the way knowledge is validated will provide a foundation for choosing appropriate teaching strategies in different domains of knowledge (science or arts, for example)
- *The biological basis of learning:* a basic introduction to how the brain works, particularly regarding memory, cognition, and emotions; this will help in interpreting the emerging field of brain research and learning
- *Learning theories* (linked to epistemology), such as behaviorism, cognitivism, the social construction of knowledge, and possibly connectivism
- *The design of teaching:* applying theory to practice, which would include an analysis of different kinds of students and their needs; an introduction to instructional design; defining learning outcomes and objectives, strategies, and activities to engage learners; and the link between learning outcomes, knowledge representation, and assessment; course evaluation methods; different types of courses (face-to-face, blended, distance); and an introduction to course and program planning
- *Learning technologies:* this would start with an assessment of the instructor's current IT skills and remediation where necessary; the relationship between technology and knowledge representation; functions and structures of learning management systems and Web 2.0 tools; relationship

between different technologies and theories of learning; strategies for media and technology selection
- *Project work:* designing, delivering, and evaluating a course

Each of these areas could be worth the equivalent of three credits except the project, which could be worth six credits, and together would lead to a postgraduate certificate or diploma in postsecondary teaching (21 credits in all). Thus the program would be completed in under a year of full-time study, preferably as part of a graduate program. To obtain a master's degree in postsecondary teaching, the learner would need to add three elective courses (making 30 credits) as follows:

- *Electives:* these might include courses on research in teaching and learning; emerging technologies; cultural and international issues in teaching and learning; planning and managing courses and programs; the application of a particular technology tool; teaching strategies for a particular subject discipline; or other topics of choice by the learner as independent study

All programs would be available in a hybrid mode, and would be offered on a state- or provincewide basis. We strongly believe that to use technology effectively in teaching, it is not enough to focus just on the technology. A basic understanding of general educational theories and practices is also essential, and training for technology needs to be embedded within educational theory and practice.

We recognize that taking the equivalent of one year out of a research degree will be too much for most institutions to swallow, which is why we believe the requirement for initial training in teaching needs to be introduced at a system level, with government, the main funding agency for public institutions, making this a requirement for state funding. This may further increase the costs of a research degree, but it is much cheaper than expanding learning technology support units or retraining tenured research faculty. However, even a shorter training program, or one spread over a longer period of time, so long as it is mandatory for all those wanting to be tenured faculty, would be a vast improvement over the current situation.

Continuous Professional Development in Teaching

As well as initial formal training, it would be beneficial to establish a more systematic approach to continuing professional development in teaching. In too many institutions, too much is left to the individual professor or instructor in deciding how to use their professional development time.

A practice developed in a few institutions could provide a model for others. In this model, every instructor is required to draw up a personal professional development plan for the next 12 months. Either the head of department or a more senior instructor reviews the outcomes of the previous year's professional development plan, and negotiates the plan for the following year with the instructor. The plan would cover teaching, research, and academic subject renewal. Ideally, this would also be linked to the academic department's three-year rolling plan. There are other possibilities of course. What matters is not so much the details, but the requirement for all institutions to provide appropriate initial and continuing training for all instructors in postsecondary teaching.

THE TRAINING OF SENIOR AND MIDDLE MANAGERS

In this section, we examine whether a more formal approach to training in technology management would have better prepared Dr. Dubrowski for the decision she had to make regarding the learning management system in the scenario at the beginning of Chapter Five.

The training of senior and mid-level administrators for technology decision making is a sensitive issue. Higgins and Prebble (2008, p. 22) comment:

> There is a continuing debate among e-learning professionals and policy-makers about the reasons for the slow take-up of e-learning by some tertiary institutions. This is blamed variously on poor infrastructure, a lack of national policy, weak institutional strategy

and leadership, and inadequate professional development of teachers. Arguably, a renewed focus on the responsibility of academic middle managers for the work of their teacher colleagues would be every bit as effective.

We have seen how technology is now permeating all aspects of administration, teaching, and research in universities and colleges. All senior and mid-level administrators are participating increasingly in decisions about technology choice, investment, maintenance, management, policies, and above all, security. Although technology specialists, such as CIOs and learning technology managers, can valuably contribute to decision making, vice presidents, deans, heads of departments, and program directors all should know what questions to ask, should have a basic understanding of technology issues and how these are managed within the institution, and should understand the implications of their decision making regarding technology.

The route by which many academics become middle or senior administrators indicates the challenge they face. They are often successful researchers or teachers with good interpersonal or political skills who have the confidence and trust of their colleagues. The appointment to these positions is often collegial in nature, in that if not directly elected, their appointment is usually made after considerable consultation with their colleagues. Senior administrators in particular tend to be older and less familiar with technology than either the students or their younger academic staff (although that is changing over time). Particularly in the case of heads of departments, the position may not be one that is greatly sought after, as there is often minimal financial reward, a great deal of administrative work that detracts from their research, and often little power over their colleagues, who can usually resist suggested changes or activities with little fear of adverse consequences.

Newly appointed administrators may or may not be sent on a two- or three-day leadership or management workshop, but if so, for most this will be their only formal training as managers. In particular, they may have no specialist knowledge of computing or information technologies, nor is this likely to be a consideration in their appointment to these positions. It was therefore not surprising that we found in the case studies that program directors, heads of departments, deans, vice presidents, and vice rectors were often struggling with decision making regarding technology.

ASKING THE RIGHT QUESTIONS

Higgins and Prebble (2008) were contracted by the New Zealand Ministry of Education to conduct a study to identify the issues of significance around e-learning for which institutional leaders must take direct responsibility. Case studies illustrating a number of these strategic options were drawn from across the New Zealand tertiary education sector. In their report, Higgins and Prebble (2008, p. 10) suggested that

> leaders need to ask the right questions about e-learning before they are in any position to assess the merit of the solutions that are being advocated. While the solutions that are being proposed are likely to be various and changing, the questions will be more generic. . . . The answers to these questions should help institutional leaders arrive at solutions that fit the needs of their own institutions rather than accepting other people's solutions to other people's problems.

The questions they identified following provide at least an initial form of training for university and college administrators regarding the use of technology for teaching and learning.

Strategy

- What are the medium and long-term strategic goals and objectives of our institution?
- How are these strategic goals reflected in our institution's learning and teaching (or academic) plan?
- How are these strategic goals reflected in our institution's more specific plans for e-learning?

Structure

- How should we organize and manage for e-learning?
- More specifically, who should be responsible for what and how should our various efforts be integrated and led?

Resourcing

- How should e-learning be resourced within our organization?
- What will it cost?

Decision Making

- Who makes the decisions about which courses and programs will use e-learning and how will they do so?

Selecting Technologies

Strategy questions

- What is the problem that this technology will solve or help us with? What sort of priority is it?
- Do our teachers/students wish to teach/study this way? How do we know students will achieve their learning outcomes?
- Will we suffer if we simply don't adopt it?

Staff development questions

- What are the implications for staff workload? Can this be managed?
- Can our teachers use and manage this technology themselves or will they be dependent on support personnel?
- What are the implications for staff development (training)?

Marketing questions

- Will the technology open up new markets (geographic, demographic, subject) for us?
- How does the technology impact on the existing mix of technologies both for supporting and delivering teaching and for administrative and support systems?
- Does this technology offer the necessary range or quality of functionality and interoperability?
- What are collaborators and competitors using? Why would we want to use the same or a different system?

Financial questions

- Is it a cost-effective solution in terms of capital and recurrent costs?

Technology questions

- Is it a robust technical solution?
- Is this technology readily scalable?
- Can we support and maintain this technology ourselves or will we be dependent on an outside supplier?
- What infrastructure will be needed to support this system?
- What level of disruption will this technology bring to our operations?
- How dependent will this technology make us on outside providers?
- Have we an exit strategy for this technology?

Intellectual property and privacy questions

- What implications does this technology have for intellectual property?
- Does this technology bring with it implications for student/staff privacy?

Building a Knowledge Base

Although this is a good set of questions, we feel they are necessary but not sufficient. If senior and mid-level administrators are to answer these questions effectively, they must have the information needed to answer the questions, or know where to get it, or have in place a process whereby all the stakeholders are involved and can agree a decision (hence the need for a comprehensive governance structure that senior administrators can depend on—see Chapters Five and Nine).

Furthermore, administrators need to have some criteria or framework for assessing the information collected. For instance, if an academic department insists that a new learning management system is required, but the IT department says that this merely duplicates existing technology and adds extra costs, how can this conflict be resolved? Administrators need to have the means by which to bring all the interested parties to the table, and know enough about the technology (and teaching and research requirements) to be able to assess competing views if agreement between the parties cannot be reached.

One way to do this would be to ensure that middle and senior administrators in academic areas have at least some experience in using technology in their own teaching as a criterion for appointment. Further, every institution should have a process by which newly appointed senior and middle level managers or administrators can be properly oriented to the main issues surrounding the use of technology for teaching and learning. This could be the responsibility of the CIO, working in collaboration with the director(s) of the learning technology support units. Such a briefing would include the following:

- A review of the institution's overall goals and strategies, and particularly its vision for the future, and where and how learning technologies fit with these goals
- A clear analysis of the existing governance structure for technology decision making, including roles and responsibilities, and the possible changes needed
- A discussion, with the relevant managers, of the roles and operations of the various units that support learning and administrative technologies throughout the organization, in particular, the IT department(s), the learning technology unit(s), and the faculty development office
- A briefing by these directors and selected faculty on key technologies currently in use, and possible future developments in technology and their implications for the institution
- An analysis of major technology strategies and projects that are already under way (essential to avoid reinventing the wheel, or canceling successful projects initiated by the previous administration), preferably with presentations or demonstrations by faculty and staff about their technology projects
- A discussion of intellectual property, privacy, and security issues
- A set of readings on the management of information and communications technologies in postsecondary educational institutions (including this book, we hope)

- A visit to at least one other organization of similar nature that has a high reputation for using technology for teaching and learning, to see how they do things

Annual open houses on information and communications technologies are useful for all faculty, students, and administrative staff, as well as for administrators; indeed, several institutions in the case studies had open houses on either learning technology, IT strategy, or both. However, the open houses in our case study institutions were not so focused or comprehensive in their treatment of managerial or administrative issues, and mostly focused on just the demonstration of technology projects, and new or possible IT strategic directions, and often even newly appointed administrators did not attend. It may be worth organizing an annual event on technology specifically for all senior and mid-level administrators, where issues such as how the projects should be evaluated (costs and benefits), funding implications, organizational issues, and the effect on student and faculty workloads can be raised.

Again, there are many possibilities for training or orienting administrators and managers in academic areas to technology issues. What is needed is a comprehensive strategy for preparing new administrators for making technology decisions, and this should be a responsibility of the executive team, with assistance from the various stakeholders. This could be combined with strategies for preparing administrators in other key areas of management, such as financial management and human relations.

WILL TRAINING BE ENOUGH TO CHANGE THE CULTURE?

It is not difficult to make the case for systematic, formal training in teaching, both before or on entry to university and college teaching, as well as continuing professional education. We would not dream of allowing doctors or pilots do their work without formal training related to their main work activities, yet this is exactly the situation regarding teaching in postsecondary education. The case for the systematic training or induction of new middle and senior managers regarding technology decision making is perhaps less obvious but equally important.

In an ideal world, the strength of our arguments would be sufficient, and we hope that is the case. We are skeptical, though, that our recommendation regarding the training of instructors and administrators will ever be implemented, because it runs against the grain of the organizational culture of postsecondary educational institutions, and in particular that of research universities.

This may be an area where government intervention will become necessary. Systematic training in teaching for all instructors is critical not just for the appropriate application of technology but for the overall effectiveness of teaching in postsecondary educational institutions. No other single action is likely to bring the required changes and improvements in the effectiveness of our postsecondary institutions. Because the stakes are so high, and because of the resistance to change resulting from the prevailing organizational culture, it may require direct intervention by government to bring about such systematic change. Governments should work with the postsecondary sector to agree to a system of training for teaching that is comprehensive and a requirement for all instructors. The ultimate government sanction would be to refuse state funding for institutions that do not provide approved training (this is discussed further in Chapter Nine).

CONCLUSION

The prevailing organizational cultures of universities and colleges present some major barriers to the changes needed to improve the management of technology for teaching and learning. The fear is that such changes will undermine the core mission and mandate of higher education institutions. However, we argue that changes can be made that in fact will not only improve the management of technology but in doing so will also further protect the mission and mandate by making the organizations more effective.

DECISION MAKING AND ORGANIZATIONAL CULTURE

Did Dr. Dubrowski and Michael Blackstone make the right decision about the renewal of the learning management system in the scenario at the beginning of Chapter Five? Probably not. They have locked themselves into an increasingly old-fashioned approach to teaching with technology for the next five years, at an increasing cost with no measurable benefits, except lack of disruption to existing faculty and programs (which is an important factor). It might still turn out to be the right decision, but the alternatives were not fully explored. How could a better decision have been reached?

First, probably a better governance structure, ensuring that the options were properly discussed by all relevant stakeholders, would have resulted in a firm and hopefully agreed on set of recommendations coming to the two vice presidents. In particular, the renewal date for the contract was known at least five years earlier. A process should have been put in place two years earlier that would have given time for a carefully researched recommendation to be developed that took into account the views and needs of all the stakeholders. We discuss in Chapter Nine an alternative way to resolve this type of problem.

Second, had Dr. Dubrowski spent some time between the announcement of her appointment and actually taking up her position being briefed about technology and other management issues, she would have increased immensely her knowledge and background for making this decision; this experience would become even more important if there were still disagreement among the key stakeholders. The need to make a decision about the learning management system would have been raised nine months earlier, and she would have had a better understanding and knowledge of the key stakeholders and their positions.

Even without a better governance structure, but with a comprehensive briefing before she started, she would have been in a better position to challenge the VP of administration and CIO's recommendation (and the dean of science's and the faculty of education's recommendations) by asking the right questions. Combined with a better governance structure, her decision would have been more knowledge- and evidence-based, and would have carried more support from the other stakeholders.

DECISION MAKING AND TRAINING

The main reason why technology has not been more integrated within universities and colleges is because the predominant organizational culture of postsecondary educational institutions acts against changes in management and teaching practices that are essential for more widespread and effective use of technology. In particular, systematic and universal training in teaching and the management of technology is needed before technology can deliver improved cost-effectiveness in our postsecondary educational institutions.

Postsecondary education is not the only professional area that has had problems with quality and standards. When real estate agents or medical practitioners have failed to regulate themselves in the best interests of the public, the government has had to step in. This has its dangers, as governments do not know professional requirements, but they do understand the need for process, for standards, and the need to protect the public. We believe that we have reached this point with teaching in public postsecondary education.

Governments should require professional certification for anyone wishing to teach in public postsecondary educational institutions. The universities and colleges should manage the certification process, setting the curriculum for training, providing the training, and issuing the certification. We would like to see at least one institution, or preferably a consortium of universities or colleges, in every state or province licensed to offer training programs for postsecondary teacher accreditation—with qualification from one of these programs being a condition of employment for all new instructors in public postsecondary education. In countries such as Canada or the United States, a regional certification program covering several provinces or states could be established by agreement between the provincial or state governments.

Governments should reserve the power to withdraw their funding from institutions that do not follow the agreed on process for the qualification of instructors. There is probably no other single step that would lead to greater improvement in the effectiveness of postsecondary education systems. If technology is to be used effectively for teaching, such action is essential. It will, however, take a brave and skilled politician to make this happen.

Chapter Nine

Building a Twenty-First-Century University or College

Ah, but a man's reach should exceed his grasp,
Or what's a heaven for? All is silver-grey,
Placid and perfect with my art: the worse!
—Robert Browning, *Andrea del Sarto*

From the E-Portfolio of Mariana Angelina Negreira, Waste Water Manager and Lifelong Learner, Gran Canaria, Spain
5 January 2025

Well, it's the new year, and time for me to update my e-portfolio. Let's start by going back to my original vision of what I wanted from a university, which I wrote in 2015 (10 years ago already!):

> My university will be my guide and facilitator for higher education throughout my life. It will not only provide me with knowledge, courses, programs, and qualifications itself, but will also help me access the learning opportunities I need from other quality providers.

Well, that's pretty much what's happened, if I look at my academic career.

Pre-University

In my last year at high school in Santiago de Compostela, one of my teachers advised me on possible programs and courses, based on my interests and abilities. Before I made a decision about a university program, I was able to enroll online as a guest student in three courses from two different universities I was interested in. Two courses, math and biology, I was studying for high school completion, and were offered by my local university in Santiago. The third course, on marine biology from the University of Tenerife, was new to me, but I really enjoyed it, and I also liked the teaching, because I could go to local beaches near Santiago, and video and photograph material for a project in the course, which counted toward my high school completion. So I went online and applied to the University of Tenerife. This was a big move for me, because I had to leave home in Santiago and travel over a thousand kilometers to study in the Canary Islands.

First Year

The best part, though, about enrolling at the University of Tenerife was that even in the first year, I could do about half of the program from home in Santiago. I decided to start all my courses in January. I stayed with a family friend in Tenerife, and went to campus about twice a week, for the first six months of the year, mainly for the practical work in the labs, so I got a small part-time job in Tenerife that helped cover some of my expenses. For the last six months, I was able to take the rest of my courses from home in Santiago, which worked really well for the biology course, as I was able to collect and record specimens from the local shoreline that were different from many of the specimens from the other students in Tenerife. Since my mother was not well, I felt really good about this arrangement, as I could keep an eye on her, although I did go back to Tenerife for the last couple of weeks of the course, just before the Christmas break.

The courses were interesting. In my group of 20 students in marine biology, there was one from a local high school in Cadiz, eight other first-year students, four second-year students, two third-year students, two fourth-year students, a graduate student, and three people who were working. These three already had degrees but had not done this course, which focused on the impact of waste management on coastal waters. The working students were great, giving me lots of help with stuff I didn't know.

A big part of the course was a research project, and the graduate student was our main guide on this. I didn't see much of the professor on campus after the first couple of weeks, but she occasionally jumped into our online discussion forums and once or twice really helped me out with my research design. However, there were about fifteen other groups that she had to look after, as well, but the grad student usually got us through, because the course was really well organized.

Most of our reading in fact was done online, accessing materials on waste management and marine biology from all over the world. Our professor and the grad student had found a lot of it for us, but toward the end we were finding lots of new stuff for ourselves that related to our specific research projects. There were only three actual lectures on this course, all from the professor, and they were terrific. I missed the middle one because I was in Santiago, but it was recorded like the others so I just downloaded it.

The prof had also made lots of short videos, showing stuff she was doing for her research, then giving us links to notes about the videos, related research articles, and her own Web site. I found this really useful when I came to do my own research design. The hardest part was writing up my research report for the end of course assessment. I had too much stuff—photos, videos, data, and real stuff, too, like oil-stained feathers, and had to leave a lot out—but I was able to get it all online in the end.

The grad student did the first run at marking our project, but because I got a really good grade, the prof also reviewed it, which enabled me to concentrate on marine biology for the rest of my degree. However, I needed a bit of money, so I took a break, then reenrolled in the April second year cohort (I just find it too hard to work and study at the same time).

I made it OK through my undergraduate program. The last year was really hard work, as my group had a really big research project to manage, and I spent quite a bit of time helping out some of the first and second year students in our group.

Master's Program

Tenerife though didn't have quite the graduate program I wanted, nor did Santiago. I was pretty clear about what master's I wanted to do, but a couple of the courses I wanted were from the University of Porto in Portugal, and another from Trondheim University in Norway. I did the research data collection mainly on the coast near Santiago, but I really wanted my prof at University of Tenerife as the supervisor for my dissertation. Fortunately the University of Tenerife has an agreement that allows me to take the courses from Porto and Trondheim, and transfer them in, so I was able to keep my supervisor. (She wanted me to do a PhD, but I wasn't ready for that yet.) As I really needed to bring some money in when my mother died, I chose to spread the master's over two years, and even better my supervisor arranged for me to work part-time as a consultant for a local waste management company in Tenerife, so even when I was working it all fed into my dissertation. I also got a little bit of money for teaching part-time in the undergraduate program, which I really enjoyed.

Out to Work

Well, in the end it took me three years to finish my master's, mainly because I was offered a really good full-time job with the waste management company in Las Palmas at the end of the first year. I'm now responsible for the city's waste water environmental control.

My prof was really disappointed that I didn't go for the PhD, but the work is really fascinating, and one day I will probably do a PhD because there's lots of stuff we still don't know in this area. In fact, I'm now taking a management program online from INSEAD, which takes about all of my spare time, but at least it's paid for by the city. Again, though, I'm able to do the face-to-face group work on change management on campus at the University of Las Palmas, over four weekends, as the group work is also a part of the Las Palmas MBA program. My prof put me on to this and helped me work it out between the two universities.

I'm also still teaching online in one of the University of Tenerife's undergraduate marine biology courses—technically, I'm classified as a mentor—but I don't do it for the money, which barely covers my expenses. I just keep learning so much from the students' projects and I like helping them out.

Taking Control of Change

In preceding chapters we have identified and critiqued a number of strategies employed by our case study institutions. In this chapter we have two aims. The first is to suggest a number of practical steps that senior managers and administrators can take to ensure the better use of technology for teaching and learning. The second is to provide a very brief summary of the main conclusions that we have drawn.

Hope and Reality

We have argued that the postsecondary system internationally is facing major challenges, and major structural changes are needed if universities and colleges are to meet the needs of learners and society in the twenty-first century. The management of technology should be a key part of that restructuring. In particular, our expectation for technology is that it can

- Facilitate an increase in the overall number of students receiving postsecondary education
- Provide more flexibility in delivery to meet the needs of a very heterogeneous student body
- Help improve the quality of teaching, through the development of twenty-first-century skills and competencies
- And do all this at the same or less cost as conventional classroom teaching

We have also argued though that to date, these expectations, with the exception of increasing flexible access to learning, have not been met. In particular

- We could find no convincing evidence, either in the case studies or the literature, to indicate that the investment in technology was leading to improved learning.
- There was evidence that technology costs are going up, especially in the areas of faculty workload, learning management systems, and learning technology support.

- In some cases, there are concerns about quality through the failure to follow best practice, the use of untrained instructors or adjuncts, or through the inappropriate use of technology, such as lecture capture for distance delivery.

DEVELOPING EFFECTIVE STRATEGIES TO DRIVE CHANGE

It would be wrong to conclude from this, though, that the use of technology for teaching and learning should be abandoned. We believe that by using effective strategies for technology management, the promise of technology for teaching and learning can be fulfilled.

We start then by describing a number of specific actions that could be taken to improve the management of technology for teaching and learning. We have been somewhat reluctant to be so specific, for several reasons. There is no one best solution out there. We need many more strategies, a range of different goals, and a variety of practices to meet an increasingly diverse and complex environment for postsecondary education. We are confident that in the very many and very diverse postsecondary institutions worldwide, there are managers and faculty who have much better ideas than ours about how to drive change through technology. However, we believe we need to give some examples, more to stimulate debate and discussion than to suggest we have all the answers.

THINKING HOLISTICALLY

A book is linear; management and, especially, decision making are not. We have written about leadership, planning, organization, quality assurance, resource management, training, and organizational culture as if they are separate, independent activities. They are not. They all interrelate.

Furthermore, technology now permeates throughout the whole organization. Faculty and students, not just IT staff, make decisions about technology. At a senior management level, it is essential to think holistically about the management of technology. Senior managers need to have the whole picture about where decisions are made about technology; this will be particularly important when it comes to technology governance, but it is also important to be clear about where decisions of different kinds are being or should be made in terms of network infrastructure, choice of teaching technologies, teaching applications, technology support, resource allocation, security, privacy, and many other areas. Figure 9.1 provides one way of looking at the whole picture of technology management in academic areas (details will vary from institution to institution).

FIGURE 9.1. AREAS OF DECISION MAKING REGARDING ACADEMIC TECHNOLOGIES

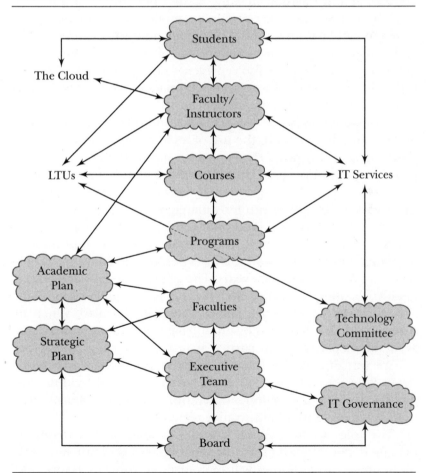

You will notice that this is not quite the same as a typical organizational chart showing line management. Nor is it top-down (or bottom-up). All the circled entities are key areas for actual decisions about the use of different technologies for teaching. We have deliberately not identified individual positions, such as VP of academic affairs or CIO, as it becomes increasingly unlikely that decisions about technology will be taken by an individual acting alone.

The rationale behind the model is that expertise in technology and its applications are spread throughout the organization. A good governance structure ensures that all the key stakeholders are engaged in decision making at the right time and the right level. In a sense, we have presented a model for knowledge management rather than a model of command and control. Such a knowledge management model fits not only the collegial culture of higher education, but also represents a model for organizations with a heavy dependence on information technologies and knowledge creation and dissemination.

The executive team and board's main responsibility lies in overall leadership (championing the use of technology for teaching and ensuring that it is properly managed) and in the governance of technology, not just the technology component but also the ways in which it is used and particularly to ensure that security and privacy issues are being properly managed.

The strategic plan should have some very broad stroke references to the importance of technology for administration, teaching, and research and the direction that technology should be taking over the next few years. The academic plan will be more detailed, setting strategies for the use of learning technology, driven by the overall academic direction in the plan, which in turn should be influenced by input from the faculties, schools, or academic departments in particular.

We will discuss the role of the *technology committee* in more detail later, but for us this would be the heart of institutional strategy, resource allocation, evaluation, and project approval for both academic and administrative technologies.

The role of *senate, faculties, schools, or academic departments* in making decisions about learning technologies is in our view relatively small. These bodies will of course approve programs, and programs will have plans for technology, but at the level of the senate, deans, or faculty approval committees, we would not expect detailed decision making about which technologies should or should not be used in a program, although they may have something more to say about the method of delivery (campus, hybrid, or distance). The main job of these bodies is to ensure that programs (and their use of technology) align with the overall institutional and departmental academic plans.

For us, the critical location of decision making about technology should be at *the program* level, which is why we have placed it at the center of the chart. It is here that the market for the program, and the vision for teaching and learning, should be determined, as well as the method of delivery, and the main technologies to be used, with strong input from central or local IT services and learning technology units to the discussions.

At the course level, *the course teams* begin to make specific decisions about the role of technology and how it will be used. *Individual instructors* will also usually have some freedom to decide on how the technologies will be used, and of course *students* will too, as they also have access now to a wide range of technologies that may help them with their studies, whether recommended by faculty or not.

Note also that individual instructors and students have access to technologies "in the cloud," such as YouTube, Facebook, and Google, that are outside the direct control of central IT services or the institution. These Web 2.0 tools are not only located on servers anywhere in the world, but are also open to those not within the institutional community of students, instructors, and staff. For this reason, the institution needs to have policies in place about the use of such technology by instructors and students, within a context where control and enforcement of policy is difficult.

It is probably contentious of us not to include either *IT services* (central or local) or *learning technology units* as key decision areas. They certainly can and should heavily influence decisions and be completely integrated into the decision-making process, but the responsibility for using technology for teaching and learning lies elsewhere, at the level of the program, course, individual instructor, or student.

Finally, such a model provides an essential component of a governance structure for (information) technologies, extending beyond a narrow definition of IT to include the application of technology to a core component of a postsecondary educational institution, namely teaching and learning. The governance structure suggested in Figure 9.1 will need to be integrated with or expanded into a similar model for administrative and research applications.

THE NEED FOR MULTIPLE VISIONS FOR TEACHING AND LEARNING IN THE FUTURE

Probably the most serious problem we have identified is the general lack of imagination about the possibilities of technology for meeting the needs of today's students. We need to move away from the dominant paradigm of the fixed time and place classroom (Andrea del Sarto's "silver-grey, placid and perfect art" in the chapter's opening quotation) as the default model for university and college teaching, and think of all the many other ways we could organize and manage teaching. In particular, we need to think very concretely about what teaching and learning could and should look like in the future. Our reach *should* exceed our grasp, driven by our assessment of the needs of students in the twenty-first century, and not by the existing institutional requirements that they must fit into. The best place to develop such a vision is at the program level, and particularly when a new program is being designed.

In the scenario that opens this chapter, we have tried to provide just one example of a vision for teaching and learning in the future. Here are some of the implications from that scenario.

1. Abolition of the semester system. In this scenario students can start—and finish—courses at different times of the year, although they are limited to three or four start and end times, to enable groups to cohere during the course. Some courses would stretch over a year, and would be worth 12 credits; others—especially foundation or prior knowledge modules— would be shorter, some as short as a week.

2. Since course materials or content are constantly changing—many sources will be off-campus—courses will be built around learning outcomes, such as research design, critical analysis, and knowledge management, within broad topic areas.

3. Courses would be designed to accommodate a range of students, from those still in high school to those already graduated. There would be a strong emphasis on collaborative learning, group work, and student mentoring. The professor will define very carefully the roles and expectations for different kinds of students and mentors in each group, and different assessment criteria would be used, depending on the experience of the students.

4. The teaching will focus on getting students to do the work: finding material, organizing it, reporting it, evaluating it, using digital technology to create portfolios of work, and peer assessment. Students would be assessed on their progress through the course, as displayed by their work.

5. Large undergraduate courses (over 250) will have one or two full professors, supported by graduate students and off-campus mentors (graduates of the program now in the workforce), an instructional designer, and digital technology support staff. The course will be designed and delivered as a team. The professor(s) will be academically responsible for the course, setting learning outcomes, determining the scope of content coverage, and managing the assessment of students. This will entail setting criteria and rubrics for the measurement of learning outcomes, and ensuring standardization in grading between the graduate students and mentors. Most assessment will be done by the graduate students and mentors in undergraduate classes, monitored by the professor(s), with some peer assessment by students as well.

6. Large classes will be broken down into small groups of 20 to 30 students, each led by a graduate student or mentor. The professor(s) will move between the groups (both in face-to-face and online contexts), monitoring the work of the mentors, and occasionally participating directly in the discussions. Professors will also create learning materials that relate specifically to their research that links to the course topics.

All such material created for teaching will be open content, except for the professors' and graduate students' own research areas. Generally for undergraduate teaching one professor will be responsible for a maximum of 250 students or 10–15 groups (and, of course, smaller classes if possible). There would be less differentiation in class size throughout the program, as students will be working through their studies in cohorts. However, the concept of a "class" will become blurrier, since students will be able to opt in and out more (see point 7), depending on their needs.

7. Assessment methods will vary, but in many cases it will be through "proof of learning," either in the form of mainly authenticated electronic portfolios of work, or by challenge. In the latter case, students may opt to take an examination when they feel they are ready. They may not follow the set curriculum, but can opt to meet the published assessment requirements through a supervised or proctored examination, or through a submission of an authenticated portfolio of work. Portfolio work will be authenticated by graduate students or mentors who have been accredited to work with students.

8. All PhD students will receive up to six months' training in teaching and learning, as well as in research techniques, as a prerequisite for tenure. Students taking master's courses who wish to act as mentors, as well as those who have graduated and are in the workforce who wish to be mentors, will receive up to three months' training in teaching, embedded within their studies.

9. Most universities will belong to consortia, which allow for automatic credit transfer of courses, modules, or credits from other consortium members into their programs. There will be many different consortia reflecting the growing diversity of higher education institutions. Many of these will be international consortia.

10. Costs will be driven down in several ways: professors focusing on overall program design, supervision of assessment, and supporting adjuncts, graduate students, and mentors in their teaching; students working within a managed learning environment, with more experienced students helping the less

experienced; use of low-paid mentors from the workforce, who benefit from the contact with the research in the university; use of graduate students, who spend as much time mentoring and teaching as researching; use of technology to improve communication, and to ensure that everyone (professor, graduate students, mentors, students) is aware of what is happening in teaching and learning within a program through an electronic system that tracks students' progress and the work of teaching staff.

We hope that you do not like this vision, so we can challenge you to come up with a better one. We need a myriad of different visions, to meet the diversity of learning environments. Above all, we need more argument and discussion about teaching models appropriate to a technology-rich environment.

A vision for how the program will be taught should be developed very early in the program planning cycle. Visioning is best done as a group activity, involving different stakeholders, and not giving too much attention to current reality and constraints. Participants should be exposed to an analysis of the current situation, examples of technology-based teaching in the topic area from both within and outside the institution, and be asked to work in teams to develop different scenarios (see Fritz, 1989, for an excellent guide to the visioning process). Students, learning technology and IT staff, as well as academics and representatives from the community should be involved in this process. It should end with some consensus on how the program will be taught, with a shared understanding of what this will look like by all those working in the program. However the details of implementation should be left to small working groups or course teams.

DEVELOPING MEASURABLE STRATEGIC GOALS FOR LEARNING TECHNOLOGY

In most of the case studies, the goals for the use of technology for teaching and learning were often too cautious or unclear, and usually not measurable. The engine room of teaching with technology is the academic program. This is where the key decisions about learning technologies should be made. At the same time, the academic programs should articulate with the overall academic and strategic plans.

Thus, to encourage and facilitate new program designs, the use of technology for teaching and learning needs to be strongly articulated in the academic plan, in the form of measurable strategies for learning technology. We provide in Table 9.1 an illustration of strategies for technology at the level of the academic plan.

Examples of other academic goals that might be identified within the academic plan where technology can play a key role are as follows:

- New learning outcomes focused on embedded twenty-first-century skills.
- Increased access for underserved, disadvantaged, or lifelong learners.
- Lower cost per graduated student.
- Increased number of courses and classes using hybrid and distance learning.
- Other goals: by definition, innovation is to some extent unpredictable. If the visioning process is successful at the program level, ideas for previously unidentified academic goals that are possible through the use of technology will emerge from the visioning process. The process suggested in Figure 9.1 (on page 215) aims to capture, support, and evaluate such new ideas.

It should be noted that the goals stated are essentially academic rather than technology goals, but academic goals where technology plays a critical role in the strategies used to achieve the goals. These goals, strategies, and performance measures should be developed through ongoing dialogue between the program areas, the technology committee, and the team developing the academic plan. We see such goal setting at an institutional level as being an amalgam of ideas both from a senior-level technology steering committee as part of the development of the academic plan, and of ideas coming upwards from the various program areas as they develop their academic plans.

The institution (through a technology committee) would track the success or otherwise of such projects, and have a strategy

TABLE 9.1. EXAMPLES OF GOALS, STRATEGIES, AND PERFORMANCE INDICATORS FOR LEARNING TECHNOLOGIES

Academic Goal	Strategies	Intended Outcomes	Performance Indicators (Within Three Years)
Innovation in teaching	1. Redesign large lecture classes	1. a. More interaction with research professors	1. a. 12 large lecture classes redesigned
		1. b. Improved learning outcomes	1. b. Student and faculty satisfaction rates improved by 15%
			1. c. Student performance increased by 20%
			1. d. Cost equal to or less than lecture class
	2. Combine virtual with wet labs	2. a. Better use of scarce lab space to handle increased enrollments	2. a. 30% increase in students in lab classes
		2. b. Better understanding of experimental design	2. b. Experimental design assessed; 80% pass rate on experimental design assessment
			2. c. Cost per student per lab hour reduced
	3. Use simulations for skills training	3. a. Better development of skills	3. a. 25% increase in employer satisfaction ratings
		3. b. More time for students to practice skills	3. b. Skills identified and assessed
			3. c. 5% improvement in completion rates
			3. d. Costs measured and contained within target

for extending successful teaching models into other relevant program areas. Again, different institutions will have different goals and priorities, but the process of identifying goals, strategies, and performance measures would be similar.

Finally, setting overall goals for the use of technology in teaching enables an institution to identify the data that needs to be collected to assess the success or otherwise of such goals. Much of this data will exist in student records, program plans, and assessments of students. Data can now be more easily identified, aggregated, and analyzed using business intelligence tools, provided that the necessary data is collected in the first place.

Develop a Systematic Annual Academic Planning Process That Drives Budgets

We see planning as ongoing and dynamic. We found in the case studies that often there was no connection between goals for technology and the budget process. Often, too, the planning for learning technologies operated relatively independently of academic planning. To avoid these problems, we suggest an annual rolling three- or five-year planning process for the academic plan which integrates learning technology and academic planning. An academic plan would extend for three or five years ahead, but is modified each year in the light of new developments. This enables ideas for new programs, modification or withdrawal of programs as a result of academic reviews, or the replacement of programs due to declining numbers or increased costs, all to be considered each year by each faculty or school, then rolled up into an institutional academic plan, which then drives or influences resource allocations (budget). (See Figure 9.2.)

When programs are being planned or up for renewal, their plans should include

- A situational analysis (current context, factors influencing program or departments)
- An analysis of strengths, weaknesses, opportunities, threats to program or department (SWOT)
- Market analysis: who needs program, changing demographics, target for enrollments

FIGURE 9.2. AN INTEGRATED ACADEMIC, LEARNING TECHNOLOGY, AND BUDGET PLANNING PROCESS

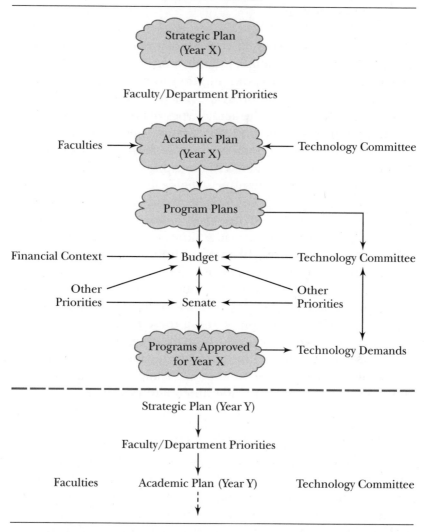

- Concrete vision for teaching and learning in the program
- Content, curriculum, and course structure
- Course development and teaching methods
- Modes of delivery (classroom, hybrid, distance) for each course

- Technology strategy and choices
- A cost and revenue analysis (see Chapter Seven)
- Evaluation strategy

Learning technology staff, IT staff, students, and even community representatives (for example, employers) should be part of the program planning process in addition to all the academics who may wish to teach in the program. The plan should also include collection of data about the actual types of courses offered (classroom, hybrid, distance) and the learning technologies actually used in each course, preferably in a standardized way so that the data can be aggregated across the institution.

The technology committee (see below) provides input to the academic planning committee about possible institutional strategies for learning technologies, analyzes program plans for technology implications, provides input to decisions on resource allocations, and analyzes changing technology demands in preparation for next year's planning process.

These plans would drive the budget process, with the academic planning team setting priorities for funding new programs, and the technology committee using these plans as guidance for spending on technology support for the programs. Again, different institutions will have different planning and budget processes, but whatever the process, it should enable technology applications and costs to be clearly identified and prioritized.

CREATE A HIGH-LEVEL TECHNOLOGY COMMITTEE

Learning technologies are only part of the technology mix in a modern university or college. Planning for learning technologies should be part of the overall planning of technology for the institution, covering infrastructure, administrative activities, student services, and research services. Decisions in any one of these technology areas can have major implications for the other technology areas. At the same time, strategies for learning technologies need to be driven by academic needs and goals.

For this reason, most institutions will require at least a high-level technology committee, with a mandate to plan technology, to set technology policy and procedures, to encourage the creative use of technology for teaching and learning, to approve projects, and to manage and oversee the governance of technology throughout the institution. This committee should also have sufficient resources to implement plans and projects as necessary. Ideally, the committee should include the VP of academic affairs, the VP of administration (either or both on an alternating basis should be the chair), VP of research or a senior research chair, the CIO, the director of the teaching, learning and technology center, and three to five academic representatives (deans or academic program directors).

The main technology committee would meet at least monthly. In larger organizations, there will be subcommittees covering resource allocation, project approvals, governance issues, and possibly an evaluation subcommittee, responsible for organizing, analyzing, and collecting data about technology use and the implementation of institutional technology strategy. The technology committee, for instance, would set up a task force to make decisions on major investments in or on choices of learning management systems.

The committee would set priorities for budget allocations for technology infrastructure, IT services, major software systems, and a central learning technology unit. It would also have funds for technology training for faculty and instructors, and funds to support innovation in technology applications, particularly in academic areas. Once allocated, resources would be managed by the relevant directors of the units.

The committee would develop each year a rolling three-year plan for technology, to be approved by the executive team. Such a technology committee is needed to determine priorities for funding across a wide range of technology applications that support goals and strategies within the institutional strategic plan and the academic plan—and also to influence these plans.

BUILDING A COHERENT GOVERNANCE STRUCTURE

The setting of goals and strategies, the identification of key decision groups within the organization and how they relate to one another, the identification of mandates, responsibilities, and powers for each of the decision groups, are all essential building blocks of a coherent technology governance structure. We have filled in only a few of the building blocks here. The other areas of technology management—administration, research, infrastructure—would also need to be added.

As stated earlier, building and managing a comprehensive governance structure is a substantial challenge for a large and complex organization such as a university. However, demands for accountability, security, and privacy of data make this necessary. More important, though, such a coherent governance structure provides the framework for the effective management of technology to transform teaching and learning in postsecondary educational institutions.

The danger is that governance is seen as mainly a technical issue delegated to the CIO and the IT specialists. Another danger is that building a governance structure becomes a hugely bureaucratic exercise, with an undue emphasis on micromanagement, form filling, caution, and the avoidance of risk. This is why it is so important for senior management and faculty to take responsibility and leadership on this issue, and also why it is so important to set a bold vision for the role of technology in teaching and learning.

Roles for Government

Generally, governments are reluctant to intervene in the internal workings of postsecondary educational institutions. Indeed, public research universities have a great deal of autonomy, despite increasing pressure in recent times for more accountability. We support a hands-off approach by government for the most part. Governments are not well placed to micromanage organizations as complex as a research university or a locally grounded community college.

However, governments can and do play a role in setting overall strategic directions for their public postsecondary education systems; indeed, when this involves extra funding for new research chairs, or more money for extra students to increase access, or closing down unaccredited private institutions, such moves are welcomed by the public institutions themselves. It is appropriate for a government to ensure that institutions have in place protocols to protect the privacy of students and the security of their IT infrastructure. It is also appropriate for governments, following extensive consultation with institutions in the system and other stakeholders, to set priorities and strategic directions for the post-secondary education system as a whole.

Our main concern is to see more innovation in the way teaching is designed, developed, and delivered. From a government perspective, some of the benefits to be obtained from more innovative teaching with technology might be: increased access to learning opportunities for working adults; increased economic development through the creation of a better-prepared work-force; more environmentally friendly learning environments; and the support and creation of new knowledge-based companies. So we set out below some areas where we think government should have a position or interest regarding the integration of technology within institutions.

STRATEGIC GOALS FOR TECHNOLOGY INVESTMENT

The government would set out its own priorities for the use of technology in the postsecondary education system. This might include improvements in the cost-effectiveness of student services, increased access through more flexible programming, better learning outcomes related to the use of technology (including ICT-skilled graduates), collaboration between institutions on online academic programming, sharing of IT systems such as open source learning management systems and server farms, and a sustainable and secure IT infrastructure. Institutions are expected to work toward these objectives.

The state of Washington (SBCTC, 2008) has developed such a policy document for its college system. The government of Alberta is going further. In collaboration with its postsecondary institutions, it is developing a comprehensive IT management control framework that includes not only strategies and goals for the use of technology in the system but also safeguards for security and privacy.

FUNDING TO SUPPORT INNOVATION IN TEACHING AND LEARNING

There are many direct and indirect ways in which governments can and do influence the strategic directions and priorities of institutions through funding. We have seen the impact of British Columbia's decision to withhold a small percentage of institutional operating grants for an innovation fund in the 1990s. Other jurisdictions provide guidelines for priority funding in advance and require institutions to put forward a strategic plan and an accompanying budget that meets the government's stated priorities. We believe now that all jurisdictions should be looking at ways to encourage more innovation in teaching and learning in post-secondary education, and using their funding mechanisms to drive this strategy.

Creation of New Institutions

The creation of universities in particular is often driven by local politics. Every city wants its own research university. We believe there is a need for new institutional models deliberately designed to exploit the benefits of information and communications technologies. We would call these hybrid institutions, in that they would be located within a community with smaller campus facilities, and a heavy use of technology to support the delivery of programs, and with perhaps a footprint centered on but wider than the local community. Such institutions would still do research, but they would focus on the needs of a knowledge-based society, and the development of local businesses and industries.

In summary, government leadership and support are needed if technology is to be fully integrated within our institutions. There is too much inertia that inhibits radical change in most institutions, and government can help those within the institutions seeking to change, without interfering directly in the academic autonomy of the institutions.

Mandatory Training in Teaching

In the case studies, we found over and over again that most instructors were merely adding technology to the current classroom-based model. We were disappointed at the overall lack of imagination and innovation in using technology for teaching. But most university and college instructors have no alternative model, no other pedagogical framework, than the traditional classroom lecture, seminar, and lab-based model. It is this lack of basic training in teaching that is preventing innovation and change in our universities. No other single action is likely to bring the required changes and improvements in the effectiveness of our postsecondary institutions. Because the stakes are so high, and because the resistance to change resulting from the prevailing organizational culture is so great, direct intervention by government is required to bring about such systematic change.

But how do we get over the problem that in a federal system, if one state or province legislates to require training, all the best faculty and graduate students will migrate to those states or provinces that don't have such a requirement? Also, good universities now recruit from around the world.

In both Canada and the United States, the federal government plays an important role in financing student aid. Without student financial aid, many institutions would lose their best students. One way to bring about radical change would be for the federal government to simply state that in three, four, or five years' time, no student will receive student aid to attend an institution where its instructors have not taken a federally recognized postgraduate training program in postsecondary teaching.

The federal government would give the institutions one year to come up with an appropriate program (or set of programs), which the universities themselves would run, but which would require approval from the federal government (who will have created a panel of experts in university teaching to make the judgment). Institutions would be given targets. For instance, a minimum of 10% of all instructors (in FTEs) must have received training by year one of the scheme and 100% by year ten for federal approval. So in 10 years, all the universities in the United States and Canada would have 100% of their instructors with at least some training in teaching. (It would certainly help if the Canadian and U.S. federal governments worked together on this, to stop country hopping—the European Commission could play a similar role in Europe, refusing to give grants to any universities without an approved training program.) Probably no other single action will improve the quality of our graduates, and the beauty of it is that it costs government virtually nothing.

How would the universities do this? The cheapest and easiest way would be to offer a 10–12 credit postgraduate certificate program for graduate students wanting a career as a university instructor, spread over one year. This program would also be open to adjunct faculty—yes, they too will need to be trained—and to already tenured faculty. It would make sense for universities to collaborate to develop a program that could be shared, and the program would involve at least some online learning. The universities will be responsible for covering most of the cost of the program, because students already pay tuition fees for graduate school. In other words, it would be partly subsidized by students spending three months of a four-year PhD on teaching, or 6% of their study, instead of all of the time on research. This is hardly likely to weaken the quality of research graduates—indeed, it may help improve their research as well.

There are lots of different ways that training could be implemented, but government has the one tool or strategy that could drive real change in the system. Is there a politician willing to take leadership on this, and withstand what will be very strong opposition from the institutions?

Evolution or Revolution?

One British vice chancellor noted: "Universities are like graveyards. When you want to move them, you don't get a lot of help from the people inside." Why should universities in particular change? They have survived for 800 years, they are recognized as essential for the social and economic development of nations, they have substantial funding from government grants, tuition fees, and endowments, and they have a great deal of autonomy.

Tierney and Hentschke (2007, pp. 13–14) argue that

> innovation in higher education has remained within a socially constructed framework where the innovators have tended to accept the parameters of traditional higher education and have worked within them. . . . As with all social constructions, deviations from these norms are relatively minor, in large part because those who participate in the construction have difficulties imagining ways much beyond the status quo.

Thus, traditional universities and colleges seek ways to integrate new technology within the parameters of the traditional model, and look for changes at the margins, in a slow and incremental manner, that sustain the existing goals and values of the organization.

There are signs of growing impatience at the slow speed and lack of radical change in universities and colleges. David White, Director General of Education and Culture, Lifelong Learning, European Commission at the 2008 EDEN conference in Lisbon, stated that

> although ICT has had a major impact on education and training at all levels, its impact has not yet been as great as we hoped and expected. The task of transforming the teaching and learning process is still just beginning. Some innovation [sic] content is there: but not enough. New business models are needed. Making the best use of new technology in education and training is not going to be achieved just by applying new methods in old contexts. In education and training, using new technology and new approaches means we must be prepared to change the model to get the best.

Similarly, the World Economic Forum's Global Advisory Committee on Technology and Education, at its meeting in Dubai in November 2008, commented:

> Education is in a state of transition from a traditional model to one where technology plays an integral role. However, technology has not yet transformed education:
>
> - Student expectations about the educational experiences (e.g., connected, participatory, engaging) are not being realized
> - Students are digital "natives" while teachers are "laggards"
> - Rather than introducing twenty-first century skills, technology is often being used to automate outdated education paradigms
> - Technology changes what students/citizens need to learn (e.g., analysis over rote memorization).

Many universities and colleges will argue that they are experimenting, innovating, and have vision regarding technology for teaching and administration, but what they are mainly doing is accommodating technology to the traditional model. What is lacking is a systematic, pedagogically based approach that fits the design and delivery of courses and programs to the needs of an increasingly large and diverse student population.

However, this cannot be done without major changes, without experimentation on a much larger scale than we have seen up to now. We do not need a standard model for teaching because our students are not standardized; they come in all shapes and sizes. Furthermore, technology alone cannot improve cost-effectiveness; it needs leadership, change management, and *above all*, new visions for teaching and learning.

BUILDING BETTER UNIVERSITIES AND COLLEGES

There is a variety of ways in which technology can be used to build better universities and colleges.

THE BENEFITS OF SUCCESSFUL TECHNOLOGY INTEGRATION

The successful integration of technology within universities and colleges, especially in economically advanced countries, will result in institutions being better able to meet the challenges of changing demographics, changing economies, changing technologies, and changing society. Successful technology integration provides an institution with increased competitiveness, resulting from

- More flexible access to learning opportunities
- Better learning outcomes and better prepared graduates
- Higher quality in teaching and administrative services, through more interaction with faculty, more individualization and customization of learning, and more flexible provision of services

It can also lead to increased cost-effectiveness, when technology is used to replace less effective processes and practices.

We need to use technology as an integral part of our teaching and learning activities to prepare learners for such a society, and to run our institutions efficiently. Instructors no longer have to create all their teaching material from scratch, and duplicate the process every year. They can increasingly select ready-made modules of free, open access online teaching materials, and organize teaching and learning around the vast resources now available over the Internet. Even better, they can give learners the freedom and responsibility to select the learning materials that they feel to be of interest and relevance.

In particular, we need to examine what is best done face-to-face, what is best done online, and for which kinds of students. We need to think about how technology could be used for personalizing learning and increasing motivation, while at the same time controlling the workload of the teacher. Technology allows work to be shifted from the teacher to the learner. Learners can spend more time on task, interacting both with digital content and with fellow students in online and face-to-face communities. We need to rethink the campus experience so that the unique benefits of the campus and face-to-face contact are fully exploited, and to rethink how the scarce time of research professors can best be used, when technology is available. In particular, we should think of lectures not as the default model for teaching, but just as one tool of many.

A BALANCED APPROACH TO TECHNOLOGY INTEGRATION

Successful technology integration requires equal attention being paid to three main elements: pedagogy (teaching methods); technology; and organization (what Sangrà, 2008, calls the TOPs model) (see Figure 9.3).

Focusing on technology alone will not lead to successful integration on the teaching and learning side. Equal attention needs to be paid to pedagogical issues, including changing the methods of teaching to get the best use out of technology, and organizational issues, such as governance, funding, and technology support.

FIGURE 9.3. THE TOPS MODEL

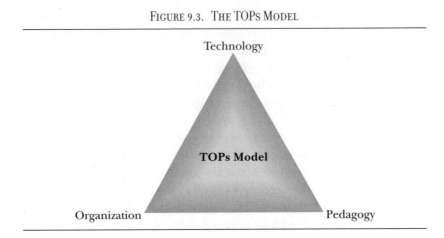

SUCCESSFUL TECHNOLOGY INTEGRATION REQUIRES PROFESSIONAL MANAGEMENT

This book is more about management than technology and has focused predominantly on the organizational side of the TOPs triangle. It may seem that we have been very critical of individuals in universities and colleges, especially senior administrators. We did find a few examples of bad decision making, poor communications, and a lack of knowledge or understanding of technology and the issues around it among some of the senior administrators.

However, technology is just one of many areas of responsibility for senior administrators. It is a relatively new area, at least for academic administrators, and one with few precedents to follow. Furthermore, Henry Mintzberg (2009) has shown clearly that management, wherever it is carried out, and no matter what the competence or experience of the manager, is a really messy business. It's just one damned thing after another, and that's no different in a university or college. The idea that an individual, no matter how charismatic, can somehow control a huge organization like a research university is inherently foolish, as any experienced president will tell you. Furthermore, senior administrators are extremely lucky if they receive more than the merest training for their new jobs. In nearly all our cases, senior administrators were doing the best they could for the institution as a whole, and some performed to the highest standards, under the circumstances.

Hence our message: *change the circumstances.* This means paying attention to organizational and cultural issues, working as far as possible with the predominant culture, but being willing to challenge it when necessary. It is important to use best practice in management (such as encouraging strategic thinking throughout the organization), but adapted to the unique conditions of higher education. Training—both for instructors and for managers—will definitely help. Much more attention needs to be paid to collecting and analyzing data for decision making, and business intelligence tools make that much easier, provided that those collecting it know what data to collect, and how to organize and analyze it. Incentives and reward systems need to be adjusted to encourage change and innovation, especially in teaching. These requirements apply to all aspects of university and college management, not just technology management.

CREATING AN ENVIRONMENT THAT ENCOURAGES INNOVATION AND CHANGE

Perhaps the biggest challenge in the successful integration of technology is the creation of a culture of innovation and change in teaching and learning. Technology allows for many different ways of teaching, and more innovation and experimentation is needed, together with careful evaluation of results. Better incentives for rewarding instructors for innovative teaching, better training in teaching, institutional strategic plans that emphasize innovation in teaching, the development of academic program plans that look for new ways to reach new target groups, and strong input from educational designers and technology specialists are all ways to encourage innovation and change.

WHAT DOES NOT NEED TO CHANGE

We do not wish to see change in the traditional mission of universities and colleges, or any activities that reduce academic freedom or the autonomy of institutions, or the use of professional managers from outside the educational world. None of this is necessary to enable technology to be effectively integrated.

Similarly, we are not arguing for the abolition of campuses or classroom teaching. However, they should be seen as one set of conditions among many that can support teaching and learning in postsecondary education.

CONCLUSION

The existing system is showing signs of strain and, more important, the trend is toward increasing pressure on the system. Institutions have adapted poorly to the massification of higher education. Our current higher education institutions are costly and inefficient, and could do a lot better if information and communications technologies are applied intelligently.

We see this book as a work in progress. Much more research and evaluation of the conditions necessary to integrate technology are needed. We know that there are other methods and approaches that could be tried that may well be more effective. What we want to encourage most of all is innovation and change in our institutions, so that the needs of students and the public are better served in the future. We want to stimulate a debate or discussion about how best to do this, so we hope readers will follow up this book by going to our Web site at http://batesandsangra.ca. At this site, you can join us in online discussion about the scenarios, be able to access a collection of resources on this topic, including many of the references in the bibliography, see reviews of this book by academics and other readers, and, above all, we hope you will be able to make your own contributions to the black art of technology management in higher education. In the meantime, we thank you for your interest and patience in sharing this journey with us.

References

Alexander, B. (2004). Going nomadic: Mobile learning in higher education. *EDUCAUSE Review*, September/October, 28–35.

Allen, I. E., & Seaman, J. (2006). *Making the grade: Online education in the United States, 2006.* Needham, MA: Sloan Consortium.

Allen, I. E., & Seaman, J. (2008). *Staying the course: Online education in the United States, 2008.* Needham, MA: Sloan Consortium.

Alsop, R. (2008). *The trophy kids grow up: How the millennial generation is shaking up the workplace.* San Francisco: Jossey-Bass.

Ambient Insight Research. (2009). *U.S. self-paced e-learning market.* Monroe, WA: Ambient Insight Research.

APQC/SHEEO. (1998). *Benchmarking best practices in faculty instructional development: Supporting faculty use of technology.* Houston: American Productivity and Quality Center.

Australian Graduate School of Management, Fujitsu Center. (1996). *Managing the introduction of technology in the delivery and administration of higher education.* Canberra, Australia: Government of Australia Department of Employment, Education, Training and Youth Affairs.

Barker, K. (2002). *Canadian recommended e-learning guidelines (CanREGs).* Vancouver, BC: FuturEd.

Bates, A. (2000). *Managing technological change: Strategies for college and university leaders.* San Francisco: Jossey-Bass.

Bates, A. (2005). *Technology, e-learning and distance education.* London: Routledge.

Bates, A. (2007). Strategic planning for e-learning in a polytechnic. In M. Bullen & D. Janes (Eds.), *Making the transition to e-learning: Strategies and issues.* Hershey, PA: Information Science Publishing.

Bates, A., & Poole, G. (2003). *Effective teaching with technology in higher education.* San Francisco: Jossey-Bass.

Batson, T. (2010, March 17). Let faculty off the hook. *Campus Technology.* Retrieved from http://campustechnology.com/articles/2010/03/17/let-faculty-off-the-hook.aspx

BCIT. (2009, November 2). *BCIT launches the CUBE: Centre for the use of 3D simulation technology taking teaching and learning to a new level.* Vancouver, BC: BCIT.

Birnbaum, R. (2000). *Management fads in higher education: Where they come from, what they do, and why they fail.* San Francisco: Jossey-Bass.

Bowen, W., Chingus, M., & McPherson, M. (2009). *Crossing the finish line: Completing college at America's public universities.* Princeton, NJ: Princeton University Press.

Bradmore, D., & Smyrnios, K. (2009). The writing on the wall: Responses of Australian public universities to competition in global higher education. *Higher Education Research & Development, 28*(5), 495–508.

Brinkman, P., & Morgan, A. (2010). Financial planning: Strategies and lessons learned. *Planning for Higher Education, 38*(3), 5–14.

Bullen, M., & Janes, D. (Eds.). (2007). *Making the transition to e-learning: Strategies and issues.* Hershey, PA: Ideas Group.

Bullen, M., Morgan, T., Belfer, K., & Qayyum, A. (2009). The net generation in higher education: Rhetoric and reality. *International Journal of Excellence in e-Learning, 2*(1), 1–13.

Burgos, D., Tattersall, C., & Koper, R. (2007). Re-purposing existing generic games and simulations for e-learning. *Computers in Human Behavior, 23*(6), 2656–2667. Retrieved from http://portal.acm.org/citation.cfm?id=1265679

The Canadian Services Coalition and the Canadian Chambers of Commerce. (2006). *Canadian services sector: A new success story.* Ottawa: The Canadian Services Coalition. Retrieved from http://www.canadianservicescoalition.com/CanadianServicesSectorANewSuccessStory.pdf

Carlton, D., & Perloff, J. (2000). *Modern industrial organization* (3rd ed.). Reading, MA: Addison-Wesley Longman.

CDW-G. (2009). *The 2009 21st-century campus report: Defining the vision.* Vernon Hills, IL: CDW-G.

Christensen, C., Horn, M., & Johnson, C. (2008). *Disrupting class.* New York: McGraw-Hill.

Christensen Hughes, J., & Mighty, J. (Eds.). (2010). *Taking stock: Research on teaching and learning in higher education.* Montreal, QC: McGill-Queen's University Press.

CIBER. (2008). *Information behaviour of the researcher of the future.* London: British Library, UCL.

Clark, D. (2009). *Donald Clark plan B.* Retrieved from http://donaldclarkplanb.blogspot.com/

Clark, R. (1983). Reconsidering research on learning from media. *Review of Educational Research, 53,* 445–459.

Coimbra Group of Universities. (2002). *European Union policies and strategic change for e-learning in universities (HECTIC Report).* Brussels: European Commission.

The College Board. (2005). *Trends in college pricing.* Washington, DC: The College Board.

Conference Board of Canada. (1991). *Employability skill profile: The critical skills required of the Canadian workforce.* Ottawa, ON: Conference Board of Canada.

Dalrymple, M. (2007). *Strategic planning in higher education.* Saarbrücken, Germany: Verlag Dr. Müller.

Daniel, J. (1999). *Mega-universities and knowledge media.* London: Kogan Page.

Davis, J. (2008). Beyond the false dichotomy of centralized and decentralized IT deployment. In R. Katz (Ed.), *The tower and the cloud.* Boulder, CO: EDUCAUSE.

Desmond, A. (1997). *Huxley: Vol. 2, Evolution's high priest.* London: Michael Joseph.

Downes, S. (2005, October 15). E-learning 2.0. *eLearn Magazine.* Retrieved from http://elearnmag.org/subpage.cfm?section=articles&article=29–1

Downes, S. (2006). Understanding learning networks. *Keynote: 4th EDEN research workshop.* Castelldelfels, Spain. Retrieved from http://www.downes.ca/presentation/52

Drucker, P. (1969). *The age of discontinuity; Guidelines to our changing society.* New York: Harper & Row.

Ehlers, U-D., & Schneckenberg, D. (Eds.). (2010). *Changing cultures in higher education: Moving ahead to future learning.* Heidelberg: Springer.

Epper, R., & Bates, A. (2001). *Teaching faculty how to use technology.* Westport, CT: American Council on Education/Oryx.

eSchool News. (2009, November 17). Stakeholders advise on national ed-tech plan. *eSchool News.*

Figlio, D., Rush, N., & Yin, L. (2010). *Is it live or is it Internet? Experimental estimates of the effects of online instruction on student learning.* Cambridge, MA: National Bureau of Economic Research. Retrieved from http://www.nber.org/papers/w16089

Financial Times. (2009, February 8). Make and mend: Reindustrialising Britain. *Financial Times.* Retrieved from http://www.ft.com/cms/s/0/e6528e46-f603–11dd-a9ed-0000779fd2ac.html

Fritz, R. (1989). *The path of least resistance.* New York: Columbine.

Gansemer-Topf, A., Saunders, K., Schuh, J., & Shelley, M. (2004). *A study of resource expenditures and allocation at DEEP colleges and universities: Is spending related to student engagement?* Ames: Educational Leadership and Policy Studies, Iowa State University.

Garrett, R. (2009). *Online higher education market update.* Boston: Eduventures.

Gilbert, J. (2005). *Catching the knowledge wave? The knowledge society and the future of education.* Wellington: New Zealand Council for Educational Research.

Government of Alberta. (2008). *Report of the Auditor General of Alberta—April 2008.* Edmonton: Government of Alberta. Retrieved from http://www.oag.ab.ca/?V_DOC_ID=911

Hanna, D. (2003). Organizational models in higher education: Past and future. In M. Moore & W. Anderson (Eds.), *A handbook of distance education.* Mahwah, NJ: Erlbaum.

Hartman, J., Moskal, P., & Dziuban, C. (2005). Preparing the academy of today for the learner of tomorrow. In D. Oblinger & J. Oblinger (Eds.), *Educating the net generation.* Boulder, CO: EDUCAUSE.

Hartman, J., & Truman-Davis, B. (2001). Institutionalizing support for faculty use of technology at the University of Central Florida. In R. Epper & A. Bates (Eds.), *Teaching faculty how to use technology.* Westport, CT: American Council on Education/Oryx.

Higgins, A., & Prebble, T. (2008). *Taking the lead: Strategic management for e-learning.* Wellington: Ako Aotearoa. Funded by the New Zealand Ministry for Education.

Hiltz, R., & Turoff, M. (1978). *The network nation.* Cambridge, MA: MIT Press.

Instructional Technology Council. (2008). *Tracking the impact of e-learning at community colleges.* Washington, DC: Instructional Technology Council.

Ito, M., et al. (2008). *Living and learning with new media: Summary of findings from the Digital Youth Project.* Chicago: The John D. & Catherine T. MacArthur Foundation. Retrieved from http://www.macfound.org/atf/cf/%7BB0386CE3-8B29-4162-8098-E466FB856794%7D/DML_ETHNOG_WHITEPAPER.PDF

Jaschik, S. (2009, May 26). The distance ed tipping point. *Inside Higher Education.* Retrieved from http://www.insidehighered.com/news/2009/05/26/distance

JISC. (2005). *Innovative practice with e-learning: A good practice guide to embedding mobile and wireless technologies into everyday practice.* Bristol, UK: JISC. Retrieved from www.jisc.ac.uk/elearning_innovation.html

JISC. (2006). *Effective practice with e-assessment.* Bristol, UK: JISC.

JISC. (2009). *Responding to learners pack.* Bristol, UK: Joint Information Systems Committee.

Johnson, N. (2009). *What does a college degree cost?* Washington, DC: Delta Cost Project.

Kamenetz, A. (2010). *Edupunks, edupreneurs, and the coming transformation of higher education.* White River, VT: Chelsea Green.

Katz, R. (Ed.). (2008). *The tower and the cloud: Higher education in the age of cloud computing.* Boulder, CO: EDUCAUSE.

Kelly, P., & Jones, D. (2005). *A new look at the institutional component of higher education finance: A guide for evaluating performance relative to financial resources.* Boulder, CO: National Center for Higher Education Management Systems.

King, J. (2008, July 11). Iconic UQ lecture theatre re-opens for business. *University of Queensland News.* Brisbane: University of Queensland. Retrieved from http://www.uq.edu.au/news/index.html?article=15298

Knapper, C. (2010). Changing teaching practice: Barriers and strategies. In J. Christensen Hughes & J. Mighty (Eds.), *Taking stock: Research on teaching and learning in higher education.* Montreal, QC: McGill-Queen's University Press.

Kozma, R. (1994). Will media influence learning? Reframing the debate. *Educational Technology Research and Development, 42*(2), 7–19.

Lamberson, M., & Fleming, K. (2008). *Aligning institutional culture and practice: The University of British Columbia's e-learning framework.* Tokyo: NIME International Symposium.

Laurillard, D. (2002). *Rethinking university teaching* (2nd ed.). London: Routledge Falmer.

Laurillard, D. (2007). Modelling benefits-oriented costs for technology enhanced learning. *Higher Education, 54*(1), 21–39.

Lee, M., & McLoughlin, C. (Eds.). (2010). *Web 2.0-based e-learning: Applying social informatics for tertiary teaching.* Hershey, PA: IGI Global.

Lokken, F., & Womer, L. (2007). *Trends in e-learning: Tracking the impact of e-learning in higher education.* Washington, DC: Instructional Technology Council.

Lorenzo, G., & Ittelson, J. (2005). *An overview of portfolios.* Boulder, CO: EDUCAUSE.

Lowendahl, J-M., Zastrocky, M., & Harris, M. (2008). *Gartner Higher Education E-Learning Survey 2007: Clear movements in the market.* Stamford, CT: Gartner.

Lyotard, J. (1984). *The post-modern condition: A report on knowledge.* Manchester, UK: University of Manchester Press.

Machiavelli, N. (1532). *The prince.* Charleston, SC: BiblioLife.

Marshall, S. (2006). *E-learning maturity model version two: New Zealand tertiary institution e-learning capability: Informing and guiding e-learning architectural change and development project report.* Wellington: New Zealand Ministry of Education.

McCarthy, S., & Samors, R. (2009). *Online learning as a strategic asset, 1: A resource for campus leaders.* Washington, DC: Association of Public and Land-Grant Universities.

McCreary, E. (1989). Computer-mediated communication and organizational culture. In R. Mason & A. Kaye (Eds.), *Mindweave: Communication, computers and distance education.* Oxford: Pergamon Press.

Means, B., Toyama, Y., Murphy, R., & Bakia, M. (2009). *Evaluation of evidence-based practices in online learning: A meta-analysis and review of online learning studies.* Washington, DC: U.S. Department of Education.

Middle States Higher Education Commission. (2002). *Distance education: Guidelines for the evaluation of electronically offered degree and certificate programs.* Philadelphia: Middle States Higher Education Commission.

Mintzberg, H. (1994a). *The rise and fall of strategic planning.* New York: Free Press.

Mintzberg, H. (1994b, January–February). The fall and rise of strategic planning. *Harvard Business Review,* 107–114.

Mintzberg, H. (2009). *Managing.* San Francisco: Berrett-Koehler.

Moore, A. (2001). Designing advanced learning communities. In R. Epper & A. Bates (Eds.), *Teaching faculty how to use technology.* Westport, CT: American Council on Education/Oryx.

Moore, J. (2005). *The Sloan quality framework and five pillars.* Newburyport, MA: Sloan Consortium.

New Media Consortium. (2008). *The horizon report: 2008 edition.* Austin, TX: New Media Consortium/EDUCAUSE Learning Initiative.

Oblinger, D., & Oblinger, J. (Eds.). (2005a). *Educating the net generation.* Boulder, CO: EDUCAUSE.

Oblinger, D., & Oblinger, J. (2005b). Is it age or IT: First steps toward understanding the net generation. In D. Oblinger & J. Oblinger (Eds.), *Educating the net generation.* Boulder, CO: EDUCAUSE.

OECD. (2005). *E-learning in tertiary education: Where do we stand?* Paris: OECD.

OECD. (2009). *Education at a glance: OECD indicators 2008.* Paris: OECD.

O'Reilly, T. (2005). What is Web 2.0? *O'Reilly.* Retrieved from http://oreilly.com/web2/archive/what-is-web-20.html

Parry, M. (2009a, November 15). Business software, built by colleges for colleges, challenges commercial giants. *Chronicle of Higher Education.*

Parry, M. (2009b, August 3). Obama's great course giveaway. *Chronicle of Higher Education.*

Parsons, C. (2008, July 13). Second Life offers healing, therapeutic options for users. *San Francisco Chronicle.* Retrieved from http://www.sfgate.com/cgi-bin/article.cgi?f=/c/a/2008/07/11/LVL211GP5C.DTL

The Partnership for 21st Century Skills. (2009). *National action agenda on 21st century skills.* Tucson: The Partnership for 21st Century Skills.

Perry, W. (1976). *The open university.* Milton Keynes, UK: The Open University.

Pollock, C., Fasciano, D., Gervais-Guy, L., Gingras, D., Guy, R., & Hallee, R. (2001). The evolution of faculty instructional development in the use of technology at Collège Boréal, Ontario. In R. M. Epper & A. W. Bates (Eds.), *Teaching faculty how to use technology: Best practices from leading universities.* Westport, CT: Oryx Press.

Prensky, M. (2001). Digital natives, Digital immigrants. *On the Horizon, 9*(5), 1–6. Retrieved from http://www.marcprensky.com/writing/Prensky%20-%20Digital%20Natives,%20Digital%20Immigrants%20-%20Part1.pdf

Prensky, M. (2006). *Don't bother me Mom—I'm learning.* St. Paul, MN: Paragon House.

Russell, T. L. (1999). *The no significant difference phenomenon.* Raleigh: North Carolina State University, Office of Instructional Telecommunication.

Sangrà, A. (2003). *La integració de les TIC a la universitat: Una aproximació estratègica.* Unpublished manuscript, Universitat Rovira i Virgili, Tarragona, Spain.

Sangrà, A. (2008). *The integration of information and communication technologies in the university: Models, problems and challenges (La integració de les TICs a la universitat: Models, problemes i reptes).* Unpublished PhD dissertation, Universitat Rovira i Virgili, Tarragona, Spain.

SBCTC. (2008). *Strategic technology plan.* Olympia: Washington State Board for Community and Technical Colleges. Retrieved from www.sbctc.ctc.edu/docs/strategicplan/strategic_technology_plan.pdf

Schaffhauser, D. (2009, June 10). Lecture capture is getting campuses talking. *Campus Technology*

Schein, E. H. (2005). *Organizational culture and leadership.* San Francisco: Jossey-Bass.

Schramm, W. (1977). *Big media, little media.* Thousand Oaks, CA: Sage.

Seaman, J. (2009). *Online learning as a strategic asset, Vol. 2: The paradox of faculty voices.* Washington, DC: Association of Public and Land-Grant Universities.

Searle, J. (1996). *The construction of social reality.* New York: Simon & Schuster.

Senges, M., Praus, T., & Bihr, P. (2007). *Virtual worlds: A Second Life's beginner's guide.* Barcelona: Universidad Oberta de Catalunya.

Siemens, G. (2004). Connectivism: A learning theory for the digital age. Retrieved from *eLearnSpace* http://www.elearnspace.org/Articles/connectivism.htm

Southern Alberta Institute of Technology (SAIT). (2006) *The SAIT strategic plan 2006–2016.* Calgary, AB: SAIT.

Stacey, P. (2010, June 7). *Architecting EdTech. Paul Stacey: Musings on the EdTech frontier.* Retrieved from http://edtechfrontier.com/

Standards Australia. (2005). *AS8105-corporate governance of information and communication technology.* Sydney: Standards Australia.

Statistics Canada. (2009). *Post-secondary participation rate, 2003–2004, by age and grade.* Retrieved from http://www.statcan.gc.ca/cgi-bin/af-fdr.cgi?l=eng&loc=/pub/81–582-x/2006001/excel/E1-E-Book.xls

Tapscott, D., & Williams, A. (2010). Innovating the 21st century university: It's time. *EDUCAUSE Review, 45*(1), 16–29.

Terris, B. (2009, September 14). University uses "clickers" to quiz students in multiple locations. *Chronicle of Higher Education.*

Tierney, W., & Hentschke, G. (2007). *New players, different game: Understanding the rise of for-profit colleges and universities.* Baltimore: Johns Hopkins University Press.

Twigg, C. (1999). *Improving learning and reducing costs: Redesigning large enrollment courses.* Troy, NY: National Center for Academic Transformation.

U.S. Census Bureau. (2009). *Statistical abstract of the United States: 2009* (Table 211). Washington, DC: U.S. Government Printing Office.

U.S. Department of Education. (2006). *A test of leadership: Charting the future of U.S. higher education.* Washington, DC: U.S. Department of Education.

U.S. Department of Education, Network for Education Information. (2009). *Accreditation and quality assurance.* Washington, DC: U.S. Department of Education. Retrieved from http://www2.ed.gov/about/offices/list/ous/international/usnei/us/edlite-accreditation.html

Wellman, J. (2010). Improving data to tackle the higher education "cost disease." *Planning for Higher Education, 38*(33), 25–37.

Wellman, J., Desrochers, D., Lenihan, C., Kirshstein, R., Hurlburt, S., & Honegger, S. (2009). *Trends in college spending: Where does the money come from? Where does it go?* Washington, DC: Delta Project on Postsecondary Education Costs, Productivity, and Accountability.

White, D. (2008). *Innovative LEARNING for Europe.* EDEN Annual Conference, Lisbon, Portugal.

World Economic Forum. (2008). *Report of the Global Advisory Committee on Technology and Education.* Dubai: World Economic Forum.

Young, J. (2009, November 22). Teaching with Twitter: Not for the faint of heart. *Chronicle of Higher Education.* Retrieved from http://chronicle.com/article/Teaching-With-Twitter-Not-for/49230/

Zemsky, R. (2009). *Making reform work: The case for transforming American higher education.* Chapel Hill, NC: Rutgers University Press.

About the Authors

A. W. (Tony) Bates has more than forty years' experience in using technology for teaching, starting in 1969, when he began researching the effectiveness of the BBC–Open University television and radio programs, as a founding staff member of the British Open University, where he became a full professor in educational media research.

In 1989, he emigrated to Canada, to take the position of executive director, Strategic Planning and Information Technology at the Open Learning Agency, Vancouver. In 1995 he moved to the University of British Columbia, to become director of Distance Education and Technology. On retirement from UBC in 2003, he started his own consultancy company, specializing in the planning and management of learning technologies in postsecondary education. He has worked as a consultant in over 40 countries.

He is the author of 12 books on learning technology and distance education, and he and his research colleagues have published over 350 papers in academic journals. He has received honorary degrees from six universities.

Albert Sangrà is a senior professor at the Open University of Catalonia, Spain, where he is currently the academic director of the eLearn Center, the research center for e-learning. He is also the program director for the university's MSc. in Education and ICT (e-learning).

He has worked as a consultant and trainer in several online and blended learning projects in Europe, America, and Asia, focusing on implementation strategies for the use of technology for teaching and learning. He is currently a visiting scholar at the Korean National Open University, South Korea.

He has been a member of the executive committee of the European Distance and E-learning Network (EDEN) (2003–2009), and of the advisory board of the Open University of Portugal (2007–2008). He is a member of the board of directors at the European Foundation for Quality in E-Learning (EFQUEL).

He has a PhD in Education from the University of Rovira i Virgili in Spain, a postgraduate degree in Applications of Information Technology from the Open University (UK), and a diploma on Strategic Use of IT in Education from Harvard University.

INDEX

Page references followed by *fig* indicate an illustrated figure; followed by *t* indicate a table.